OXFORD STUDIES IN AMERICAN LITERARY HISTORY

Gordon Hutner, Series Editor

The Latino Continuum and the Nineteenth-Century Americas

LITERATURE, TRANSLATION, AND HISTORIOGRAPHY

Carmen E. Lamas

OXFORD

UNIVERSITY PRESS

OXFORD
UNIVERSITY PRESS

Great Clarendon Street, Oxford, OX2 6DP,
United Kingdom

Oxford University Press is a department of the University of Oxford.
It furthers the University's objective of excellence in research, scholarship,
and education by publishing worldwide. Oxford is a registered trade mark of
Oxford University Press in the UK and in certain other countries

First Edition published in 2021

Impression: 3

Published in the United States of America by Oxford University Press
198 Madison Avenue, New York, NY 10016, United States of America

British Library Cataloguing in Publication Data

Data available

Library of Congress Control Number: 2021930452

ISBN 978-0-19-887148-4

DOI: 10.1093/oso/9780198871484.001.0001

Printed and bound by
CPI Group (UK) Ltd, Croydon, CRO 4YY

For John and AJ

{ ACKNOWLEDGMENTS }

The idea of a Latino Continuum began with the conceptualization of the Americanized-*criollo* in *Revista Hispánica Moderna* (2008) and was introduced in *The Latino Nineteenth Century* (2016). I thank Rodrigo Lazo and Jesse Alemán, editors of *The Latino Nineteenth Century*, for including my essay "Raimundo Cabrera, the Latin American Archive and the Latina/o Continuum" in this ground-breaking collection. The full concept of the Latino Continuum is articulated in the present volume.

The primary sources for this book can be found at the New York Public Library, Harvard University Library, the Cuban Heritage Collection at the University of Miami, Butler Library at Columbia University, the Recovering the US Hispanic Literary Heritage archive at the University of Houston, Van Pelt Library at the University of Pennsylvania, the Library Company of Philadelphia, the Historical Society of Pennsylvania, and the University of Virginia Special Collections Library. I also accessed (in Spain) the Archivo General de Indias in Seville and, through the assistance of Gerald E. Poyo, the Archivo General de la Administración, Alcalá de Henares. Chapter 5 of this book could not have been completed without his generosity. Isis Campos and Carolina Villareal also accessed much-needed documents for this chapter. In Cuba I thank Silvia Godoy, who, with the help of Mabel Cuesta, made access to the Fondo Familia Guiteras at the Archivo Nacional de Matanzas possible. Chapter 3 could not have been written without their assistance. Letters of introduction from Lillian Guerra made it possible for me to access the Archivo Nacional de la República de Cuba in Havana. Olga Portuondo Zúñiga and Arturo Soregui made possible my early work in the Archivo de La Ermita de Nuestra Señora La Caridad del Cobre and the Arzobispado de Santiago de Cuba. Miguel A. Valladares-Llata was invaluable in accessing difficult-to-find texts at the Biblioteca Nacional de Cuba José Martí. Without his help and that of Carmen Moreno (Luis A. Retta Libros) and Gonzalo Baptista (Emory and Henry College) the chapter on Eusebio Guiteras could not have been written. Miguel also collaborated with fellow librarians across the country and antiquarians in Spain to obtain difficult-to-find sources. The filmmaker Luis Pérez Tolón was instrumental in the completion of Chapter 2: his beautiful film *Emilia: An Untold Cuban-American Story* (2017) is an invaluable contribution to Latinx history and established a much-cherished friendship.

Support from multiple universities and organizations aided in the completion of the book. At the University of Virginia, a Sesquicentennial Fellowship during 2019–20 made it possible for me to dedicate myself full-time to writing this book. Appointment as a Mellon Fellow and a member of the Global South Lab facilitated multiple conversations with colleagues at UVA and across the country that enriched the book. Also at UVA, the Institute for the Humanities and Global Culture, the Americas Center, the English Department, the American Studies Department, the Spanish Department, and Environmental Humanities @ UVA provided funding to invite such scholars as Frances Aparicio, Patricia Gherovici, Albert Laguna, Antonio López, and Randy Ontiveros to UVA's Grounds for enriching conversations. Funds from the English Department secured with Steve Arata's support, together with that of Francesca Fiorani at the A&S Dean's Office and support from the Office of the Vice President and Provost, made possible my participation in the National Center for Faculty Diversity and Development (NCFDD) Faculty Success Program in the Spring 2018, which facilitated completion of the chapter on Latina/o historiography. I have continued to participate in the NCFDD Faculty Alumni Program with Michelle Ramos, my colleague at California State University, Fullerton, and I thank her for many years of encouragement and camaraderie.

The UVA A&S Dean's Office, the Institute for the Humanities and Global Culture, and the Americas Center provided invaluable financial support for the Latina/o Studies Association (LSA) Conference in Washington DC in July 2018. The conversations I had there, along with those at other LSA conferences in Pasadena, CA, and Chicago, IL, are weaved into this book. Keisha John, Brie Gertler, Alison Levine, and Christian McMillen in the Dean's Office have likewise offered material and other support that facilitated the completion of this manuscript. I also thank our Dean of the College and Graduate School, Ian Baucom. In addition to the many years of advocacy for Latinx studies by faculty in the American Studies program and UVA students, it is because of Ian that scholarship on the Latinx experience has found a permanent institutional place at UVA. UVA's Greater Caribbean Studies Network and the Carter G. Woodson Institute for African-American and African Studies have provided network opportunities and intellectual exchanges through their support of faculty lunches, bringing scholars to Grounds, and theme-focused symposia, for which I thank in particular Alison Bigelow, Njelle Hamilton, Anne-Garland Mahler, Deborah E. McDowell, and Charlotte Rogers.

Also at UVA I thank Anna Brickhouse, Jennifer Greeson, Sylvia Chong, Steve Arata, and John O'Brien for their leadership of the American Studies Department and the English Department, both of which supported this project. Anna Brickhouse also generously read through the manuscript and provided invaluable editorial suggestions, as well as mentorship. This book could not have come to fruition without her support, much of which is invisible in nature. Indeed, she is one of the primary reasons that Latinx Studies exists at UVA. Marlene Daut generously read through Chapter 5 and provided much-appreciated mentorship and laughter. Her brilliant scholarship is always an inspiration. Camilla Fojas has provided insight into the workings of university life, for which I am deeply grateful. I also thank the amazing scholars of the C'Ville Coffee Pomodoro Writing Group: Anna Brickhouse, Geeta Patel, Janet Horne, and Penny Von Eschel. Meeting with you multiple times a week kept the project on track. Lisa Goff and I met every two weeks to ensure we were moving forward in our respective writing projects. Our accountability to one another and her encouragement made the completion of this work possible. I also thank Tamika Carey, Lisa Woolfork, and David Vander Meulen. Their hallway conversations and mentorship have been invaluable. Not least, I thank my students at UVA: Alex Cintrón, Natalia Heguaburo, Kayla Dunn, Brian Zuluaga, George Villacis, Gabriela Mendoza, Angie Aramayo, Hector Quijano, and Asha Chadla. Your support, courage, and activism are constant sources of inspiration.

Colleagues and friends from across the country have supported my scholarship in a variety of ways, among them Rita Barnard, JoAnne Dubil, Greg Urban, Jean-Michel Rabaté, Ignacio Javier López, Henry Schwarz, and Roderick M. Hills (for his love of Emerson's writings). I thank Lisa Jarvinen for her friendship and for introducing me to Brother Miguel A. Campos FSC during my time at La Salle University. Brother Miguel gifted two boxes of his books that are the foundation of the chapter on Félix Varela. That chapter is dedicated to him. I also thank Thomas Keagy for his support.

Colleagues in the field of Latinx Studies have been interlocutors as we presented our work, organized and participated in the Latina/o Studies Association, marched together for social justice, and collaborated to advance the study of Latina/o history and experience in the academy. I thank John Alba Cutler, Jesse Alemán, Frances Aparicio, José Aranda, William Arce, Raúl Coronado, Lee Bebout, Lori Celaya, Jennifer Hartford Vargas, Ylce Irizarry, Albert Laguna, Laura Lomas, Marissa López, Tony López, Elena Machado Sáez, John Morán González, José Navarro, Randy Ontiveros, William Orchard, Yolanda Padilla, Mérida Rúa, Antonio Saborit, Kirsten Silva Gruesz, Lourdes Torres, Silvio Torres-Saillant, Alberto Varón, and Maria Windell. Other colleagues who have been a source of inspiration and encouragement are Iván Acosta, Sharada Balachandran Orihuela, Daylet Domínguez, Kenya Dworkin, Erica Edwards. Maia Gil'Adí, William (Billy) González, José Gurpegui Palacios, Lauren Frances Guerra, Laura Halperin, Olga Herrera, Jesse Hoffnung-Garskof, Renee Hudson, Jenny L. Kelly, Marisol Legrón, Lázaro Lima, Agnes Lugo-Ortiz, Lucas Marchante, Manuel Martín-Rodríguez, Marisel Moreno, Ricardo Ortiz, Guillermo de los Reyes, Israel Reyes, Ralph Rodríguez, Marion Rohrleitner, Deborah Shapple, Ivonne del Valle, Deb Vargas, and David Vázquez.

I thank Rodrigo Lazo for his important scholarship. His works paved the way for my own writings. Nicolás Kanellos founded the Recovering the US Hispanic Literary Heritage Project. He has dedicated his life to archiving Latina/o writings and created an important intellectual hub for all scholars working on the Latino Nineteenth Century. The imprint of his many years of dedication is on this volume. I thank Nicolás, Gabriela Baeza Ventura, and Carolina Villareal for organizing the biennial Recovering the US Hispanic Literary Heritage Conference, an event I consider my intellectual home.

I thank Gordon Hutner for his dedication to American literary scholarship and for sharing his editorial experience with me. He took an interest in this project and ensured its publication, providing invaluable advice throughout the process. At OUP I thank Katie Bishop for guiding this project through the many complex stages of review and production at the Press. Deva Thomas was an exemplary project manager, and Donald Watts an expert copyeditor. I also thank the anonymous reviewers of the manuscript, whose feedback has truly made this a better book.

Patricia Gherovici, Kristina Arriaga, Mirta Ojito, and Laura Middlebrooks have supported this project in many ways. I recall when Patricia kindly asked me to read the early drafts of *The Puerto Rican Syndrome*. This gesture gave me the confidence to pursue this career path. Her professionalism, productivity, and compassion have always been an inspiration. Kristina has fought endlessly for women's rights across the globe. Her kindness when we lived in DC and then her intellectual support throughout the years will always be with me. Mirta is one of those women who sets the world on fire with her amazing journalism and keen sense of the human experience. Her dedication to social justice is exemplary. Laura has known me since graduate school. Her insightfulness, loyalty, and deep spirituality are without measure. *Mis amigas, no saben cuánto las aprecio*. These four brilliant women are a reminder daily that we can change the world.

Alison Sparks and Ilán Stavans have been dear friends through the years. I also thank my much-loved friends, Amy and Mike Miller, and my oldest friends Young-Ju and James Kim. They have nourished me with their kindness and thoughtfulness. My kindred spirits at La Colombe also had a part in this volume: Gus Laessing, Angie Chung, and the guru of Rittenhouse Square, Donald Goodis.

I thank my parents Manuel and Elba Lamas and my sisters María Lamas and Elva López. I appreciate the many sacrifices they made to support my professional aspirations. Though my mother's beautiful smile is no longer with us, it is forever imprinted on my heart. I also thank my aunt, María Fasco, whose unwavering affection has supported me through the years.

I thank my partner John Nemec. He kindly read through every part of this manuscript multiple times and offered invaluable support. AJ has been patient, supportive, and kind. I missed quite a few summers with them due to my many hours at the library and my research travel. Whenever I expressed my guilt about not being available, they hugged and encouraged me. This book was written for the two of you.

{ CONTENTS }

Introduction

THE LATINO CONTINUUM

In May of 1892, the Cuban exile Nestor Ponce de León (1837–99) delivered a lecture titled "Los primeros poetas de Cuba" (1892, 385) (The First Cuban Poets) at a meeting of the Sociedad de Literatura Hispano-Americana in New York City. Despite the name of the society and the ostensible focus of Ponce de León's talk, this meeting was not simply a gathering of friends and visiting authors from Latin America who found themselves in the vicinity of New York and who happened to love Cuban literature and the wider culture of belle lettres in the Americas. Ponce de León was surrounded by fellow exiles planning revolution. In the audience sat one of the founders and a former president of the Sociedad, José Martí (1853–95), who had stepped down from leading the New York literary society in order to organize the Partido Revolucionario Cubano. As was so often the case among nineteenth-century Latina/o intellectuals (and their Latin American counterparts), literary and political practices were mutually informing and hard to separate into neat categories of their own.

Ponce de León's lecture opened with a discussion of the epic poem *Espejo de paciencia*, then and now considered the first major literary achievement in Cuba. But his purpose was not to elucidate or praise the poem, as today's readers might surmise; rather, he sought to inspire those present to join the Cuban independence movement. For in citing the poem, and relating its history, Ponce de León was in fact inextricably tying Cuba to New York and vice versa, the history of the poem's transcription and transmission paralleling the life experiences of the many exiles present in the room. Discussing the piece did more than remind those gathered that Cubans deserved an independent nation, as evidenced by its long literary tradition; it also tied the people in the room to the political group that discovered the piece in the 1830s in Havana, Cuba, to begin with—a dissenting

The Latino Continuum and the Nineteenth-Century Americas: Literature, Translation, and Historiography.
Carmen E. Lamas, Oxford University Press (2021). © Carmen E. Lamas. DOI: 10.1093/oso/9780198871484.003.0001

faction that had seen their filibustering attempts foiled by the Spanish authorities as well as the US government. While the early nineteenth-century filibusterers had failed in liberating Cuba, those men of letters who had gathered in New York to hear about the poem now had the opportunity to finish their work. It was their moment to write literary and political history, and this time they would free the island to which the poem belonged. Fittingly, this New York event, the poem referenced, the scholar who discussed it, those who heard the lecture, and finally the text's contested transcription and transmission histories collectively represent the phenomenon described in this book: the Latino Continuum.

The poem, which supposedly dates from 1608, was originally authored by Silvestre de Balboa Troya Quesada, a native of the Canary Islands who arrived in Cuba in the late sixteenth century and remained there until his death in 1647. Written in *octavas reales* that depict a group of Cubans fighting off a French pirate attack, the early modern poem had been lost to literary history for centuries until— as Ponce de León explained to his New York audience—it was willed to him by José Antonio Echeverría (1815–85), a Cuban reformer who had recently died in exile in New York without seeing his homeland again. Echeverría had discovered the poem in the library of the Sociedad Económica Amigos del País, the leading scientific, commercial, and cultural institution in Cuba at the time. It was transcribed into the work *Historia de la isla y catedral de Cuba*, handwritten by Bishop Pedro Agustín Morell de Santa Cruz (1694–1768) in the 1760s. Echeverría, finding the *Historia* in a deteriorated state, had transcribed it fully in his own hand and, when subsequently fleeing the colonial authorities, had brought this transcription of a transcription with him to New York, saving it for posterity, and willing the priceless treasure to Ponce de León for safekeeping—until it could be returned to a Cuba freed from Spanish rule. This is how Ponce de León found himself in front of his fellow exiles piecing together Cuba's literary heritage as a means of planning the upcoming war of independence, literally building the nation from abroad, as Cubans and Latin Americans alike had done since the early 1800s.

Ponce de León's lecture in fact simultaneously retells and expands an article written by Echeverría in 1838, which was originally part of a series titled "Los historiadores de Cuba," and in which he narrated the details of the discovery and the contents of the poem, which included a prologue dedicated to the seventeenth-century readers of the poem, a *carta-dedicatoria* to Bishop Juan de las Cabezas Altamirano, six sonnets by local townspeople praising Balboa's literary enterprise, and the actual epic poem. Citing Echeverría, Ponce de León in his New York lecture described how the poem narrates the kidnapping of Bishop Juan de las Cabezas Altamirano by French pirates, the paying of his ransom by the townspeople, and the bishop's subsequent release after the leading French corsair villain is violently defeated, indeed decapitated, by the heroic and enslaved Salvador Golomón. In creating a centuries-old Cuban history in and for the 1830s, Echeverría's article spoke directly to the budding nationalism then occurring in Cuba—just as, almost sixty years later, Ponce de León sought to reanimate that same early modern Cuban history for his own revolutionary moment. Yet neither Echeverría's article nor Ponce de León's lecture in any way addressed the notorious slave uprisings of the 1830s throughout the island. For while many of the *criollo* nationalists believed in ending the slave trade and the institution of slavery on the island, they did not support immediate emancipation in the 1830s and struggled with the role of Afro Cubans in the future Republic. Afro Cubans, perhaps not surprisingly, were absent from both Echeverría's and Ponce de León's respective narratives—even though *Espejo de paciencia*, the poem through which they sought to kindle a flame of independence, so prominently featured a "negro valiente," Salvador Golomón, as its epic hero.

While they are absent by design from the article and the lecture, Afro Cubans, enslaved and free, were active participants in all of the separatist movements of the nineteenth century. They sought political change for the island and individual and collective freedom through the means available to them—escaping into the mountains, burning sugar cane fields, and fomenting outright rebellion. Plácido, the martyred poet, composed poetry;[1] Manzano, who wrote the only known Spanish American slave narrative, told his story.[2] The political actions of both of these groups, *criollo* nationalists and Afro Cubans alike—as well as the disavowal by the former of the latter—are obliquely but indelibly memorialized in the article and at the lecture. For neither of these literary-historiographic texts could fully erase the true epic hero of the poem, Salvador Golomón, an enslaved African *criollo* born on the island who kills the leader of the pirates. Though Golomón is marginally addressed in the article and the lecture, neither Echeverría nor Ponce de León pays tribute to his foundational role in Cuba's first historical-literary enterprise.[3] This, too, constitutes an element integral to the phenomenon of the Latino Continuum that is explored in the pages that follow: the disavowal of Afro Cuban political action in the nineteenth century—and all too often in our own.

*   *   *

We tend to think of a continuum as a smooth progression from one end to the other, an arc or line without disruptions, bumps, and breaks. Yet the etymological resonances of the term provide a much richer set of connotations. In a technical sense, a continuum is a sequence or collection of discrete, yet related things; according to a standard dictionary definition, a continuum is "a coherent whole characterized as a collection, sequence, or progression of values or elements varying by minute degrees." A continuum, in other words, has a lot in common with an archive, a coherent and intentional, yet somewhat haphazard whole consisting of documents, records, books, and other objects that are highly varied in their collectivity, yet unique in their material instantiations.

As a simultaneously historical and imaginative archival assemblage, the Latino Continuum is vast in its reach across the centuries, and inexhaustible in the possible sequences of meaning it can afford those who take up its invitation to study. The term continuum in relation to *latinidad* has appeared in Latinx studies. For example, Frederick Aldama (2013) speaks of "a continuum of literary production" when he refers to how such writers as Gary Soto, Rolando Hinojosa-Smith, and Jimmy Santiago Baca began writing in the 1960s and 1970s and continue to publish to the present day. He believes that, in this extended literary production, these authors are "transgressing period[s] bound by historical dates and offering instead a continuum of Latina/o literary production" (91). Ramón A. Gutiérrez (2012) similarly speaks of placing Latino male sexuality on a continuum. In addition, Wendy Roth (2012) refers to a continuum in relation to how concepts of race are redefined when the contemporary migration of Puerto Ricans and Dominicans to New York City is studied.

I propose a different deployment of the term, however, in that I speak of a continuum that is constituted and comes about simultaneously in and beyond space and time, suggesting that Latina/os, their lives, and their texts, represent a sort of identity that is not entirely

Latin American and not entirely US American. Nor is it merely transnational, which is ultimately still tied to the geographic/spatial; rather, it is a sort of identity that simultaneously occupies multiple spatialities while inhabiting and crossing diverse temporal moments. It had, to be sure, a significant hand in shaping *latinidad* in the nineteenth century and up to the present day. I first made this argument in "Raimundo Cabrera, the Latin American Archive and the Latino Continuum" [2016].[4]

Yet this intersection of geographic, political, linguistic, cultural, and temporal juxtapositions remains largely unexamined, despite the valiant efforts of a small body of specialists who have dedicated their careers to early Latina/o literary recovery over the last twenty-five years, since the inauguration of the Recovering the US Hispanic Literary Heritage Project in 1992. It also remains largely undertheorized—despite groundbreaking interventions on this front by such scholars as Kirsten Silva Gruesz, who links Latina/o writing to transnational and hemispheric studies. Her book *Ambassadors of Culture: The Transamerican Origins of Latino Writing* (2002) argues for the recognition and theorization of the network of trans-American texts and lives that are part of Latina/o literary production in the nineteenth century. Proposing the concept of an enlarged America, she contends that scholars of American literature must take into account the impact of Latina/os and their Latin American experiences on US nation-building when writing about nineteenth-century US literature. In a similar vein, Anna Brickhouse in *Transamerican Literary Relations and the Nineteenth-Century Public Sphere* (2004) addresses the inextricable ties between US, Caribbean (Anglophone, Hispanophone, *and* Francophone), Latin American, and Latina/o literature. Moving beyond the recognition of Latina/o writing as integral to US literature, Brickhouse demonstrates how the trans-American nature of Latina/o works was integral to the development of a public sphere in the United States.

Engaging the US literary tradition while showing its narrative dependence on Latina/o literary production, John Morán González in *The Troubled Union: Expansionist Imperatives in Post-Reconstruction American Novels* (2010) concentrates on US expansionism from the Civil War to Reconstruction, placing such Latina/o works as María Amparo Ruiz de Burton's *The Squatter and the Don* (1885) in critical dialogue with Henry James and Helen Hunt Jackson. Meanwhile, David Luis-Brown proposes a link between sentimentalism, primitivism, and ethnography in such Latina/o writers as María Amparo Ruiz de Burton in *Waves of Decolonization: Discourses of Race and Hemispheric Citizenship in Cuba, Mexico and the United States* (2007). Comparing the political writings of such figures as José Martí, W. E. Du Bois, and Teresa Urrea (the Santa de Cabora), he explores romantic racialism, sentimentalist discourse, empire, and black agency in these works. Jesse Alemán and Shelley Streeby (2007) focus on popular fictions written by such US authors as Ned Buntline, George Lippard, and Mary Andrews Denison. They demonstrate that the use of the term "antebellum" as well as the general acceptance that the origin of US empire begins in 1898 with the Spanish American War is challenged when US popular writing of the nineteenth century is taken into account, and, thereby, they highlight the need to rethink US literary periodization as one that disavows the wars against indigenous peoples and against Mexico.[5] In *The Literatures of the US-Mexican War: Narrative, Time, and Identity* (2010), Jaime Javier Rodríguez concentrates on dime novels, novelettes, poems, and other genres to recover writings about the US-Mexico War of 1846–48. Including Mexican, Mexican American, and canonical works from the United States, Rodríguez argues that these writings provide insight into contemporary issues and concerns.

Scholarly engagement with nineteenth-century *latinidad* that concentrates more finely on Latina/o texts exclusively occurs in *When We Arrive: A New Literary History of Mexican America* (2003). Here, José F. Aranda traces a history of Mexican American literary production (from the nineteenth century to the Chicano movement) in order to demonstrate its importance for the development of US literature, advocating the need for comparative study. Another work that recovers the literature of Chicana/os in the nineteenth century is *The Emergence of Mexican America: Recovering the Stories of Mexican Peoplehood in U.S. Culture* (2006) by John-Michael Rivera. Chapters on Lorenzo de Zavala, María Amparo Ruiz de Burton, and Antonio Otero, Jr., speak to malleable cultural narratives that construct Mexican Americans as a people. Likewise concentrating on one national-origin group, Rodrigo Lazo in *Writing to Cuba: Filibustering and Cuban Exiles in the United States* (2005) links a burgeoning Cuban nationalism in the US with the rise of US imperialism. His focus on the Cuban exile community in New York and its print culture in the antebellum US through the figure of the nineteenth-century *filibustero* continues to be a methodological primer for contemporary scholars who study "The Latino Nineteenth Century," a term coined by Rodrigo Lazo and Jesse Alemán for their 2016 landmark edited volume of the same title.

Concentrating on Chicana/o works in order to theorize the hemispheric impact of Chicana/o writing, Marissa K. López in *Chicano Nation: The Hemispheric Origins of Mexican American Literature* (2011, 12) proposes the concept of a transamerica, one that expands the geographic and genealogical scope of Chicana/o literature.[6] Beginning with a discussion of the travel writings of Domingo Sarmiento (Argentina), Lorenzo de Zavala (Mexico), and Vicente Pérez Rosales (Chile), López rereads Mariano Guadalupe Vallejo's five-volume late nineteenth-century *Recuerdos históricos y personales tocantes a la Alta California*...(1875) in order to place it in an international network of textual relations. Another important intervention is Raúl Coronado's *A World Not to Come: A History of Latino Writing and Print Culture* (2013). In this field-shifting work, Coronado explores how the conflict between Protestant and Catholic worldviews impacted Texas Mexicans before and after the US-Mexico War and produced a new social imaginary that must be taken into account to understand Latina/o and US writing in the nineteenth century and up to the present moment. Most recently, Alberto Varon's *Before Chicano: Citizenship and the Making of Mexican American Manhood, 1848–1959* (2018) links the long-standing presence of Mexicans and Chicanos in the US to "the emergence of a national category now identifiable as Latino" (3).

Finally, when thinking about a Latino Continuum and its constitution in the nineteenth century, the landmark volume *The Latino Nineteenth Century* (2016) edited by Lazo and Alemán has served as an inspiration for the different stages of this work, especially in its forceful argument against "the logic and practice of an English-only approach to American literary history" (viii). As I will show, the Latino Continuum decenters the notion of US American or Latin American literature as leading referents by conceiving instead of Latina/o literature as the original point of reference for the emergence of a new history and literary practice, since it is the experience of Latina/os and the manner in which they brought this experience to bear in their lives and/or in the texts they produced that created and continues to create a new historiography, through time and space, that moves beyond that of the Western hemisphere.

The Latino Continuum excavated here is indeed largely archived in Spanish, and it addresses a range of concerns palpably felt within (and integral to) the United States and beyond. At the same time, however, English-language works also find a place on this continuum and in some cases turn out to have real implications for political and cultural life beyond the US, while Spanish-language works in some cases address concerns of hispanophone *and* anglophone communities in the United States. Moreover, the central role of translation practices continually speaks to the global *and* the local nature of the continuum. For the Latino Continuum embeds layered and complex political and literary contexts and overlooked histories, situated as it is at the crossroads of both hemispheric and transatlantic currents of exchange that are often effaced by the logic of borders—national, cultural, religious, linguistic, and temporal. To recover this continuum of *latinidad*, which is neither confined to the US or Latin American nation states nor located primarily within them, is also to recover forgotten histories of the hemisphere, and to find new ways of seeing the past as we have understood it.

As such, the writings explored in this study have been largely lost to both US and Latin American literary history because they are located in the intersections between archives or, more properly, between our methods for working within them. US literary history has ignored these writings because they are either written in Spanish or written by figures perceived to be "Latin American." As Alemán writes in the preface to *The Latino Nineteenth Century*, Latina/o literature "is not the same as the one emerging from New England. Rather it displaces the center of American literary history across the US, from Florida to Philadelphia, New York to New Mexico, and Texas to California. It also dispossesses American literature from the US, traversing Mexico, Cuba, Argentina, Chile and Guatemala" (viii). Simultaneously, Latin American literary history has ignored nineteenth-century Latina/o works because they are often produced within and sometimes largely about the US. In the introduction to *The Latino Nineteenth Century* Lazo reminds readers that one of the goals of Latina/o historical scholarship is to show how nineteenth-century concerns are "in dialogue with contemporary concerns of Latino studies and respond to the limitations of nationalist US literature and regionalist Latin American studies" (3). As an interpretive category and archival mode, the Latino Continuum thus asks us to reconsider the still existing divides between US, Latin American, and Latina/o literatures and histories.

Even more significantly, though, this continuum opens resources for shaping a critical Latina/o historiography—one that recovers not only the individuals who composed or translated the texts in question, but also the actual and potential readers who played powerful roles in different stories of reception. Individually and collectively, the works that comprise this Latina/o historiography have much to say about the manner in which the present and past were narrated in the nineteenth century, and about the nature of historical writing more broadly: how sources are chosen and interpreted, whose voices are privileged, and what futures are imagined or foreclosed. This is so perhaps most visibly with works of translation, which cross not only borders and language communities but also historical moments of publication and reception. In some cases, the works under consideration had a double use in the nineteenth century, as history text-books and language primers designed to teach native Spanish speakers English and native English speakers Spanish. Considered particularly in relation to their original function as historical narratives, such texts comprise part of a powerful and unexamined reception history, one that shows us how both translators and their readers, regardless of national origin or site of reading, become part of a broad Latino Continuum that exceeds the requirements of residency or even physical travel to the actual space of the US and Latin America itself. The travels of these historical texts reveal not only the impact that the US would have on Latin America and the hemisphere and vice versa, but more importantly the impact that Latina/os had on the US and on Latin America. For, as I suggest in the Conclusion, there is always a *Latinx Return*, a phrase that captures both the physical and textual return of authors and their texts and translations to their home countries, and, as was often the case, back again to the US.

The implications of the readings I offer here are relevant for today's historical moment, since a defining feature of the Latino Continuum is the continued impact of Latina/os on US and Latin American culture and politics down to the present day. The implications also reach backward, allowing us to conceive the long centuries after the European invasion of the Americas through the lens of the Latino Continuum—a lens that discerns the entanglement of imperial histories in the Americas rather than their siloed disciplinary unfolding. But the book itself is squarely situated in the nineteenth century and ranges from the Haitian Revolution to the establishment of the Cuban Republic in 1902. Moving in roughly chronological

order, this study takes into account the importance of the early
nineteenth century, when Latin American revolutionaries found
their way to the US in order to advocate for Latin American independence or to flee Spanish colonial despotism. It follows this history to the period after the Spanish American wars of independence
(1820s–1850s), when Latin American statesmen and businessmen
continued to travel to the US to learn firsthand its democratic form
of governance and to establish political and economic relations with
their northern neighbors.[7] The consequences of all of these events
may be traced to their influences upon the present day.

But the Spanish American historical narrative of this book is carefully interwoven with its anglophone, US contemporaneous coun-
terpart. The writers under discussion engage the antebellum period
with its debates regarding the future of the institution of slavery in
the country and its attendant discussion regarding the influx of Irish
and German immigrants. Both this debate and this migration of
populations from Europe to the US played significant roles in establishing urban centers in the Northeast and in US western expansion,
including the participation of immigrant peoples in the US-Mexico
War of 1846–48 and the Civil War. While the most significant numbers of European immigrants arrived on US shores in the 1870s–1890s
and at the beginning of the twentieth century—a matter also
addressed in this work—US immigration was also on the rise in the
1830s–1850s, and along with it came pronounced anti-Catholic sentiments, made evident by the establishment of Nativist parties and by
the Protestant-Catholic debates and ensuing violence of the era.
These debates spoke directly to the impact that immigrants had on
US national life, as well as the place of Latina/os, many of them
Catholic, in the body politic. And all of this occurred concurrently
with the Carlist Wars in Spain and their simultaneous impact on the
remaining Spanish colonies, including Cuba, Puerto Rico, Guam,
and the Philippines. The Latino Continuum, I argue, makes it possible to map the intersections of these historical contexts, as well to
recognize, whether implicitly or directly, the effects of the concerns
of the period on contemporary political and cultural life in the
United States and beyond.

But the Latino Continuum is also historically constituted by the
broader contexts of violence against—and genocide of—indigenous
people throughout the Americas, as well as the hemispheric presence of enslaved and previously bonded peoples in the nineteenth

century. While scholars of US and Latin American history and literature have done groundbreaking work on indigenous and African diasporic history, disciplinary boundaries have not allowed for a truly integrated approach. The scholar of Cuban slavery knows little about the unfolding of Apache history in the US Southwest, and vice versa. Yet the framework of the Latino Continuum, which follows the travels of texts, writers, and readers where they take us, insists that multiple histories come together in and through the Latina/o experience in the Americas—histories through which the truly hemispheric and often global concerns and influences of the day may newly be understood.

Consider, for example, the overlapping but very different experiences of Latina/os, Native Americans, and African Americans during the US-Mexico War and the US Civil War. Individuals from these very different groups were key actors on both sides of what would become the US-Mexico border, and on both sides during the War Between the States.

Their disparate histories come to new light, however, when examined within the framework of the Latino Continuum. For the writings of Latina/os during these periods speak directly to the continued disenfranchisement of Native American people in the US, a disenfranchisement effected by way of their removal from their ancestral lands and their forced settlement on reservations, followed by the privatization of their land and the establishment of Native American Boarding Schools and Indian Mission Schools. Latina/os both participated in and wrote about these programs, variously supporting or criticizing them, while they also played a corresponding role regarding the multiple nationalist programs legislated in Latin America to incorporate the *indígena* into the nation by way of such culturally devastating policies as enforced citizenship.

Simultaneously, Latina/o writers spoke to the importance of the black experience in the Americas. As the Ten Years' War (1868–78) raged in Cuba, Afro Cubans fought side by side with *criollos* and US Americans, who also took part in the conflict. During the campaign and after its failure, Afro Cubans fled to the US, ultimately to work in cigar factories, and as personal servants, cooks, and tailors, among other professions. They experienced Reconstruction and Post-Reconstruction firsthand, leaving in writing their perceptions of these historical events on US political history and race relations in particular.

The methodological approach of this book is perhaps best explained with the phrase *archival juxtapositions*. When studying the
lives of nineteenth-century Latina/os and their works, I have followed their biographical and textual footprints to multiple archives—
both physical and, in some cases, imagined by the writers themselves. These archives quickly demanded the crossing of various
disciplinary boundaries. I have found it impossible to enter Latina/o
texts and their authors' lives merely from the position of a literary
scholar trying to understand the form and function of a literary piece
or its place within a genealogy of genre. Likewise, I have found it
limiting to approach straightforwardly as a historian trying to piece
together cause and effect during a specific moment or event in time.
Instead, while working at the crossroads of these disciplines, I have
focused largely on the juxtapositions of texts *and* their multiple temporal moments: not only the moment of an individual writer's lived
or represented experience but also the multiple lives of a particular
work as it travels both physically and conceptually, in translation or
its original language. These accumulating textual lives have served as
guideposts for navigating the histories their authors created and, via
continued readerships, continue to create. As readers will see in the
following pages, Latina/o authors were actively *writing* history,
though not necessarily through the historiographic venues one
might currently imagine. The role of translation, especially, was vital
for imagining alternative histories, which is the subject, in particular,
of Chapter 3.

Across all the chapters, we find Latina/o authors interpellating
their readers (both contemporaneous and future ones) into a broad
project of recognition: of witnessing often little-regarded lives and
experiences, traces of which are found in their creative and non-literary
productions, and in the fragments that make up their biographies. In
short, it is through the project of archival juxtaposition—across the
disciplinary siloes that keep US, Latin American, and Peninsular
historiographic sources separated—that the Latino Continuum
emerges. In the historical interpretation of these sources, and in
drawing the connections that link disparate works of various
genres—novels, textbooks, historical works, opinion pieces and
journal articles, travelogues, and other texts written in Spanish and
English—within the overlapping historical contexts of the US, Latin
America, and Europe, we begin to see how the lived experiences of
the writers in question, and those they represented, bequeath us a

truly intersectional grasp on the historical period, and one that can serve us well in an age of what is still too often oversimplified narratives of "minority" history.

At the same time, while one must squarely situate events and people in the moment in which they lived and wrote, considering along the way the *places* where their work was written, published, and then circulated, the reality is that we cannot but read their works and study their lives *now*. This temporal commonplace is not a challenge to overcome, I argue, but a source of inspiration: one that speaks directly to how the framework of the Latino Continuum can allow for more nuanced and creative interpretive work, work that moves fluidly across time and place, beyond the when and where of the original text, beyond the limited lifespan during which it was written. As I argue, the reader's act of interpretation, as well as their location, is also fundamental to the constitution of the Latino Continuum. For what a scholar writes about a nineteenth-century author whether during or after that author's life, indeed whether immediately after the writer's death or perhaps a century later, also lies on the Latino Continuum: scholarly work too comes to comprise the discontinuous, never smooth progression of *latinidad* in a centuries-long dialogue including the original author of a text, the original author's represented subjects and contemporaneous readers, and present and future readers of the scholar and thereby the original author. As this continuum moves across time and space, it links not only past and present worlds to those future ones we have yet to imagine, but also those "worlds not to come," as Coronado has memorably called them: those histories that might have but did not unfold also bear on the broad historiographic project of the Latino Continuum.

If this approach strikes some as ambiguous or esoteric, we might pause to recall the manner in which national borders functioned in the nineteenth century. The border between what would become the US and what was French America, Spanish America, and then Latin America continually shifted across the nineteenth century with the Louisiana Purchase, the Adams-Onís Treaty, and the Treaty of Guadalupe Hidalgo, to name only a few of many fluctuating territorial demarcations of the period. Simultaneously, though, many indigenous groups and Afro-diasporic groups such as the *cimarrones* did not recognize these borders, before or after they were redrawn, and moved across them at will, defying US, French, Spanish, and

Mexican laws in doing so, often triggering thereby the potential for violent repercussions. Likewise, the texts comprising the Latino Continuum often operated along pathways that official maps do not record. Indeed, whatever their individual politics, when these Latina/o writers authored histories, memoirs, and literary texts that spoke to their experiences in and outside the US, their works entered subterranean networks of resistance that are not always recognizable when approached through well-established disciplinary lenses. As I hope this book will show, the porosity of borders—both physical and textual—continues to the present day, just as the *histories* of those borders continue to be negotiated, reinterpreted, and—indeed—lived in their consequences. Similarly, the broad practice of reading early Latina/o lives and works both recovers and creates histories that are pertinent to the reality of the lives and communities of Latina/os today, in their many manifestations. For the physical borders take on significance in part by way of their being imagined as borders, and the acts of imagination that can harden borders are ones that draw on memories and texts, fusing the past and the present, reading not only the captured ideas and feelings of historical works into the present, but also present-day emotions into the archives we have of a shared past.

The particular sources that embody the Latino Continuum, as I conceive it here, are housed in archives physically located in the US, Spain, and various countries of Latin America; collectively, they comprise what can be referred to as an *Americas* archive, one whose Latina/o component demands alternative accounts of both the nation and the so-called transnational. For the Latino Continuum— despite the extent to which its individual authors often represent elite perspectives across the nineteenth century—necessarily inter-sects with the history of marginalized communities in and outside the US. The writers studied here intuitively understood this emer-gence of marginalized groups; they self-consciously sought in their work to forge national, hemispheric, and ultimately global change, pressing continually toward what Eusebio Guiteras (1823–93) memo-rably called the "universal sentiment" of human dignity and free-dom. At the same time, this largely lost body of literature collectively subverts some of the generic conventions that shape our understand-ing of the past, pressing against the constraints produced by national ideologies and their attendant literary forms. A writer such as Félix Varela, the subject of Chapter 1, explicitly disavows genre altogether in *Cartas a Elpidio*, a philosophical-religious work, which he produced during a long, lived experience as resident rather than visitor in the US. Yet, as he well understood, this significant political and social intervention would not be recognized by his readers as such, and this important genre-crossing text—it can be read as a travel diary, an instruction manual, and/or a memoir simultaneously—, which so clearly depicts the Latina/o experience in the antebellum period, entered the dustbin of oblivion.

As I conceive it here, the Latino Continuum speaks to the regional as global and vice versa, unfolding along hemispheric and transatlantic axes: encompassing not only legislative procedure in Washington, DC but also the Spanish *Cortes*, engaging not only the Cuban independence movements and the Spanish American revolutions, but the foundational (and in some ways foundationally opposed) US and Haitian ones. The Latino Continuum also refuses the logic of *both* the binary opposition and the bridge between the US and "Latin America," revealing instead their fundamental interdependence, politically, socially, culturally, and aesthetically.

At the same time, this continuum—comprised of the experiences, writings, and translations of and by the individuals I study—continually bears witness to the incomparable histories and lived experiences of its various actors, from the most elite beneficiaries of colonialism to the most dispossessed lives in an ongoing structure of coloniality. If a continuum implies a progression, the Latino Continuum does not make its way *toward* the US, nor does it move toward some essential identificatory quality: toward becoming more Latina/o and less, say, Mexican or Honduran. Instead, the progression of the Latino Continuum is broadly historical, a set of dense imbrications interlocking Latin America and the United States, through flows of people, objects, ideas, and even affect and memories, that grows in intensity across the nineteenth century and into the twentieth-century emergence of "Latino" as an ideological formation, arriving perhaps in the future of (what may well one day be called) our own Latina/o—or Latinx—century.

Here—at the seemingly untroubled slide from Latino to Latinx—a word about nomenclature is in order. Like most scholars of what has recently been called the "Latino nineteenth century," I follow the standard practice of employing the masculine suffix in my title in keeping with the temporal moment under examination in this study. Claudia Milian (2019) referred to the ascendency of the twenty-first century use of the term "LatinX" and its inherent quality as a point of departure: "LatinX plunges into what is currently happening and what may be coming. Its primacy—a present tense based on a quotidianness that reverberates in the future—is simultaneously in conversation with the tension, iteration, and situation that make X possible" (6). Agreeing with Milian, John Alba Cutler also finds a place for the x in Latinx in the nineteenth century:

> The *x* in *Latinx* helpfully indexes the fragmentation and fugitivity of the archive, gesturing toward everything missing and everything we cannot know about the periodicals, the literature, and the writers... *Latinx* thus works both to indicate an archive that was always capacious and transnational and to remind us that important aspects of the archive have become unknowable.
>
>   (John Alba Cutler, personal correspondence,
>   February 19, 2020)

The writers I take up here are, however lamentably, all men—a fact that tells us much about the masculinist framework of the broad revolutionary moment I study. Where applicable, when referring to the wider context that these male writers document in their writing, I use the more inclusive "Latina/o"—though not, for the purposes of this particular study, "Latinx," an indispensable term emerging from a theoretical context that far postdates the period under consideration here. In this sense, the term "Latino" also represents both a historicist concern and an implicit argument, one that recognizes Latino, as Jesse Alemán puts it "not, as some might assume, an anachronism, but a marker of nineteenth-century transnationality" (2016, vii). However, when referring to the academic discipline, I use Latinx studies, this to stress the contemporary and ever evolving nature of the discipline in its necessary (yet still insufficient) inclusion of Central American migration—as well as the important scholarship on Latinx LGBTQ+ literary works and histories that have transformed Latinx studies.[8]

But the stakes in using the term "Latino" go well beyond historicism, particularly in the case of my own study, which centers on a group of nineteenth-century and largely elite writers born in Cuba. Lazo has aptly called these individuals the "trans-American elite" (2020, 72). I concentrate on the lives and works of Cubans in the nineteenth century in part because of the relatively voluminous archives available to scholars today, which hold the particular kinds of sources most relevant to my interests in this study. Indeed, the long-standing presence and participation of Cubans in US social and political life, as well as the presence of US Americans in Cuba since the eighteenth century, led these authors to read the national experience of the island, both directly and indirectly, in light of US history, and in doing so they also addressed, both directly and implicitly, the experiences of other Latin American states, and other Latina/o groups that were negotiating and confronting US expansionism, including *californios*, *tejanos*, *nuevomejicanos*, as well as Central and South Americans. In other words, to apply the term "Latino" to a seemingly coherent group of writers born in Cuba signals a particular intervention of this book, both political and methodological.[9] For it is a term explicitly rejected by a significant portion of the scholarly fields of Cuban and Cuban-American literature—just as the term is also rejected by particular political constituencies defined around Cuban identity and living in the US today—a disavowal silently but powerfully based on race. To be "Cuban" not as a subset of, but rather than, "Latino" is to be, quite often, associated with whiteness, and thereby disassociated from blackness. While I construct the Latino Continuum based on Cuban lives and texts from the nineteenth century, my hope is that scholars of other Latina/o national-origin groups, as well as those in American and Latin American studies, will deploy the methodological approach of the Latino Continuum to further uncover the integrated and mutually imbricated literatures and histories of the Americas, one solidly emerging from the Latina/o experience.

This book's embrace of the term "Latino" thus also signals one of its central aims: to recover, where possible, nineteenth-century Afro Latina/o voices, and to bring new light, where possible, to the female and enslaved historical figures silenced by the archive but glimpsed and sometimes given voice in the body of writing recovered here. The arc of this book thus bends toward what the Afro Cuban Latino writer and political thinker Martín Morúa Delgado envisioned as potentially liberatory futures for the hemisphere. In his words, "la justicia es grande, alcanza para todos; el amor es inmenso, puede colmar el corazón de todos" (*Cuba y América* 1903, 320). (Justice is great, it is available to all; love is immense, it can fill the heart of all.)

* * *

As noted, the book moves more or less chronologically across the long nineteenth century—from 1791 and the outset of the Haitian Revolution to the founding of the Cuban Republic in 1902—and examines the changing roles of translation, historiography, and literature (the novel in particular) in chapters on five nineteenth-century Latina/o writers: Félix Varela, Miguel Teurbe Tolón, Eusebio Guiteras, José Martí, and Martín Morúa Delgado. Chapter 1, "Félix Varela's Hemispheric Interventions," recovers the hemispheric interests and influences of the Catholic priest Félix Varela (1788–1853), who lived nearly thirty years in the United States and was nicknamed the "Father of the Irish" during his lifetime. In doing so, it challenges the fractured reading of Varela's archive in the scholarly literature, where he is normally studied only as an influential Cuban philosopher, his profound influence on American history having passed almost entirely without note. The chapter serves to fill this lacuna by illustrating the manner in which Varela played a key role in the US Protestant-Catholic debates of the 1830s and 1840s and in the secularization of the public school system of New York City, outlining both how these debates facilitated the emergence of minority politics in the United States and, simultaneously, the important role of Latina/os in that emergence. The chapter also illustrates the influence of Varela's US experience on his intervention in Spanish American (and particularly Cuban) social, religious, and political life, paying special attention to his 1826 annotated translation of Thomas Jefferson's *Manual of Parliamentary Practice* (1801). I argue that Varela's rendering of the work, which highlights the ways in which Jefferson's procedures actually threatened the rights of the minority (most notably around the question of abolition and also immigrant rights), exhibits a hemispheric reach and significance precisely because it was intended for Spanish-speaking residents of the US, for citizens of the nascent republics of Spanish America, and also for Cubans living under Spanish colonial rule. Given his dexterity with multiple genres, including his translation practice, his literary, philosophical, religious, and educational texts, and his journalistic contributions, Varela presents an exemplary figure from which to begin to access the concept of the Latino Continuum.

Chapter 2, "Latina/o Translations as Historiography," explores a Spanish-language, Latina/o translation of Emma Willard's then best-selling and now classic antebellum textbook, *Abridged History of the United States* (1830s–1860s). Miguel Teurbe Tolón (1820–57) translated the work into Spanish in 1853, during his residence in New York City. The chapter argues that when his role as the editor of the bilingual annexationist newspaper *La Verdad* (published in New York) is taken into account, classifying his rendering of Emma Willard's textbook as merely a translation meant for the Spanish American market cannot capture its full value or potential effect. For his translation did not so much import the "foreign" culture of the source language or seek to transform that of the target language, but it negotiated a complex historical and political moment, one in which the divisions between such linguistically circumscribed cultures (and the political formations for the most part associable with them) were not only in flux, but were also not so simply distinguishable. It is not merely to translate but to negotiate this complex cultural and political world, both for himself and for his various audiences (in the US, in Cuba, in Spain, and in Spanish America), then, that Tolón's Latina/o rendering did its work: it offered not a transposition of one cultural world to another, but the negotiation of a single, if varied, cultural and political continuum. In a word, it offered a historiography: a study of the intersection of these national histories, of how that intersection was written out of the record, and of how it might be restored.

"Archival Formations and the Universal Sentiment" (Chapter 3) examines the life and writings of Eusebio Guiteras (1823–93), who lived for twenty-five years in Philadelphia. In this chapter, I juxtapose Guiteras's observations about American life and culture, found in his travel diaries of the 1840s–1880s, with a relatively unknown translation by Guiteras of *Rudo Ensayo* (1761–62), a work by the eighteenth-century priest Juan Nentvig (1713–68) that details the evangelization mission of the Jesuits in what is now the American Southwest (after the US-Mexico War of 1846–48), but was then northern New Spain. Contextualizing the production and circulation of the multiple editions of Nentvig's text in the nineteenth century, specifically one by the well-known antiquarian Thomas Buckingham Smith (1810–71), I argue that this Latina/o translation in fact advocates for a constructive place for the Catholic Church in both the US and Cuba. This advocacy, however, must be understood in light of the translation's underlying racial politics. Following his source text and the political designs of the editors of the *Records of the American Catholic Historical Society*, in which the translation was published in 1894, Guiteras simplistically depicts the evangelization of Native Americans in New Spain as a compassionate enterprise led by morally and spiritually dedicated priests. But in his travel diary, *Un invierno en Nueva York* (n.d.), Guiteras in turn transposes this spiritual enterprise to the Cuban context, in which the place of Afro Cubans was being debated in the 1880s and 1890s, both on the island and in the US. In doing so, he envisions Catholic priests and Catholicism as agents for the pacification and assimilation of Afro Cubans in Cuba's future republic while also arguing for a parallel and positive role for the Catholic Church in fashioning a culturally integrated United States. In the face of nativist, anti-Catholic voices in the US, Guiteras proposed a Latina/o religious institution built in large part of racial paternalism.

Chapter 4, "The Black *Lector*: Forging a Radical Revolution" directly addresses race relations in Cuba and the United States by examining the life and works of Martín Morúa Delgado (1856–1910), the son of a first-generation enslaved woman. Morúa lived in Key West and New York in the 1880s. The first black reader, or *lector*, in cigar factories in Havana, Key West, and New York, he labored incessantly for workers' rights on both sides of the Florida Straits. I argue that Morúa's novels, *Sofía* (1891) and *La familia Unzúazu* (1901), and his translation into Spanish of James Redpath's 1863 rendition of John R. Beard's *The Life of Toussaint L'Ouverture: The Negro Patriot of Hayti* (1853) reveal a concern not simply for black Cubans on the island but for Afro Latina/os and African Americans then living in the United States under the violence of post-Reconstruction racism.

I juxtapose Morúa's rendition with José Martí's 1887 translation of Helen Hunt Jackson's *Ramona* (1884). *Ramona* speaks specifically to US expansionism and its effect on Native American populations, but it does not directly address Cuba's pertinent question at the time— the possible role of black Cubans in the wars of independence and in the future republic—since the indigenous population had been made extinct in Cuba through conquest, disease, slavery, and colonization in the sixteenth century. It also did not address the violence experienced by African Americans in the North and in the Jim Crow South. This chapter questions the significance of each author's translation choice and the importance of the same for articulating their respective understandings of race relations in Cuba, the US, and the hemisphere more broadly. Juxtaposing Morúa and Martí in this way reveals how two key figures in the Cuban independence movement simultaneously unite and collide on the Latino Continuum.

Chapter 5, "Morúa's Continuum: Redeeming the Americas," extends the study of Chapter 4 by providing a close analysis of Morúa's translation of James Redpath's rendition of Beard's 1853 biography of L'Ouverture. Morúa completed this translation in New York City in 1883 and subsequently titled it *Biografía del Libertador Toussaint L'Ouverture por John Beard. Vida de Toussaint L'Ouverture (Autobiografía)* (Morúa 1957, 1–2), publishing it in Havana in 1892 in his Cuban edition of *La Nueva Era*. Read alongside Morúa's journalistic contributions of the 1880s and 1890s (both in the US and Cuba), these texts allow us further to understand the reasons Morúa disagreed with José Martí's approach to Cuban independence. They also bring to light Morúa's long-term belief that only full racial integration would bring true political, economic, and social equality to Cuba and to the Americas more broadly, including the US. Indeed, Morúa believed not only that a leader modelled on the likes of Toussaint L'Ouverture could serve to protect the Americas from the voracious cultural, social, economic, political, and ideological expansionism of the US, but that the black experience in the Americas could serve as a cultural and political model for the US itself—one that could redeem the US from its own racist origins, made conclusively evident in Morúa's time by a system that codified in law a "separate but equal" policy of segregationism.

The book's conclusion, "The Latinx Return," turns briefly to Raimundo Cabrera's (1852–1923) periodical *Cuba y América*, which he founded in New York (1897–98) and then continued to publish from Havana (1899–1917) upon his return to the island. Like Varela, Cabrera wrote extensively about Cuba and did so across multiple genres; but unlike Varela or other writers explored in this study who lived for extended periods of time in the US, Cabrera spent less than two years in the United States. I argue for classifying him as a Latina/o nonetheless by questioning both the concept of "exile" and the notion that a specified minimum time in the US is necessary for a figure to be categorized as a Latina/o. Simultaneously, in Cabrera's recovery of writings by New York Cubans in his Havana edition of *Cuba y América* (1899–1917), he incorporates Latina/os into the new Republican Cuba instead of leaving them on the US side of the political border. To put it differently, while he physically returns to Cuba, in his publication of these writers—many of whom remained in the US—he extends his and their US experiences into Cuba.

This act of return, I conclude, adds a new dimension to our understanding of the Latinx experience, which has historically been depicted as a one-way migration to the US or as a one-sided border crossing the Southwest and California. Instead, I argue that the Latinx return is integral to that original experience, challenging scholars to include these comings and goings in any theorization of the Latinx experience (past, present, and future) and its concomitant impact on American, Latin American, and hemispheric literature and history more broadly. In other words, I argue that we must recognize how the multidirectional movement of peoples, in its many manifestations across borders (geographic, temporal, ideological, aesthetic), constitutes, emerges, and lies on the Latino Continuum.

Félix Varela's Hemispheric Interventions

The Cuban Catholic priest Father Félix Varela (1788–1853) lived, worked, and wrote prolifically in New York City for almost thirty years. Scholars of Cuban and Latin American history have studied him as one of the earliest proponents of Cuban independence, while scholars of early Latina/o literature know him primarily for his supposed authorship of the novel *Jicoténcal*, a novel about the sixteenth-century Spanish conquest of Mexico that is also the earliest known historical novel written in Spanish in the Americas, published in Philadelphia in 1826. But a deeper reading of Varela's *oeuvre* reveals more distinctly contemporaneous and US-focused political concerns, revealing the priest and historical novelist as an early theorist of Latina/o political activism who worked tirelessly on behalf of an identifiable and organized minority in the United States from the 1820s to the 1840s. During these years Varela and other Latina/os in New York City were embroiled in the Protestant-Catholic debates that were inflaming the city—a fraught and ultimately violent context that converted Varela and his Latina/o community from their status as exiles, primarily concerned with the political fates of lost homelands, into distinctly US political agents who confronted the anti-immigrant factions threatening the city. To recover this history requires going beyond the literary narrative that celebrates the "first-ness"[1] of his novel and engaging the deeper intellectual contexts of his religious-ethical work *Cartas a Elpidio* (1835, 1838). This recovery marks Varela as far more even than an influential figure in US Catholicism, though he was certainly that, but instead as an intellectual activist working at the crossroads of religious and political philosophy, and engaged in interventions at both the US national and hemispheric levels.[2]

What unfolds from reading across Varela's writings, and in particular his US archive, is a Latina/o intervention into US history,

The Latino Continuum and the Nineteenth-Century Americas: Literature, Translation, and Historiography.
Carmen E. Lamas, Oxford University Press (2021). © Carmen E. Lamas. DOI: 10.1093/oso/9780198871484.003.0002

centered on the rise of minority politics in the United States. At the same time, however, one also witnesses Varela's concerted attempts to influence Latin American and particularly Cuban political and social life *on the basis of his experiences in the United States*. Nowhere is this more evident than in Varela's (1826) annotated translation of Thomas Jefferson's (1801) *Manual of Parliamentary Practice*, examined closely in the final section of this chapter. And yet, even this intervention exhibits a hemispheric reach and significance, as the translation was intended not just for Spanish-speaking residents of the United States, but also for readers in the nascent Spanish American republics of Latin America as well as in colonial Cuba.

A deeper examination of Varela's US archive and wider body of writings, then, fundamentally challenges scholars to rethink the still existing divides between American, Latinx, and Latin American studies—a challenge that lies at the heart of this book. To take up this challenge requires locating Varela, like the other authors explored in this study, on a still-emergent Latino Continuum—an archival and theoretical framework that reveals these early Latina/o writers as cultural actors shaping the very foundation of US history and interacting with the US body politic, while also engaging broader ideas in Latin American political and cultural life.

Varela's Life and Works

Born in Havana, Cuba, in 1788, Félix Varela was raised in colonial St. Augustine, Florida, which remained under Spanish rule until 1819. At the age of thirteen, he returned to Havana, choosing a religious career instead of a military one because "he wished not to kill men but to save their souls."[3] He taught at the Seminario de San Carlos, where he held the chair of philosophy. In 1822 he traveled to Spain as a Cuban representative to the Cortes, but had to flee the following year once Ferdinand VII re-established monarchical rule, disbanded the legislature, and exiled his opposition. Varela fled to the United States in 1823, where he lived first in Philadelphia for a year, before moving to New York, where he lived for the next twenty-five years. In 1850, in declining health, he retired permanently to St. Augustine, the city of his childhood, now no longer a colonial Spanish northern outpost but a part of a new US State of Florida, admitted to the Union in 1845.

In this vastly changed political space Varela resided until his death in 1853.

Varela's interest in philosophy began early in his life. During his youth in Cuba, Varela wrote philosophical texts that defended the New Science emerging from Europe. While he did not reject scholasticism outright—he was an ardent reader of Thomas Aquinas—he advocated for induction in scientific inquiry and the use of the Cartesian method.[4] The first to teach in Spanish instead of Latin at the university level in Cuba, Varela considered himself a modernizer. After arriving in the United States, he wrote in both Spanish and English, and quickly set to work translating Thomas Jefferson's *Manual of Parliamentary Practice* into Spanish in 1826. In these early years, he also published *El Habanero* (1824–26), a political newspaper he founded in Philadelphia that espoused independence for Cuba and cautioned against US intervention in Latin American affairs. Varela questioned Spanish American interference in Cuban affairs as well, and for this reason he has often been considered to be the first advocate for Cuba's political independence.[5] He also published US editions of his earlier philosophical writings, *Lecciones de filosofía* (*Philosophical Lessons*) and *Miscelánea filosófica* (*Philosophical Miscellanea*), which were originally published in Havana in 1818 and 1819, and then in New York in 1827. Finally, he co-edited *El Mensajero Semanal* (1829–31), a weekly that addressed literary, political, and scientific topics, with his student José Antonio Saco.[6]

To understand the significance of Varela for New York City and for Latina/o literary history more broadly, we must be aware of his surprisingly large corpus in English. For example, a portion of his extant writings are preserved in English in US Catholic newspapers and magazines of the era, periodicals that in many instances he founded and edited himself, all in New York. He edited and published many dozens of articles in the *Catholic Expositor and Literary Magazine* (1841–44) and *The Protestant Abridger and Annotator* (1830), which he founded and edited in response to the publication of *The Protestant*, an anti-Catholic weekly in New York City, and its arguments against Catholicism. Similarly, he published articles in the *Truth Teller* (1825–55), a Catholic newspaper in New York that responded to the accusations of popery published in *The Protestant*. He published and contributed to the first bilingual magazine in New

York: *El Amigo de la Juventud/The Youth's Friend* (1825), a children's magazine. And he was the founder and editor of the *New York Weekly Register and Catholic Diary* (1834–35) and the *New York Catholic Register* (1839–40). The latter was absorbed by the *New York Freeman's Journal*, which ran until 1918. This newspaper became *the* voice of Archbishop John Hughes in his successful fight against the New York Public School Society, which ultimately led to the removal of religious teaching from the public-school curriculum in New York City.[7]

Varela was a critical early figure in these debates. In fact, he had started the *Catholic Register* in order to keep Archbishop Hughes apprised of the status of the public-school debate while the latter travelled to Europe. During Hughes's absence, Varela asked the Public School Society to bring all of their textbooks to him, so he could highlight the parts that misrepresented Catholics or Catholicism. His evaluative readings required the society to edit the books in order to make education more inclusive. According to his US biographers, Joseph and Helen McCadden, Varela, like the editors of the *Truth Teller*, wished for religion to be taught in schools, but he opposed the demonization of Catholics. In a dramatic moment in the history of religion in the US, Varela's early advocacy led to the end of the use of the King James Bible as a text in the public schools (McCadden and McCadden 1969, 106–7). And yet, although he and the other editors sought to collaborate with the Public School Society, General Vicar John Powers and Archbishop John Hughes intervened to excise religion from public schools altogether while obtaining access to state funds for Catholic education. The latter but not necessarily the former was a position Varela also advocated. The cumulative effect of this debate contributed to the secularization of the US public-school system.[8]

Varela was prolific on the role of religion in the US, in other words, and his writings were key to US Catholic history. Why, then, have so few US historians heard of or written about him? The answer lies in how scholars approach the archive, and in the extent to which assumptions about transnational figures shape scholarly interest. The transnational, multilingual approach to archival research that has characterized Latinx studies scholarship can bring to nineteenth-century American, Latin American, and Caribbean studies key historical and literary contexts that have long been overlooked. The "archive" that constitutes the Latino Continuum embraces the disparate physical archives found throughout the United States, in Spain, and in Latin American countries and especially Cuba (in this case), which house texts that are usually thought to be field- and nation-specific, due to the languages in which they are written and/or the nationalities of their authors or publishers. For example, while a Cuban author's work might be housed in a US location—Yale University, the Cuban Heritage Collection at the University of Miami, or the New York Public Library—that author and his work regularly figure only in Cuban or Caribbean historical narratives. Recovering that same figure in the broader, multilingual contexts of the author's readers, lived experience, political action, and travels often reveals layers of history that call into question some of our most basic assumptions about key developments in history and literature: from the origins of secularization to the rise of minority political identities.

The archive, in the broadest sense, also includes the historiographical sources that have been written by area studies scholars invested in national formations. These sources are built around academic fields and disciplines such as American studies or Latin American and Latinx studies. Such secondary works create their own historical record—that is, they may be read themselves as primary sources that illustrate the views of their authors and record the trends and biases in their respective historiographies. Moreover, a broad conceptualization of the Americas archive will always exceed what has been recorded in print culture. To fully acknowledge this, we must attend to the lived experiences of individuals who were not able to narrate their experiences and their historical moment. We must find their presence and lives, their impact on history, indirectly through what others directly or inadvertently wrote about them or what can be found in statistical reports, legal cases, and other documents recording fragments of lost perspectives. Accessing their lived experiences through these texts allows us to recover and reconstruct their important, though previously erased, participation in the history they helped to forge.

The argument at hand in this book, then, is that scholars in American, Latin American, and Latinx studies have much yet to learn from these archives, and from developing a practice of reading both primary and secondary sources that is transnational, trans-American and transatlantic in scope. This approach, located at the intersection of multiple nationally configured archives, invites scholars to ask different questions about the material emerging therefrom, and it brings forth a new and more complex narrative of the Latina/o experience and of the academic disciplines of American and Latin American studies. In what follows, I show how entering Father Félix Varela's Americas archive from this perspective invites an epistemological shift in how we study Latina/o literature, beckoning us to approach it not merely as a bridge traversing the American and Latin American studies divide, but as an integral part of both histories—the exclusion of which has led to the formation of dangerous lacunae on both sides of the imagined border between "our" and the "other" America.

Varela's Reception in Latinx, Latin American, and American Studies

Most Latinx studies scholars know of Father Félix Varela from Luis Leal's 1960 article "*Jicoténcal*, primera novela histórica en castellano."[9] This article claimed that it was Varela himself who wrote this work, which is often regarded as the first historical novel in Latin America, though it was, provocatively enough, published in "la famosa Filadelfia" in 1826, a site we know, through the work of Rodrigo Lazo in "'La famosa Filadelfia': The Hemispheric American City and Constitutional Debates" (2008) and *Letters from Filadelfia: Early Latino Literature and the Trans-American Elite* (2020), as key to nineteenth-century Latina/o literary history. As such, while Father Varela had previously been regarded as a key figure in Latin American philosophy by Latin American intellectuals, Leal's article claiming Varela as the novelist behind *Jicoténcal* placed him at the very center of both American and Latin American literary history, at a key juncture for Latinx studies: the first historical novel in Latin America—a novel that condemned the conquest of Mexico by Hernán Cortés—now could potentially be claimed as part of Latina/o literary history.

It took nearly forty years following the publication of Leal's article for *Jicoténcal* to be published in the United States: it was not until 1995 that Arte Público Press—under the Recovering the US Hispanic Literary Heritage Project—released *Jicoténcal* in Spanish. While Leal had simply recovered Varela as the ostensible author in 1960, now he and his co-editor Rodolfo Cortina clearly situated Varela as a Latino author and the novel as a Latina/o one:

En ese espacio entre dos mundos, el de los EE.UU. en el cual se ignora la producción literaria de los hispanos, y el de la América hispánica que solo ve a los escritores *en* el Norte y nunca como *del* Norte, cabe lo que hasta muy recientemente ha sido el saco roto de las letras hispánicas: la literatura hispana de los EE.UU.

(Leal and Cortina 1995, xxxiv; emphasis mine)

(In that space between two worlds, of the United States in which the literary production of Hispanics is ignored, and that of Hispanic America [Latin America] that only sees writers *in* the North and never *from* the North, fits what until recently has been the broken sack of Hispanic letters [Latin American letters]: the Hispanic literature of the United States.)[10]

Four years later, the University of Texas Press published an English translation for wider use in the university classroom. With these publications, the anonymously written *Jicoténcal* was now canonized in Latinx studies, with excerpts appearing in the emerging market of anthologies of Latina/o literature of the 1990s. Today the novel is a standard work in anthologies of Latina/o literature and in introductory Latina/o literature courses, its authorship invariably attributed to Félix Varela. And yet, while this attribution guarantees Varela's name is at least known in Latinx studies, it is the novel's narrative content—its critique of the conquest of Mexico and the abuse of indigenous people at the hands of the conquerors—that takes center stage. Its anonymous production continues to relegate its supposed author, and the balance of his writings, to a certain obscurity.

Take, for example, the manner in which Varela is treated in the seventh edition of the *Heath Anthology of American Literature* (Lauter 2014). While the importance of including *Jicoténcal* in the anthology must not be dismissed, Varela, as in other anthologies that include him, is literally an aside: no effort is made there to consider the biography of the author in relation to his significance in Latina/o or US history. That is, the *Heath* finds importance in the book only in its arguments regarding the conquest of Mexico and its depiction of La Malinche as the mother of the mestizo nation in particular, as this is the section of the novel they choose to anthologize. What this means, in other words, is that the *Heath* highlights the presence in the narrative of a key symbol for the Chicana/o movement of the 1960s and 1970s in the United States, and does nothing to explore the significance of the Cuban identity of the text's supposed author within either his Cuban or his US contexts. One must laud the *Heath* editors for including *Jicoténcal* in their anthology,[11] and Raúl Coronado, the author of the entry, for selecting such a representative excerpt from the novel. Nevertheless, the lack of contextualization of Varela's life and works calls for a wider reading, a way to address the lacunae surrounding the supposed author of the first hispanophone historical novel of the Americas.

The Norton Anthology of Latino Literature (2010), in turn, moves closer to giving Varela his rightful place in Latina/o literary history, since the editors anthologize excerpts from *Cartas a Elpidio*, a work by Varela that speaks directly to his US experience and ministry. Nevertheless, they also frame Varela as an exile who happened to be "an insightful observer of American life" (Stavans et al. 2010, 173) and thereby, implicitly, not an integral or active part of it. Varela chose not to return to Cuba when a general amnesty was offered in 1832 to those who had been exiled in 1823—yet he also refused to take US citizenship, even while remaining in the United States. His own sense of national affiliation is thus ambiguous, and scholars have accordingly demurred from the conceptual challenges he raises by simply labeling him an exile. Yet this ascription, which only partially captures Varela's lived and political experience, has also served to augment the aforementioned lacunae, leaving significant portions of his literary and political work unexamined. Indeed, nowhere in the showcasing of *Jicoténcal* in Latina/o literature or of *Cartas a Elpidio*, in the case of the *Norton Anthology*, is any measured consideration given to Varela's *entire* body of written work, nor is the significance of his biography in relation to it.

On the other hand, when examining the scholarly reception of *Jicoténcal* in Latin American studies, we find scholars unanimously unsupportive of the ascription of authorship to Varela—a strong irony, given that his supposed authorship of the novel accounts almost entirely for interest in Varela in American and Latinx studies. Shortly after the publication of the first Spanish-language edition of *Jicoténcal* in the United States in 1995, González Acosta dedicated an entire book to what he called *El enigma de Jicoténcal* (1997), attributing the authorship of the text to the Cuban romantic poet José María Heredia, since a copy of the work was found in his papers upon his death. Heredia had also traveled north during his exile from Cuba, but chose to live in Mexico from 1825 instead of staying in the United States, where he had lived from 1823–25. González Acosta also challenged the classification of the work as the first historical novel in Latin America, arguing that its US site of publication, Philadelphia, precluded this status, and citing other possible novels by authors that he deemed truly Latin American. In turn, Anderson Imbert, the well-known Argentinian anthologist of Latin American literature, went so far as to ask, "¿Es legítimo incluir *Jicoténcal* en una historia de la literatura hispanoamericana?" (Imbert 1995, 221) (Is it legitimate to include *Jicoténcal* in a history of Hispano-American literature?). Imbert agrees to do so, ultimately including it in his anthology of Latin American literature, but qualifies his choice by listing the reasons that the novel resembles European literary productions of the time, and thereby implicitly suggesting that a Spaniard may have authored the piece in the first place, rather than a *criollo* or "Latin American" author. Indeed, one of Imbert's rationales for questioning the Mexican and/or Latin American origins of the writer is that the novel is discursive instead of descriptive and that the discourse itself translates the conquest of Mexico into "*términos europeos*" (Imbert 1995, 222) (European terms). At the most, he argues, *Jicoténcal* is the product of a Latin American novelist so deeply under the influence of European literature as to render the novel's Latin American status negligible.

More recently, Gustavo Forero Quintero (2012) published a new edition of *Xicotencatl* in Mexico. In the introduction, he argues that *Xicotencatl* could be read as offering a model for a Mexican Manifest Destiny, one in which Mexico and not the US is the chosen nation that would lead the newly independent Spanish American colonies toward republican governance (11):

> *Xicotencatl* no constituye una simple traducción de los hechos de la conquista en términos europeos...su autor se apoya en la teoría del destino manifiesto para establecer su visión romántica de México y un paradigma para el futuro nacional y continental.
> (Forero Quintero 2012, 12)
>
> (*Xicotencatl* does not constitute a simple translation of the conquest in European terms...its author bases his narrative on the theory of Manifest Destiny in order to establish a romantic vision of Mexico and a paradigm for a national and continental future.)

He adds that the anonymous authorship of the novel in fact makes possible a more fruitful reading of the text's political significance in the 1820s, since it highlights the already existent territorial tensions between the United States and Mexico in the context of the border disputes related to the Adams-Onís Treaty of 1819 (when Spain ceded Florida to the US). He explains:

> En este contexto, la publicación de una novela como *Xicotencatl*, que habla justamente del tema del territorio nacional, objeto principal de disputa entre la nación americana y española, después mexicana, se produce en un ambiente ambivalente en el que los propios Estados Unidos apoyan la independencia de las colonias hispanoamericanas de la metrópoli europea, sin renunciar a sus propios intereses en estos territorios.   (Forero Quintero 2012, 22)

> (In this context [the border disputes between first Spain and then Mexico and the US], the publication of a novel like *Xicotencatl*, that speaks precisely of a national territory, a principal object of dispute between the American, Spanish, and later Mexican nations, generates an ambivalent atmosphere in which the United States supports the independence of the Latin American colonies from the European metropolis, without renouncing their own interest in these territories.)

For Forero Quintero assigning authorship is irrelevant. It is, in fact, the novel's authorial anonymity that allows contemporary scholars to understand the political significance of the author's argument for Mexico's national and continental destiny.

I would argue, however, that this negation of Varela's authorship erases an emerging Latina/o political discourse regarding a hemispheric American (versus solely a US or solely a Latin American) political present and future. And, indeed, when Forero Quintero explains that the ideals of the Protestant ethic are present at the foundation of the concept of Manifest Destiny, disputing Leal and Cortina's argument regarding Varela's authorship, he in fact places Félix Varela as the most likely candidate for authorship. For Varela had a clear understanding of Protestant theology as a result of his role as an official apologist for the Catholic Church. And he took up this role, in public forums and in print, to counter religious attacks against Catholicism by Protestant clergy in New York and New England.

After declaring the ascription of authorship as unnecessary and irrelevant, Forero Quintero's argument for returning to the Nahuatl spelling of the namesake of the novel (*Xicotencatl*) from its hispanicized original spelling (*Jicoténcatl*) marks an important intervention. He brings to the forefront, like Guillermo I. Castillo-Feliú before him—the translator of the 1999 English-language edition published by University of Texas Press (Varela 1999)—the important but forgotten role played by the Tlaxcalans in the Spanish conquest of Mexico. And yet his corrective simultaneously erases emerging nineteenth-century Latina/o voices who contributed to the political dialogues surrounding Spanish American and US American post-independence narratives, and whose perspectives should be counted as foundational for the historiography surrounding the emancipation of the Spanish colonies from the metropolis as well as that of the US from Britain. For in assigning authorship to Varela, discussion about Manifest Destiny in the novel could be put into dialogue with Varela's own political views of US interventions in Spanish America and serve to bolster an even more pronounced conceptualization of Spanish American emancipation and post-independence political and economic sovereignty from a different perspective, one that emerges from "the belly of the beast," as José Martí would later describe the position of Latina/o subjects writing from the United States in his foundational essay "Nuestra América" (1891) (Martí 1963, 6: 15–23).[12]

In the field of Cuban studies, *Jicoténcal* is simply non-existent. Instead, both before and after the 1959 revolution, scholars of Varela on the island have concentrated almost exclusively on his early philosophical works. As early as 1862, Mestre y Domínguez in *De la filosofía en la Habana* writes of the importance of Varela's philosophical texts for Cuban history, but he excludes Varela's US works. Likewise Rexach (1950), Roig de Leuchsenring (1953), Vitier (1970), Serpa (1983), and Piqueras (2007) concentrate almost exclusively on Varela's philosophical texts without addressing *Cartas a Elpidio* or Varela's political activist writings in US newspapers. While his Cuban biographer, Travieso (1949), in turn, who combed through US sources in DC, Philadelphia, and New York, speaks to Varela's US activism and writings, he dedicates most of his biography to his Cuban writings. And his earlier book on Varela, *Varela y la reforma filosófica en Cuba* (1942), concentrates on his philosophical works.

Meanwhile, *El Habanero* (1824–26) has become a resource for scholars, since a complete compilation of its articles was published in 1997 by Ediciones Universal in Miami, Florida. This edition includes the once lost seventh issue of the newspaper. Yet, while stressing the importance of Varela's writings for Cuban political history, the introduction to this important compilation does not include a review of the significance of Varela in a US context. EduardoTorres-Cuevas, the general editor of Varela's (2001) complete works, writes:

> [El pensamiento de Varela] proyecta la búsqueda del deber ser de su sociedad y no la justificación del ser que aún no es. Sus ideas no son una justificación de la sociedad colonialista, o colonizada, y esclav-ista, o esclavizada, son de una sociedad éticamente superior y libre. Es, en resumen, una filosofía del deber ser de la cubanidad, que no es aún; de la sociedad soñada pero no lograda.   (Varela 2001, xxxv)

> ([Varela's thinking] maps the search for what his society should be and not the justification of a reality that has not been attained. His ideas are not a justification for the colonial or colonized, and slave-owning or enslaved society. They are of a society ethically superior and free. It, in sum, is a philosophy of what *cubanidad* should be, one that is not as yet; of a society dreamed of but not attained.)

Moreover, his US biographers, José Ignacio Rodríguez (1878) and Joseph McCadden and Helen McCadden (1969), speak to Varela's importance in relation to US Catholicism but do not contextualize his life from a Latina/o perspective. Indeed, the former, in particular, dedicates most of his book to Varela's work originally published and/or written in Cuba and Spain.

Varela's US archive is generally excluded from Cuban historiography. While the University of Havana, under the direction and editorship of Torres-Cuevas et al., published Varela's *Obras* in three volumes in 2001, unfortunately, due to lack of access to US sources, the editors were not able to compile and include all of Varela's articles from US Catholic newspapers. This omission is a misfortune given that the socially progressive ideology of the Cuban Revolution would have found resonances with the ideas Varela develops in his US publications (although Varela, as a Catholic priest, would have de-nounced the manner in which the revolution has approached both religion—and Catholicism in particular—and the role of the state in civic life).

Another serious omission is Varela's 1826 translation of Thomas Jefferson's *Manual of Parliamentary Practice* (1801). Varela's rendi-tion is an annotated translation with thirty-five footnotes in which he dialogues with the *Manual* and his readers, noting that his translations and annotations are "un servicio a los nuevos estados americanos" (iii) (a service to the new American states [meaning the recently emancipated Spanish nations]). In these footnotes Varela juxtaposes British parliamentary practice, the procedures then in effect in the Spanish Cortes, and the emerging practices in the US Congress, in order to present them against his own "ideas teoricas" [*sic*]: the opinion he has formed based on his political experiences in Spain and the United States (iv). Not surprisingly, *Jicoténcatl* also does not appear in the Torres-Cuevas's *Félix Varela: Obras* (2001) either. And in these omissions we find a missed opportunity to understand an emerging Latina/o intervention in contemporaneous political issues that spoke not simply to Spanish American and Cuban concerns, but to those of the US as well.

Finally, American studies, generally speaking, does not consider *Jicoténcal* to be a part of the US literary heritage, except insofar as it figures in the Latinx studies curriculum.[13] It is not a work counted in the broad literary historical narrative as integral to our understanding of American history, as is the case when we read Washington Irving or William Prescott and their respective histories of the discovery and conquest of the New World, for example. Yet this exclusion is problematic, since, after all, Varela (assuming he is the author of *Jicoténcal*) also wrote about the conquest of the New World in this historical novel, and particularly since he lived in the United States for more than thirty years. Is not his historical novel *also* a relevant New World colonial narrative of the kind so central to nineteenth-century US-American literary history? Do we not have still to learn from this early Latina/o perspective?

The story of *Jicoténcal* across the disciplines offers but one example of how the segmentation we see—in Cuba, in Latin America, and in the United States—in the reading and study of the writings of Latina/o intellectual and historical figures obscures the greater links that exist across these geographic and cultural regions. The methodological approach I here propose, one that in itself helps to constitute the Latino Continuum, illuminates the role of Latina/os not only in US politics and history but also in Cuban and Latin American cultural and political histories. Varela's life and ministry exemplify this continuum, and further highlight what we gain in understanding by attending to its presence and importance.

The Protestant-Catholic Debates of the 1830s and 1840s

When we appreciate that Varela's life and ministry took place over the course of some thirty years in the infamous—and mainly Irish— Five Points neighborhood of New York City (referred to as such because Cross, Orange, and Anthony Streets came together to form a five-point intersection in what is now between SoHo and Chinatown in Manhattan), we begin to see his embeddedness in New York and US history in the early nineteenth century.[14] For example, Varela is credited with founding a Catholic school for children in 1828 at Christ Church as well as a vocational school for women, mostly for Irish immigrants who populated the Five Points area, in order to help them enter the workforce and support their families. He was also the founder of the Half Orphan Asylum (1835–52), a refuge for children who had only one parent or relative, and he established the New York Catholic Temperance Society (1840), the first of its kind in the city. As vicar-general of New York, he pastored and/or founded St. Peter's, St. Patrick's (the original cathedral), Christ Church, St. Mary's, and the Church of the Transfiguration (which is still serving parishioners, though as of 1853 at a different location than where Varela first founded the church in 1836). His dedication to his mainly Irish parishioners has led to him being called the "Father of the Irish," and he is today considered to be the founder of New York Catholicism.[15]

But Varela shaped US history more broadly as an apologist for the place of the Catholic Church in American life. In his day, various Protestant groups held public meetings that called on Catholics to defend the church, demanding they prove that the church was not the "whore of Babylon," was not religiously intolerant, and was not calling for a new Inquisition in the US (in a move parallel to that of the Carlists, who at that time were advocating for the Inquisition's return to Spain). Varela addressed the moral and religious themes so prevalent in US political life in his little-studied *Cartas a Elpidio*, a series of letters written to a friend, "Elpidio." Written in Spanish in New York and published there in two separate volumes in 1835 and 1838 respectively, the *Cartas* record his prominent role in these debates. In addition, the volumes, titled *Impiedad* (1835) and *Superstición* (1838), speak to events in Spain, as well as the growing despotism of Cuba's governor and the concurrent repression on the island. Yet their main theme is religious intolerance in the United States.[16]

In the second volume, for example, Varela describes in detail his confrontation with the Presbyterian clergyman and nativist ideologue W. C. Brownlee in a public debate. Brownlee approached the event as a monologue, forestalling Varela's participation in the debate by interrupting him repeatedly whenever Varela attempted to respond. Remembering the farcical nature of the encounter, in which he was hardly permitted even to speak, Varela describes a particular moment of theological impasse:

> No admitiendo la existencia teológica, por decirlo así, de ninguna religión, mal pueden admitir la verdadera tolerancia, que necesariamente supone la existencia de las cosas toleradas. No se hubiera disputado tanto sobre esta materia si hubiera habido una verdadera tolerancia de sentimientos, quiero decir, si hubiera habido más caridad y menos soberbia.   (Varela 1944, 2: 151)

> (Not admitting to the theological existence of any religion, to say it this way, they [the Protestants] cannot admit to true tolerance that necessarily presupposes the existence of things tolerated. We would not have argued so much on this matter if there had been a true belief in religious tolerance. I mean, if there had been more charity and less arrogance [on the part of the Protestants].)

We must stop here and ponder the word "arrogance." Varela expresses a theological concern. He understood that the nineteenth-century Catholic Church saw itself as the one and only church, the only path to salvation. He also knew that the Catholic Church admitted that exceptions would be made for non-Catholics who, in their ignorance or incapacities, could not see or properly know the church. Although not Catholic, these exceptional souls could also attain salvation. Furthermore, Varela also understood his Protestant opponents to maintain the same theological view, just as he knew that they also were aware of the theological parallels between Protestant and Catholic doctrines of salvation.

Yet, as Varela notes in *Cartas*, his Protestant (primarily Presbyterian) opponents hypocritically attacked Catholicism for its intolerance, while ignoring the exceptions Catholics allowed for non-Catholics to attain salvation. More than this, Varela lamented that his Protestant opponents ignored the existence of their own theological exceptions, because they could not yield to his differing beliefs. Instead, as he objected in *Cartas*, they repeatedly sought to convert him to Protestantism. As he saw it, they could not tolerate a

Catholic remaining Catholic in their midst, even though their theology
allowed for just that. And he lamented that, despite the known parallels in their theologies, his Protestant interlocutors could not tolerate
his Catholicism precisely because they wrongly demonized the
Catholic Church as exclusivist. He concludes ironically by saying,
"Créeme, Elpidio, que el argumento más fuerte contra la tolerancia es
el mero hecho de disputarse tanto acerca de ella" (Varela 1944, 2: 151).
(Believe me, Elpidio, the strongest argument against the existence of
any tolerance is the mere act of having to argue so much about it.)

Varela's indictment in *Cartas* and in his newspaper articles followed from his experience with religion in the United States, since
he wished to warn his readers against erroneously praising the pluralism of Protestant denominations, as if they reflected a concomitant tolerance for diverse political or even religious views. Though
noting that religious pluralism was enshrined as a legal right in the
US Constitution, in *Cartas* he argued that, in practice, no concomitant social or theological tolerance accompanied this legal right.

For this reason, Varela warns his readers in the United States and
Latin America not to see the North American model as a foundation
for their democratic projects:

> Habrás oído mucho acerca de la libertad religiosa de este país, acom-
> pañada de una armonía social y una paz admirable...temo que no
> hayan adquirido ideas correctas sobre este punto, y que te hayas
> dejado llevar de las exageraciones de unos y de la injusticia de otros.
> (Varela 1944, 1: 100)
>
> (You may have heard a lot about the religious liberty in this country
> accompanied by social harmony and an admirable peace...I fear that
> these individuals may not have acquired correct ideas on this point,
> and that you may have allowed yourself to be taken up by the exag-
> gerations of some and the injustice of others.)

In order to impress on his readers the serious nature of his warning
in *Cartas*, he concludes: "Hace tiempo que conocía a los impíos, pero
aquí he venido a conocer a los protestantes. Unos y otros acusan a la
Iglesia de intolerante, y unos y otros la exceden en intolerantismo"
(Varela 1944, 2: 136). (I have known the impious for a long time, but
here I have come to know Protestants. One and the other accuse the
[Catholic] Church of being intolerant, and one and the other exceed
the Church in their intolerance.) Directly linking his discussion of

religion to political and social concerns, including discrimination, Varela also explicitly cautioned that it was not his identity as a Catholic priest that led him to write about Protestantism; rather, it was the eminently political nature of religion in the United States that led him to write about politics by way of discussing religion. He decries the veracity of judgments formed in haste by short-term visitors who perceived the United States as a model for the Spanish American republics:

> La experiencia que tengo del corazón humano me anticipa que mis pruebas pasarán por delirios de un interés religioso, porque mi lenguaje es distinto del que se encuentra en los libros de mero cálculo político; y del que usan muchos que creen conocer este país, solo por haber paseado las calles de algunas de sus ciudades y haber asistido a una u otra tertulia.   (Varela 1944, 2: 171)

> (The experience I have of the human heart warns me that my examples [of religious intolerance] will be passed over as the delirious rantings of religious interest, simply because the language I am using for my argument is different than what is found in books of mere political calculations. That language [of a political nature] is used by many who believe they know this country, simply because they have strolled through some of its cities and attended one or another social gathering.)

Given his views of the limits of US tolerance, it is no surprise that Varela supported Cuban independence over annexation, and by doing so as early as 1823, is regarded, as mentioned earlier, as the first Cuban to do so.[17]

But perhaps most notable in the last quotation is Varela's distinction between the casual visitor to the United States, specifically to New York (here he may be referring to well-known Cuban figures such as Domingo del Monte), and the experience of others, such as himself, who had come to know the country intimately as a resident over the course of decades. Indeed, he was more than merely a Cuban exile in New York, as most anthologists and biographers have called him, but rather an actor integral to US history.

In *Cartas* Varela divided religious tolerance into three categories: the legal, the theological, and the social. He concluded that tolerance of religious diversity in the US exists only in the form of the first, as a legal category. While he framed his critique of theological ignorance through his debates with such ministers as Brownlee, Varela recorded a similar absence of religious tolerance in everyday social practice. Most poignantly, he did so in his role in the events surrounding the burning of the Ursuline Catholic Convent outside of Boston in 1834, which in turn triggered rioting in New York. While both Protestants and Catholics criticized the violence perpetrated against the young women who studied in this convent school, mostly attended by daughters of Congregationalists, the perpetrators were never convicted. In *Cartas*, Varela notes the significance of the event:

> La experiencia probó, mi Elpidio, que los sentimientos de la ciudad de Boston eran contrarios a la religión católica, y muy ajenos a esa tolerancia de que tanto se habla y tan poco se practica. Un incendio siempre excita compasión... mas los bostonianos se contentaron con sus lamentaciones de gaceta y no creyeron que debían hacer algo por una casa de educación reducida a cenizas por uno odio religioso, que de este modo se probó que era casi universal.
>
> (Varela 1944, 2: 155–56)
>
> (Experience showed, my Elpidio, that the beliefs of the city of Boston were opposed to the Catholic religion and very foreign to that supposed tolerance of which so much is spoken but so little is practiced. A fire always incites compassion... but the Bostonians were happy with their expressions of grief and condolences in the press (*lamentaciones de gazeta*) and did not believe they should do anything else for a place of education reduced to ashes due to religious hatred, which was proven by the newspapers themselves, as a universal fact.)

And as Varela notes later, while Bostonian newspapers spoke against the anti-Catholic sentiments that fueled the fire, Bostonians publicly celebrated when those accused of the arson were exonerated for the crime (Varela 1944, 2: 157–58).[18]

Moreover, Varela objected to the decision of the state of Massachusetts to deny the convent reparation funds to rebuild it, funds that had been set aside specifically for such purposes (Varela 1944, 2: 155). In her groundbreaking study, *Roads to Rome: The Antebellum Protestant Encounter with Catholicism* (1994) Jenny Franchot contextualizes the significance of this denial, highlighting the fact that the convent was situated close to Bunker Hill, and that writings of the time stressed that it was inappropriate for a Catholic institution ever to have been built so close to such an essential

American historical site. In the end, the convent was never rebuilt (Franchot 1994, 135–54).

Two important dimensions of American sociopolitical life are linked to this event, and scrutinized in *Cartas*. The first involves the disenfranchisement of the working class in early America, for the arsonists were Scots-Presbyterian bricklayers who found themselves competing for jobs with the Irish and having to move west in order to subsist and find work (Franchot 1994, 135–54). The second is the disestablishment of mainstream Protestantism and its impact on US religion and politics. In *Superstición* Varela amply lists and critiques the many Protestant groups (Methodists, Baptists, Quakers, Shakers, etc.) emerging from and populating the US religious landscape.[19]

After another event that confirmed his indictment of so-called religious freedom in the United States—a planned attack in 1835 against New York's St. Patrick's Cathedral—Varela mobilized the Catholic community to resist. In *Cartas* he describes the manner in which he helped to thwart the attack. The attackers had developed a detailed conspiracy theory claiming that the Pope was sending Catholics to the United States in order to take over the country, and that a new Inquisition was being secretly administered in St. Patrick's Cathedral. Varela describes how one of his parishioners overheard the would-be arsonists: a group of Protestant butchers at the local market allegedly had described their plan to destroy the cathedral. Varela warned the church trustees, who in turn reached out to the governor for protection in response. According to *Cartas*, he then joined 500 Catholics in surrounding St. Patrick's to greet the arrival of the 200 to 300 rioters, who were turned back by the sheer numbers present who were willing to defend the building. The presence of this mobilized minority group along with the governor's threat to interfere, stopped the planned arson (Varela 1944, 2: 159–61).

Varela was thus deeply involved in the beginnings of US minority political history—a history that emerged far earlier than the twentieth century, as Kyle Volk (2014) has shown, and in fact dates back to a concerted reaction by immigrants, African Americans, and Catholics to the rise of majority rule in the United States in the 1820s. One of the core controversies between Protestants and these groups centered on temperance. Varela, who established the first Catholic temperance society in New York, was an influential voice in this early controversy too. Following the Second Great Awakening, and the positive reception of Lyman Beecher's *A Plea for the West* (1835), Protestant reformers of the period began arguing more broadly that moral rectitude was key to the survival of the American republic. Lobbying to convert a broad public to observing the Sabbath and inscribing temperance into law, these reformers quickly learned the power of political majorities. As Volk notes, during the broad shift from minority to majority rule in American politics, reformers in particular used majority rule to impose their mandates on the US populace. They did so through grassroots campaigns that mobilized the masses: "By involving millions of predominantly middle-class men, women and children, reform associations emerged alongside political parties as a major force of democratization" (Volk 2014, 27). But this force of democratization often depended, and still depends, upon minority scapegoating. In the case of the nineteenth-century Protestant reformers, they mobilized by singling out immigrants, African Americans, and Catholics as the driving force behind the moral depravity of the nation that would in turn lead to the collapse and end of the American republican project (Volk 2014, 25). As Volk concludes:

> Their exertions would continue to transform public life in the nine-teenth century, not least by giving rise to popular debates about American democracy's central postulate—that the majority should rule—and by rousing a range of new grass-roots political action on behalf of minority rights.   (Volk 2014, 35)

In the dialectic of American democracy, these mass Protestant mobilizations in turn led to the rise of a robust minority politics.

One example, cited by Volk, was the reaction by minorities after the nativist James Harper won the mayoral election in 1844. Harper proposed the exclusive use of the Protestant King James Bible in public schools, opposed the funding of Catholic schools, and sought tougher naturalization legislation (Volk 2014, 43). As minority groups understood immediately, these attempts to regulate morality via majority rule were fundamentally opposed to working-class and immigrant rights and culture—and to the very premise of religious freedom established in the constitution:

> Countering Sabbath reformers and other advocates of Sunday legisla-tion, these critics advanced cultural pluralism and religious liberty as

cornerstones of American democracy. In their view, governmental protection of religious worship would ruin the republican experiment. The implication of their position reflected not only the diversifying ethno-religious order but also the everyday changes accompanying the ascension of market capitalism.   (Volk 2014, 43–44)

Varela was deeply involved in these debates and events as both a priest and an intellectual. Though an advocate of temperance, he ultimately chose to protest against temperance societies that were totalitarian in nature (Travieso 1949, 421–23); and though a staunch supporter of Catholic schools, he took an active role in debates about the destiny of public schools.

When inaugurating the New York Catholic Temperance Society in 1840, Varela wrote (in English):

> The object of the New York Catholic Temperance Society is to abolish intemperance without imposing unnecessary privations...each person is solely impelled to avoid intemperance, and not to deprive himself completely of liquor.... We do this in this manner because we consider imprudent the establishment of a general rule when each case is, in its very nature, different. He that during his meals always drinks a glass of wine without feeling the effects of intemperance, we will not force him to break his custom, because others are drunkards.
>   (Quoted in Travieso 1949, 421–22)

Varela threads a difficult needle here. In creating a temperance society in the first place, Varela submits to the demands of the social norms in New York City at that time—norms based on a Protestant and distinctly ethno-religious critique of Catholics (i.e., the Irish and Germans) drinking on Sundays. But Varela makes sure to highlight here that drinking is only a problem for those who cannot control themselves; otherwise, he suggests, it is fine to drink on any day, including Sundays: the vice lay not in the practice but in those unable to control themselves.

At the same time, Varela traces the origin of intolerant and superstitious religious views and practices in the United States to the Puritans, invoking the infamous Blue Laws of Connecticut, compiled by Samuel Peters in 1781 (Varela 1944, 2: 127–29). Though the laws were, in fact, fictitious, the idea of their existence was still widely believed in the nineteenth century, and during the religious and political debates of the 1830s, many, including Varela, cited them to illustrate the absurdity of Protestant critiques of Catholicism. Varela includes an extensive, yet selective rendering of the Blue Laws in the appendix of *Superstición*, and in the body of *Cartas* itself, he cites them as examples of the contradiction that exists between religious freedom and social restrictions enforced by religious belief in the US and also of how these social restrictions, in turn, are irrational and stand as an affront to individual freedom and ultimately democratic governance. He writes:

> ¿Qué ataque más directo a la libertad que prohibir hasta que un hombre pueda hacer pasteles y comérselos en su casa? ¿Que una madre bese a su hijo en domingo, como si una expresión de cariño por la misma naturaleza, pudieses ofender al autor de ella, cuando más bien podría considerarse como una acción de gracias por el beneficio de haber recibido un hijo de manos de la Providencia y homenaje de respeto apreciando una criatura que Dios mismo la manda apreciar?   (Varela 1944, 2: 129)

> (Can there be a more direct attack against freedom than to prohibit a man from baking pastries and eating them in his home? That a mother kiss her child on Sunday, as if an expression of affection inspired by nature itself could offend the great author of that nature, which in fact could be considered as an act of thanks for the blessing of having received a child from the hands of Providence and an homage of respect in cherishing a child that God himself tells her to cherish?)

As Varela continues, however, his critique of Protestant intolerance expands into a complex commentary on the relation between religion and political governance more broadly, in both hemispheric and transatlantic contexts:

> Creo haber manifestado con raciocinios y comprobado con hechos que la superstición influye de distinto modo según la naturaleza de las instituciones populares y las ideas religiosas admitidas; que donde florece la verdadera religión toma a superstición el principio de la autoridad para abusar de ella, y en los países donde reina el desorden religioso, o lo que es lo mismo, una multitud de religiones, se vale de la razón para abusar igualmente de ella.   (Varela 1944, 2: 132)

> (I believe I have shown with reason and proven with acts that superstition influences in different ways according to the nature of popular institutions and the religious ideas admitted by them. In those countries where the true religion flourishes, superstition takes the

principle of authority to abuse authority, and in countries where religious disorder reigns, or what is the same, a multitude of religions reign, superstition takes advantage of reason in order to similarly abuse reason.)

Though he does not say so explicitly, Varela in this passage criticizes Spain, where bloody civil wars would rage throughout the nineteenth century, and where religion was being deployed by different political groups in the 1830s. On one side, the Spanish Decree of 1832 had secularized the properties of the Catholic Church, which Varela opposed. But on the other, the absolutists who favored a return to an *ancien régime* also opposed the abrogation of the Inquisition, an institution they wished to see re-established.

The political and religious situation in Spain during this time, with its concurrent impact on Cuba, is important to understand, since it is these historical intersections that constitute the Latino Continuum and simultaneously allow us to find new histories from their juxtaposition. In the Spanish context, after Ferdinand VII took the throne in 1823, a debate regarding succession to the Spanish throne commenced. Two factions took part in the disagreement, leading to bloody civil wars throughout the nineteenth century. On one side were the Cristinos, named after Ferdinand's last wife, María Cristina de Bourbon, and the mother of his two heirs. Supporters of Ferdinand VII, they believed that Ferdinand's infant daughter Isabella II (b.1830) was the rightful heir to the Spanish Crown, this based on the unpublished Pragmatic Sanction of Charles IV in 1789, which in turn was based on precedent laws of Castile and León that sanctioned women to rule the kingdom. Ferdinand VII supported this law and established the Pragmatic Sanction of King Ferdinand VII in 1830 to ensure his daughter's ascendancy. On the other side were the Carlists. They supported the succession of Don Carlos of Bourbon, the younger brother of Ferdinand VII, noting that the Sanction of Charles IV was never made public and therefore was of questionable authenticity. Consequently, on the basis of the Salic Law of Succession of 1713 (which was established to prevent any monarchical union between Spain and France), they argued that no female could be named successor to the throne. Apart from opposing María Cristina's rule (1833–40), as regent of the kingdom, and that of Isabella II (1833–68), the Carlists and Don Carlos were absolutists and wished for a return to an *ancien régime* based on strong Catholic values.

The Cristinos were both radical and moderate liberals. They believed in Enlightenment ideals and were thus seen by the Carlist traditionalists as expounding French values. In order to pay for the failed war against Latin American independence and to manage Spain's bankruptcy, caused in part by the failed war in Spanish America, the Cristinos drafted and enforced the Decree of 1832, which allowed the government forcibly to confiscate church property, a move that had a negative impact on the peasantry across Spain, since it disrupted a way of life in which small farmers worked for the church estates and thereby earned their sustenance. After the Decree, they were left property-less, as the land was privatized. The Carlists opposed these moves to centralize Spanish landownership and control, as they did the abrogation of the Inquisition, an institution they keenly wished to see re-established. In religious matters, the liberals or Cristinos sought clerical reforms, while the Carlists were conservatives with strong ties to the Roman Catholic Church. The Carlist banner was "God, Country, King," and they waged wars against the Cristinos from 1833 to 1876. With this history in mind, then, one may identify in *Cartas* both an attack on those liberals in Spain who opposed Catholicism (radical Cristinos) and one on extremists who used it as a political weapon (Carlists).

Simultaneously, Varela criticized the contemporaneous state of the Church in Cuba, which had become particularly pro-Spanish. In Varela (1989) Felipe Estévez notes there were three key circumstances in the church in Cuba that posed threats to Cuba's continued political union with Spain: (1) liberal ideas had won over the intellectual and affluent classes; (2) the church had not evangelized enslaved Africans, nor freedmen and freedwomen; and, counterintuitively, (3) most of the clergy was aligned with Spain and not Cuba, since they did not seek independence but supported Spanish rule. Consequent on the last was the fact that many Cubans saw the Catholic Church as "irrelevant" and instead supported the ideals of the French Revolution, along with its irreligiosity. For Varela, this constituted an intolerable use of religion as a political weapon. But if Spain was suffering a crisis of "authority abus[ing] authority" (Varela 1944, 2: 132), the US had a problem with its religious pluralism, which, as he saw it, could not be disentangled from religious disorder and led to "reason abus[ing] reason" (Varela 1944, 2: 132). The US, Spanish, and Cuban contexts were linked, however, by the problem of superstition: the source of all trouble, whether directly or indirectly.

During his long residence in the US at the height of Protestant-Catholic debates, then, Varela developed a nuanced position on the interrelationships of religion, government, reason, and authority from which he could analyze religious and political events in Spain, Cuba, and the US. Simultaneously, he observed and lamented the state of the church in Cuba, his natal land, and the island over which the two empires, Spanish and US, would go to war by the century's end. Though he abhorred the growing irrelevance of the church in Cuba among liberals and intellectuals, he also detested the results of the church's increasingly hardened pro-Spanish position, especially the failure to embrace enslaved Cubans and freed people of color.

Varela's Translation of the *Manual of Parliamentary Practice*

If Varela's thirty years in the United States speak to his deep engagement in US life, as an agent in important events in the life of the American Catholic Church and in US history more generally, it is also the case that the Protestant-Catholic debate in which he took part enabled him to speak in complex ways beyond the limits of a US context. Varela's engagement with American social, political, and religious life summarized in this chapter was at times written in Spanish, as we have seen, which suggests that he self-consciously targeted *Cartas* to a broad Cuban audience, including Cubans settled permanently in New York, Cubans visiting the United States, *and* Cubans in Cuba. His narrative about American Protestantism also articulated another narrative, one meant to express concern for a Cuban understanding of American political, religious, and social life.

Varela's consistent strategy—while ostensibly writing one story in *Cartas*, about American intolerance—is to write multiple stories simultaneously. American legal tolerance of multiple religions did not extend to a theological or social inclusivism in the United States, in Varela's view, as we have seen. It was thus crucial that Cubans in Cuba, who often read into the legality of religious pluralism in the United States a concomitant tolerance for social and political difference, come to an understanding that this erroneously imagined inclusivism would not extend to them (Travieso 1949, 412). Varela's narrative about American intolerance, in other words, constituted a warning to Cubans in the US and Cuba and to Spanish Americans more broadly that neither immigration to the US nor annexation would bring the sort of inclusivism and social harmony they imagined.

Early in Varela's residence in the US, he registered these concerns—nowhere more fittingly than in his translation of Thomas Jefferson's *Manual of Parliamentary Practice*. Varela lauds Jefferson's work as "judicious and meritorious" (Varela 1826, iii), but he apparently saw room for improvement, for he went far beyond a literal translation of the *Manual*. Instead, Varela fashioned an annotated one. He explains that this decision to append notes to the translation occurs when the text is "en controposición ó mis ideas teoricas, ó los datos que me ha proporcionado una corta, pero azarosa y sostosisima practica" [*sic*] (Varela 1826, iii–iv) (they appear in those places where what is in the work is in contraposition to my theoretical ideals, or to the facts that a short but perilous and maintained practice have provided) (Varela 1826, iii–iv). The "contrapositions" lead to thirty-five footnotes that establish a dialogue between Varela, his reader, and Jefferson's work—a dialogue that ultimately corrects and expands Jefferson's text along the way.

What these "contrapositions" signal is never specified directly, but they indicate not only Varela's support of the newly formed Spanish American republics but also his apprehension about the entire hemisphere blindly accepting a US-style of republicanism *in toto*. Committed to the free flow of ideas across languages, Varela offers his translation of Jefferson, but nevertheless indicates that there are aspects of Spanish forms of governance in the political past to be considered, laudable practices to be taken from Spanish American histories as well as Anglo ones. To illustrate just this, Varela includes observations regarding practices at the Spanish Cortes that he deemed preferable to those engaged in the US Senate—for example, when he questions the prohibition against final readings of edited bills on the US Senate floor. Varela notes that the practice could lead to confusion as to the actual final content of the bill. Jefferson himself admitted this probability by including in his *Manual* a paragraph regarding the dangers of this practice (Jefferson 1820, 85). Yet Varela gives Spanish Americans and Jefferson his own suggestion regarding this practice by including the following at the foot of the page:

Para evitar este inconveniente se leia en las Cortes de España nuevamente la minuta del decreto, ley ó mensage conforme la habia corregido la comision de correccion de estilo, y se habia copiado en la Secretaria. Preguntabase entonces á las cortes si estaba conforme con lo resuelto, y si algun diputado objeccionaba, volvia el documento á la Secretaria para confrontarse con el original de la discussion. [*sic*]

(Varela 1826, 65)

(In order to avoid this problem, in the Spanish Cortes the details of the decree, law, or message were read anew in conformity with the corrections of the commission, and how it was copied in the Secretariat. It was then asked of the Cortes if they were in conformity with the result, and if any deputy objected, the document returned to the Secretariat so it could be compared with the original under discussion.)

Varela does not directly correct Jefferson's work or US congressional practices, but he does remind his Spanish American readers not to reject their own political traditions outright.

A deep concern with protecting minority interests from majority rule is also in evidence each time the annotations call for taking into account the place of minoritized points of view in democratic governance. Specifically, Varela warns his readers against the ways in which hidden political intentions and interests can impact Republican governance. He frames this discussion around the right to "read" a speech in front of Congress. After translating a line that states that a legislative member has no right to read his own discourse without permission but may only speak extemporaneously on the topic, Varela intervenes in the annotation:

No comprehendo por que pueda negarse el permiso de leer su discurso al que no quiere, ó no puede hacer otra cosa. Se dirá que esto es aplicable á los discursos ya pronunciados? La regla nada dice; mas aun en este caso, ¿por que si se permite como antes se ha dicho hablar dos veces sobre una materia no se permite leer dos veces, cuando acaso se han hecho mas alteraciones, y con mas reflexion en el discurso escrito que en el improvisado? [*sic*] (Varela 1826, 68)

(I do not understand why the permission is not given to read a speech to those who do not wish to or are unable to do anything else. Is this understood to be applicable to all speeches already given? The rule does not address this; and even in this case, if it is permitted, as previously said, to speak twice on a topic, why is it not permitted to read aloud about it twice, when maybe some additional alterations have been made with more reflection in the speech that is written versus one that is improvised?)

Varela's questions appear straightforward, yet raise complex issues regarding the nature of speech and textuality, improvisation, and alteration: to speak twice, in his view, is no different from revising a text, which is also a form of speech. As the different procedures for presenting a bill to congress are delineated in Jefferson's text, Varela interposes: "confieso que todo esto me parece enrredo de enrredo; otros veran mas claro" [sic] (Varela 1826, 77). (I must confess that all of this appears to me as a tangle upon a tangle; maybe others will see more clearly.) In the end, Varela addresses these contradictions by hailing his ideal reader, the "prudent and patriotic man" who must always be alert so injustices are not committed, especially in parliamentary practice (Varela 1826, 79–80). He warns:

> Tambien hay otros casos en que una mocion conveniente y justa se conoce que no ha de tener buen suceso por la intriga de un partido, y que si se decide negativamente, ó se deshecha por algun otro medio produce un efecto funestisimo, autorizando por una decision del cuerpo deliberante el mal que se intentaba remover. [sic]
>
> (Varela 1826, 79)

> (There are also other cases when a convenient and just motion is recognized as not being successful because of the intrigue of a party, and if it is decided negatively, or it is undone by some other means, it produces a terrible effect, authorizing by a decision of the deliberating body the evil it was meant to remove.)

This fear that parliamentary procedures could serve to disenfranchise those who wish to present motions that may be good for the country but in opposition to other—majority—political parties speaks doubly to Varela's own positions, first as a colonized Cuban subject during his time as a representative in the Spanish Cortes and later as a Catholic immigrant and priest in the US. Similarly, Varela was particularly concerned about the role of legal precedents in deciding legal cases as well as the legal implications they could have in the future. Specifically, he feared that precedents would not take into account the historical and political moment at which they were established and therefore would blind the court to any political intrigues occurring at that time that worked against the defendant (Varela 1826, 140). The concept of precedence, as he observed, superimposes temporal moments in ways that always disadvantage one interest over the other—a recognition that surely came in part from his movements across the discrepant times of the Americas, colonial and settler-colonial alike.

Elsewhere, Varela was troubled by several rules of procedure that limited, or abrogated, the rights of protest of minority actors. First, he was disturbed by the need for a rule allowing a representative to be forced to attend a session of Congress. He believed that the rule spoke not only to a lack of commitment among representatives to execute their legislative obligations, but also a lack of commitment to the public good. More than this, he was troubled by the notion that the governing body, controlled by a majority, could force a member representing a minority view to attend a legislative session, even if the dissenting member declined to attend for legitimate reasons of protest (Varela 1826, 79).

Varela was similarly troubled by the ways in which American procedures allowed secrets to be held: he was troubled by the fact that a doorman and sheriff could be privy to state secrets (being in the room while they were deliberated), even while some members of Congress—likely from the minority—could be barred from attending the same closed sessions. He writes: "Es una regla universal que la seguridad de un secreto está en razón inversa del número de personas a quienes se comunica, y aunque la ley debe desear la moralidad de los hombres, no debe suponerla; sino prevenirse como si no la tuviesen" (Varela 1826, 170–71). (It is a universal rule that the security of a secret is inversely related to the number of persons to whom it is communicated, and even though the law should desire the morality of men, it should not assume it; instead it should anticipate their lack of it.) In other words, he understood the true purpose of the rule not to be the preservation of a secret per se; it was designed, rather, to allow the majority to exclude the minority from particular legislative deliberations.[20]

If these annotations collectively comprise Varela's critique of US democratic governance as articulated in his contemporary setting, it is his exclusion of Jefferson's preface that furnishes the most radical of interventions. For Varela does not merely exclude Jefferson's preface but also substitutes it with his own. Jefferson's preface ends with the following sentence: "But I have begun a sketch, which those who come after me will successively correct and fill up, till a code of rules shall be formed for the use of the Senate, the effects of which may be accuracy in business, economy of time, order, uniformity, and impartiality" (Jefferson 1820, x). On first blush, one may understand Varela's exclusion of the preface through the lens of this last line, which signals the document's unfinished quality and its very particular purpose within the US legislature. In other words, one may read it as evidence that Varela sought to generalize the document and remove those qualities suggesting an authoritative, if unfinished manual for precise political governance—qualities that might unduly influence readers in the new Spanish American republics for whom Varela was translating. Indeed, as noted earlier, there are suggestions within the annotations that Varela may have envisioned an alternative genealogy for parliamentary practices for the new Republics; he may have left out the preface accordingly to shape the meaning of the document as a general resource rather than a guide—as a historical document, that is, the first of its kind in the hemisphere, and one to which the Spanish American republics might refer but were not to adopt or assimilate without deep reflection. In short, Varela excluded Jefferson's preface because he understood that Spanish America had its own very different political history and cultural legacy.

Yet Varela substitutes for Jefferson's preface, not his own words, but an allusion to Jeremy Bentham, followed by direct quotations from Étienne Dumont's introduction to Bentham's *Tactique des assemblées législatives* (1816). The choice of Dumont is significant on multiple levels, for Varela spoke and wrote fluently in English and could easily have cited directly from Bentham had he wished. By citing Dumont instead, Varela highlights the importance of the *translator* in the dissemination of a work. As Varela well knew, had it not been for Dumont and his French renderings, Bentham's writings might never have reached the wide audience they did in the nineteenth century—including, most importantly, Bentham's essays regarding the Spanish colonies, which significantly influenced Spanish American revolutionaries, most of whom read French with more familiarity than English. Moreover, Dumont, like Bentham and unlike Jefferson, was an abolitionist. Substituting Jefferson's words with Dumont's in effect reframed the translation, bringing it into alignment with Varela's own politics in the 1820s regarding the slave trade and the institution of slavery.[21] At the same time, Varela's translation of Dumont's introduction includes multiple expressions that allowed the document to speak obliquely to the new Spanish American republics rather than the US legislators to whom Jefferson's original was addressed:

Garantizar la libertad de todos los miembros, proteger la minoria...
conseguir por ultimo una espresion fiel de la voluntad general...
Siempre estan a sus puertas dos grandes enemigos, la oligarquia por
la cual un corto numero domina a la mayoria, y la anarquia en la cual
cada uno celoso de su independencia se opone a la formacion de un
voto general. [*sic*]   (Varela 1826, v–vi)

(Guaranteeing the freedom of all of its members, protecting the
minority... obtaining in the end a faithful expression of the general
will... At its doors there are two great enemies, the oligarchy, by
which a small group dominates the majority, and anarchy, in which
each one is jealous of his own independence and is opposed to the
formation of a general vote.)

In this translation of Dumont, we see Varela speaking directly to the
perils facing the new Spanish American republics. Through Dumont
he warns the new republics to beware the interests of the oligarchy,
who owned the means of production and would continue subordi-
nating the Spanish American masses, most of them indigenous or of
African descent, and he likewise warns them of the anarchists or
those who only thought of independence without taking into account a system to ensure its success, thereby jeopardizing the independence project in the process. Inclusion of the Dumont preface,
moreover, also addresses those in Cuba who sought political change
and who looked to the US as a model. The "oligarchy" consisted of
the island's plantation owners, slave traffickers, and traders, who
conspired with the colonial government in Cuba to continue the institution of slavery on the island, thereby ensuring the colonial status
of the island for fear of slave revolts. In quoting Dumont, then, Varela
offers a veiled warning to the rising educated classes, including his
former university students, that if they were to seek independence
for the island and set up a parliamentary system to ensure its democratic governance, they must also take care to understand these two
challenges—from above and below—that could end their democratic aspirations.

Varela also foresaw yet another set of perils in this moment: the
possibility, as US sectionalism was consolidating, that the northern
republic might annex Cuba to extend its slaveholding territories.
Varela opposed slavery openly during these years, and he did not
wish to see the institution reinforced in the US by the incorporation
of the island into the Republic, particularly given that slavery was so
deeply ensconced in Cuba. His annotation of Jefferson's parliamentary

procedures also must be understood, then, in this context: he thought they served to abrogate the rights and influence of the minority—a minority of Catholics, of immigrants, and of those outright opposed to slavery—and rendered thereby the American republic less democratic than advertised. Some of those in the minority in the US, who spoke and wrote only in Spanish, were also warned by Varela's intervention regarding the dangers of majority rule. In a word, Jefferson's procedural manual represented for Varela a resource worth translating—but Jefferson, and all he stood for more broadly, had to be carefully reframed to highlight dangers to minority interests both within the United States and across the hemisphere.

*   *   *

At the intersection of Varela's multiple archives lies a lost Latina/o history, one that shapes our broader understanding of those Latina/os who lived (and those who continue to live) their lives crossing borders, both physical and metaphorical. Varela's life and biography give voice to those who, like him, cannot return to their place of origin or refuse to do so, but who, at the same time, cannot find themselves fully at home in the world of the United States. Varela, who refused to return to Cuba and at the same time refused to take US citizenship, exemplifies the double bind of a Latina/o history that lies between political exile and social assimilation, between the possibility of natal return and immigrant belonging. Or perhaps his life exemplifies the expanded political possibilities of refusing the narrow parameters of both colonial and national delimitation.

Indeed, from his intricate positionality, Varela could speak with an unusual complexity about issues that too often invited simplistic one-sidedness. He voiced his misgivings about the manner in which the business of the Catholic Church was sometimes conducted in Cuba, particularly in its failure to minister to enslaved Cubans and free people of color. He lamented the church's weakness in siding too closely with Spain and its colonial control of the island. Yet he defended the ongoing work of the Catholic Church in the United States, where it performed precisely the sort of charity that he felt was lacking in the land of republican freedoms: service to the poor, including the multitude of immigrants who were deeply in need. In Varela's view, the Catholic Church had a capacity to imagine itself, beyond mere theological superiority, in relation to other ways of thinking and believing. It had a capacity for tolerance that he did not see reflected in the daily political and social life of a country supposedly premised on religious tolerance. The church had something indispensable to offer to both Cuba and the United States, as Varela saw it, but it needed to address the different political and moral "superstitions" of both societies to transcend its own failures and limitations.

At the same time, Varela used his particular vantage point to address the failures of the United States in upholding the values it was supposed to present and to organize on behalf of an emergent minority politics. He called for a place to be found for the poor, non-white Catholic minority of New York and the nation at large: the Irish who were not yet "white," at least prior to the Civil War, and other Catholic immigrants and minority groups that hailed from across the world. Varela spent his literary career in the US reminding his readers that these immigrants should have been and yet were not welcomed.[22]

Varela made a decision to live between worlds, which allowed him to address and engage multiple worlds *simultaneously*. And in reading across the disparate, nationally delimited archives that house his writings, we find a methodology, a way of locating the literature and lives of those like Varela on the Latino Continuum, where their lives and works speaks to multiple worlds of thought even as their historical experiences evidence the discrepant spaces and times of living across US, Caribbean, and Latin American contexts.[23] Ultimately, Varela is an exemplar of the many Latina/o writers who were actively integrated into American life in the nineteenth century, yet who continued simultaneously to address and shape politics and ideas in contemporaneous Cuban, Latin American, and Spanish contexts. Varela's life and *oeuvre* present us with a series of intersections and flows, networks and relations, as Silva Gruesz (2001) and Brickhouse (2004) have respectively demonstrated, that are within, and yet also move beyond, their own space and time, yielding what we now speak of as Latina/o history.[24] Indeed, this history unfolds on a continuum, one that is constituted by the discrepant spaces and times of its actors across US, Caribbean, and Latin American contexts. But all too easily that continuum is obscured by the siloed reading of the evidence, housed as it is in what is restrictively imagined as national archives and often separated by linguistic divides.

In Chapter 2, I turn to a different Latina/o literary history, this time to explore the work of translation as historiography in a translation project that speaks to US interests in the Southwest while also bequeathing a record of Latina/o resistance to the concepts of Manifest Destiny and divine right. Here again, we find early Latina/o literary history drawing upon the vantage point of US location to address the new Spanish American republics, in this case warning them that the production of history itself must be read historically for its implication in hemispheric imperialism, while simultaneously cautioning US English-language readers against complicity in forging that history.

Latina/o Translations as Historiography

Miguel Teurbe Tolón (1823–57) is a figure well-known in Cuban history, in particular for his landmark contribution to the island's cultural and political life: he is credited with designing the nation's flag. While no anthology of Cuban literature would exclude Tolón, he nevertheless is generally received as a minor literary figure: his poems, the best-known—and most commonly anthologized—of his writings, belong to a short-lived romantic movement in Matanzas, Cuba, and his inclusion in anthologies is generally explicable more by the fact that he designed the Cuban flag than by any reputation he may have held as a consequential Cuban author.

While Latin American studies scholars may be justified in deeming Tolón's literary contributions to be relatively peripheral, Tolón nevertheless captures our attention for three principal reasons. First, his work as a translator; for he rendered for the first time in Spanish one of the most influential and consequential histories of the US that was published in his day, Emma Willard's *Abridged History of the United States*. The cultural significance of translation work, more broadly, is by now well understood in general terms, as it has been theorized extensively, the influence of translation having been measured as an extension of the form and meaning of a rendered work, for example, what amounts to a sort of fulfillment of the work's destiny (as Walter Benjamin (2007) would have it in the "Task of the Translator"). Lawrence Venuti (1995), in turn, has mapped in detail the influence of the translator's particular editorial decisions and the circumstances in which he or she works on the cultural influence of their rendered works. Susan Bassnett and André Lefevere (1990) draw our attention to the "cultural turn" in translation studies, reminding us that the translator inhabits, influences, and is influenced by his or her cultural world, while Edwin Gentzler (2008), by contrast, sees translation not as culturally embedded, but rather as

The Latino Continuum and the Nineteenth-Century Americas: Literature, Translation, and Historiography.
Carmen E. Lamas, Oxford University Press (2021). © Carmen E. Lamas. DOI: 10.1093/oso/9780198871484.003.0003

generative of culture. These theories inform the following analysis of Tolón's work.[1]

The second reason, which is related to the first, is that the specific circumstances of Tolón's historical moment signal the cultural importance of translation, and his translation of Emma Willard, in particular. For advancements in print technologies rendered published works more affordable to mass audiences. Concurrently, a continued interest in post-independence Latin American countries in American political and other works, such as Thomas Paine's *Common Sense* (1776), facilitated a robust and competitive mass market for English to Spanish translations. Translation, then, offers an important site, historically significant as it is, for understanding the manner in which *cultures influenced cultures* in the US, Cuba, and Latin America in the nineteenth century. Translation is a site for identifying not only the movement of cultural ideas across supposed cultural bounds, but also the mutual imbrication of supposedly different cultural worlds.

Tolón's translation and the act of contextualizing his historical moment signal the third reason for our interest in his writings: it is through an analysis of Tolón's rendering of Willard's *Abridged History* that we find him and his works situated on the Latino Continuum; and, noting in particular Willard's intended audience for this translation—a textbook for Spanish-speaking inhabitants of the newly acquired Southwest territories as well as a book for learning Spanish for US readers—, we may better discern the manner in which the Latino Continuum is articulated as a cultural phenomenon in American and Latin American history. Tolón's translation practice, in fact, sits on a continuum, moving between English and Spanish and between Cuba, the US, and Mexico. By critically engaging the vision expounded by Willard of the newly acquired Southwest and California territories, he provides an early political critique of US expansionism through his translation practice.

A measured study of his biography, historical context, and written works and translations, then, allows for Tolón's recovery as a key figure in US cultural and political history, while simultaneously revealing him to be not merely the author of a Cuban national icon but a figure whose US experience influenced him deeply, and through him Cuba as well. Finally, as I will argue, a study of Tolón's rendering of Willard's text reveals precisely that his is a Latina/o translation that, in fact, constructs a Latina/o historiography.

Matanzas, Cuba, to New York City and Back Again

Miguel Teurbe Tolón was born on September 29, 1820 in Matanzas, Cuba, a lively nineteenth-century intellectual center that came to be known as the "cuna" or cradle of Cuban poets. His parents too were from Matanzas, though his grandparents were Spanish but with genealogical ties to France. Tolón was educated in the local school in Matanzas and by private tutors but did not attend university. At this time of his life, he traveled within Cuba, visiting Havana on various occasions, but, probably for financial reasons, did not go abroad to Europe or the US as many of his contemporaries were doing at the time.

He exhibited an early interest in languages—he learned Latin, Greek, French, German, Italian, and English both autodidactically and from tutors—and voraciously read European authors in the original languages. This led ultimately to a professional career, beginning in the early 1840s, as a translator at the Real Hacienda, or what today we would refer to as the Chamber of Commerce, this being explicable in part by the fact that Matanzas had a concentration of US residents in Cuba at the time.[2] Tolón's work as a colonial translator was short-lived, however: he left this post in 1843 to dedicate himself to teaching and literary activities. After publishing his first collection of poems, *Los preludios* in 1841, he wrote a drama titled *Un caserío* in 1843. In 1844 he married his first cousin, Emilia Teurbe Tolón, who was only 16 years old at the time, in what was not a common practice in his day.

The Teurbe Tolón family was a revolutionary one. Their uncle, José Francisco Teurbe Tolón, was well known for his anti-colonial activities, including his organization of and participation in the Gran Legión del Águila Negra conspiracy of 1829, which led to his capture and indictment for conspiracy against the Spanish Crown. He avoided execution, however, by receiving a royal pardon from the Spanish monarchy. (Ferdinand VII, in an effort to garner support for the ascendency to the throne of his daughter Isabella II issued a general pardon in 1832 to all Spanish subjects who had engaged in revolutionary activities on the island.) Upon his release, José Francisco, unrepentant in his revolutionary ambitions, left the island to live in Mexico. There, he was named vice consul of Mexico in Philadelphia, where he continued to plan a Cuban revolution until his death in New Orleans in 1834.

Miguel Tolón also participated in revolutionary activities. He regularly attended the local *tertulia* in which authors from Matanzas and elsewhere in Cuba (such as Havana and Camagüey) would meet to share their work and, oftentimes, plan for Cuban independence. Like Tolón's uncle, they envisioned a Cuba independent of Spanish colonial rule by way of annexation to the United States as a fully incorporated state.

In Cuba Tolón wrote and published his poetry in multiple newspapers and literary magazines such as *El Faro Industrial, La Prensa, La Piragua, La Floresta Cubana, Brisas de Cuba*, and *El Duende*. He also published a *costumbrista* novel titled *Lola Guara. Novela cubana* in 1846.[3] At the same time, he edited with José Victoriano Betancourt a compilation of poems well known in Cuban studies, *Aguinaldo Matanzero* in 1847.[4] Eventually, the political activities of the Matanzas literati caught Tolón up in their revolutionary agendas, and he was forced to flee to New York in 1848 to avoid persecution at the hands of Spanish authorities for his anti-colonial activities.[5]

In the US, Tolón continued his journalistic career as the editor of *El Herald* of New York. He also edited the pro-annexation newspaper *La Verdad* from 1848 to 1852, which led to his being sentenced to death *in absentia* by Spanish authorities, this due to *La Verdad*'s call for Cuban independence through annexation to the US (Tolón's long-held political position, one that, intriguingly, he seems to have abandoned precisely around the time when he set himself to translating Willard's *Abridged History*). His wife Emilia stayed in Cuba when Tolón fled to New York, but also found herself implicated in these activities. Ultimately, she was exiled from the island in 1850, joining her husband in New York in April of that year. In fact, hers was the first exile order issued to a woman, and she is thus often counted as the first female Cuban exile (Chávez Álvarez 2010, 31).

Emilia divorced Tolón in October 1854 in the State of New York and was remarried two months later in Savannah, Georgia to one Dr. Juan Luis Rey, a fellow Cuban who had practiced medicine in Matanzas from 1847 to 1853. Emilia and Juan Luis married in the Protestant Christ Church in Savannah, Georgia, their nuptials officiated by the Reverend Stephen Elliot, who was the thirty-seventh bishop of the Protestant Episcopal Church of the United States and was eventually appointed the Presiding Bishop of the Protestant Episcopal Church of the Confederate States of America. Subsequently, and after the official dissolution of her marriage to Tolón by the

Catholic Church, Emilia and Juan Luis were married in the Catholic Church in New Orleans in 1857. Tolón also remarried, wedding one Sara Jean Wallace, a woman with whom he was most likely already involved in New York when Emilia arrived in 1850. Marrying one month after his divorce from Emilia was finalized, they had a daughter together in 1856, Estrella, who died from tuberculosis in Cuba in 1875 at the age of 19, this in the midst of the Ten Years' War (1868–78), Cuba's first organized attempt at independence. Sara Jean Wallace had died earlier in Matanzas from yellow fever, a year after Tolón's own death from tuberculosis (Chávez Álvarez 2010, 41). (While the present analysis concentrates on Tolón, it is important to recover the lives of such Latinas as Emilia and Estrella, since they help us recover the lives of Latinas in the nineteenth century.)

In New York, Tolón aligned himself politically with annexationists who supported Narciso López's filibustering activities. López was born in Venezuela, fought against Simón Bolívar, and left Venezuela in 1823, when it separated from Spain. In Cuba, he married the sister of the high-ranking Spanish official and plantation owner with vast slaveholdings, el Conde de Pozos Dulce. After the dissolution of their short-lived marriage, López moved to Spain and fought against the Carlist rebels until 1841, when he returned to the island. In Cuba, he was a part of the Spanish colonial administration until he became disenchanted with Spain's political and economic abuses. He too had to flee Cuba in 1848 out of fear of punishment at the hands of the Spanish authorities for revolutionary activities that aimed at separating Cuba from Spain. In New York Tolón not only aligned himself with the López filibusterers, but was also a part of the Consejo Cubano, headed by Gaspar Betancourt Cisneros and Cristóbal Madán. Madán was a plantation and slave owner who married the sister of John O'Sullivan, the supposed originator of the concept of Manifest Destiny and editor of the *The United States Magazine and Democratic Review* (1837–59).[6]

Narciso López mounted several armed campaigns to liberate Cuba by invasion. He was captured and then executed by Spanish authorities on September 1, 1851 during one of these attempts. As a consequence, the Cuban exiles in New York found themselves without a leader. The lack of support on the part of President James Polk and Congress, coupled with John Quitman's own last-minute cancellation of a filibustering mission—John Quitman had been named López's successor after the death of the latter—led to the dissolution of the Consejo Cubano and curtailed future filibustering activities. Ultimately, the death of López occasioned the formation of the Junta Cubana in 1852, though it disbanded in 1855 due to internal dissension among *Junta* members. With the demise of the Junta Cubana the annexationist movement itself fell apart, this according to a contemporary of Tolón's, Pedro José Guiteras (2001, 142). Tolón, himself a member of the Junta, became disillusioned with the politics of the Cubans in New York and left the group in 1854. It is also around this time that he increasingly chartered his own path in pursuit of revolutionary activities. After leaving *La Verdad* in 1852, he founded and published his own newspapers. In 1855 he founded *El Papagayo*, later renamed *El Cometa*. He also published political opinion pieces in various local Latina/o newspapers such as *El Mulato*.

The demise of annexationism had other, material consequences in Tolón's life. Several of his financial patrons were wealthy Cubans who lived between New York and the island, and being slave owners continued to advocate for joining Cuba to the United States. This they did with the intention of strengthening the institution of slavery on the island by forming a political alliance with the Southern slaveholding states. The loss of their patronage meant Tolón's economic situation took a turn for the worse, and he found himself having to sell his poetry for profit in order to survive financially. Around this time, he also published *The Elementary Spanish Reader and Translator* (1853) and translated Emma Willard's *Abridged History of the United States or Republic of America* as *Compendio de la historia de los Estados Unidos o república de América* (1853). Tolón published poems in English in the *Waverly Magazine* in 1852, and in 1856 he published, in New York, his *Leyendas cubanas*, a collection of Cuban *costumbrista* pieces written both on the island and in New York City.

A general amnesty was granted to exiled Cubans by the Spanish Crown in 1854. Tolón, however, waited until he was on his deathbed to return to the island, which he did on August 23, 1857. After his return to Matanzas he published *Flores y espinas*—a collection of his poems written both in Cuba and in New York—and died shortly afterwards, on November 16, 1857, from tuberculosis (Ropero Regidor 2004, 66).[7]

A few months after his passing, his friend Emilio Blanchet published an article on Tolón that presented him as a sort of persona, the tragic romantic poet who sacrifices for the Cuban nation, at the cost in particular of personal betrayal, this at the hand of his first wife

Emilia. On May 13, 1858 in the Matanzas newspaper *Aurora del Yumurí*, in a review of *Flores y espinas*, Blanchet writes, "Amó con delirio a una mujer quien tan cruelmente le traicionó, de tal desencanto y hastío supo llenarle el alma que, huyendo los brillantes salones a donde con ansias era llamado, buscó el olvido en la embriaguez, en pasatiempos insensatos, y al fin cayó rendido en la tumba" (quoted in Chávez Álvarez 2010, 48) (He loved with delirium a woman who cruelly betrayed him, his soul filled with disenchantment and weariness to the point that, fleeing the excellent salons to which with longing others beckoned him, he searched for forgetting in intoxication, in imprudent pastimes, and in the end fell defeated on his tomb). While I will not here examine *Flores y espinas*, nor Blanchet's complete review of the collection, suffice it to note that *Flores y espinas* is filled with untranslated epigraphs in English and contains poems dedicated to the likes of Cirilo Villaverde, a longtime Cuban exile/Latino who was a friend of Tolón's. These linguistic, spatial, and affective connections place Tolón and his work on a continuum. The significance to the Latino Continuum of *Flores y espinas* is signaled as well in his dedication to this collection, titled "Al lector," which dramatically reflects his views regarding his New York exile:

> En la patria i en estrañas tierras; en dias de felizidad i en noches de infortunio, he recojido este haz que al fin dejo caer ante el umbral del público, como el fardo de pobre peregrino fatigado. Las flores son pocas i ya marchitas; pero pocas son tambien las espinas, porque muchas se han quedado clavadas en mi frente. [*sic*]   (Tolón 1857, 5)

> (In the homeland and in foreign lands, in days of happiness and nights of misfortune, I have gathered this sheaf that I finally let fall before the doorstep of the public, like the bundle carried by the poor fatigued pilgrim. The flowers are few and already withered; but few also are the thorns, because many have been nailed on my forehead.)

In referring to the homeland and to foreign lands, meaning Cuba and the US respectively, Tolón thus recognized the places from which he composed his work, as well the impact these spaces had on his writing. *Leyendas cubanas* (New York 1856) and *Flores y espinas* (Matanzas 1857) in particular demonstrate the comings and goings of Tolón and Latina/os and their works as simultaneously constituting and existing on the Latino Continuum. Tolón published works written in both Matanzas and New York in both of these collections as well as translating some of these texts for the *Waverly Magazine* (1852 5: 8-10) and using others for his *Elementary Spanish Reader and Translator* (Tolón 1853). This circulation of texts creates a continuum between Matanzas and New York and then back again that exemplifies how time and space are conflated on the Latino Continuum, calling for a re-evaluation of how Latina/os impacted the US, their home countries, and the Americas more broadly. It is to such sites as Matanzas and New York, in particular, the context in which Tolón's translation was crafted, that we now turn. For in the linguistic and spatial crossing and recrossing of his life and his translation, Tolón's *Compendio* provides a warning regarding US expansionism to his Latin American readers and to those Mexicans and *californios* now forced into (or out of) the US national imaginary. But, it also provides a corrective to US readers of their own erroneous history-making enterprises, thereby inviting them to read the violence of their expansionist histories more accurately.

Historical Context: US-Mexico War and Cuba

Tolón arrived in New York in 1848, the year that the US-Mexico War ended. Two years later California was admitted to the US as the thirty-first state. Three years earlier, Texas was admitted to the Union as the twenty-eighth, this after having declared its independence from Mexico in 1836 but prior to Mexico ceding the territory to the United States in 1848, which only occurred after the US military occupied Texas in 1846. Florida too joined the Union in 1845, bringing the US border to the Straits of Florida and the doorstep of the island. As is well known, the period in which Tolón found himself in the US (he left New York in 1857) was one defined by territorial expansion that was guided by the doctrine of Manifest Destiny and shaped by debates about slavery and its future in the Union. As an annexationist Tolón would have looked optimistically at what appeared to be flexible options for Cuba's incorporation into the United Sates: Texas was admitted as a slave state and California as a free state. More importantly, Texas found its way into the Union via a sort of filibustering: the territories acceded to the US were counted by Mexico as an integral part of that country at the time of accession, and it is only with the US military invasion in 1846 that Mexico ceded the Texas territories. Tolón, on his arrival in New York, had good reason, then, to imagine a Cuba annexed to the US as a slave state, for such ambitions were consonant with the political events of the day.

Unfortunately for Tolón, his time in the US led him to learn the common lesson that history is not always remembered or memorialized as it occurs. Despite the events of the day, Tolón in his roles as editor of *La Verdad* and translator of Willard's *Abridged History* realized that the Cuba and US imagined in these two textual worlds excluded a place for his own conception of Cuba as part of the United States. Willard's history, in particular, was crafted with a singular telos in mind: to defend and justify the divine right of American expansionism and, more than this, to do so in a way that would foster or support the continued union of American states, even in the face of severe disagreement regarding the future of the institution of slavery therein. In pursing this aim Willard systematically wrote any violence or conflict surrounding the institution of slavery out of her narrative and systematically erased any record of the presence of Mexican nationals in the newly acquired territories of the Southwest. Willard's strategy, then, was to focus on the newly acquired territories, emphasizing Manifest Destiny in order to eclipse the deep fissure that the future of slavery was causing in the Union. In what follows, I offer a contextualized reading of Willard's *Abridged History*, which charts her deployment of the events of the US-Mexico War in her whitewashed historiography. It is this historiographic intervention that I propose most struck Tolón, because it is one that elided or erased any awareness of Latina/os in the newly expanded Union, as it did any cognizance of Catholicism among those peoples, this in a pattern with her treatment of Native Americans in her historiography. To put it differently, Willard's history denied any recognition of a Latino Continuum, which is restored by Tolón in his translation.[8]

Emma Willard's *Abridged History of the United States* was based on her bestseller *History of the United States, or Republic of America* (Willard 1848). Willard began to publish her *History* in 1828. The *Abridged Histories* began to appear in 1831 and continued into the 1860s. The *Abridged History* was so popular that it was adopted as a textbook in multiple states. The longer *History* was sold to private libraries and academies, while the *Abridged Histories* were sold to individuals and common schools. Thus, Nina Baym (1991, 5) in "Women and the Republic" concludes that Willard's audience was "the entire literate population" of the US, since, in addition to her textbooks, entire sections of her book were reprinted in other histories of the nineteenth century. A descendant of revolutionaries, Willard included in her early editions a poem that dedicates the book to her mother, a testament to her desire to preserve revolutionary history in the face of the fact that participants in the Revolution were disappearing and were no longer able to tell their stories (Baym 1991, 11). Willard's goal, Baym explains, was to keep the memory of the American Revolution alive for the American reading public (Baym 1991, 10). Yet Baym, while admitting the importance of Willard for US history, stresses that Willard was not a historian inasmuch as she used no secondary sources. Rather, she suggests, Willard was a writer of history (Baym 1991, n1 19).

This designation of Willard as a writer of history speaks directly to the type of narrative that she created, one in which "explicit military history" (Baym 1991, 15) frames and constructs US national history. And one in which "the US-Mexico War—which excited her territorial imagination with an intensity second only to the American Revolution—enlarges the military segment of the American histories after 1850" (Baym 1991, 15). Baym's discerning analysis of war as Willard's paradigm for the creation of the US concludes with the observation that Willard's narrative presents women and children as figures merely to be protected from the effects of war rather than as active participants in it, a conclusion I will argue against (Baym 1991, 15).

Susan Schulten's (2012) *Mapping the Nation: History and Cartography in Nineteenth-Century America*, in turn, while echoing Baym's assessment of Willard's historiographical practices, meaning she understood them to be not official histories per se, concentrates not on the role of war in her narratives but on Willard's use of maps:[9] "US history was synonymous with growth [after the War of 1812], and the present could be framed as the fulfillment of past struggles" (Schulten 2012, 11). Growth was best depicted spatially, and Schulten draws an important distinction between geographical and historical maps in evaluating the popularity of Willard's renderings. The former record the contours of terrain and geography with precision, while the latter do not and merely record historical events pictorially. Willard exclusively published the latter in her textbooks. Schulten asks, "If these maps did not explain American historical geography in any useful way, why were they so popular?" (Schulten 2012, 12). She answers:

> In fact, it was their *lack* of detail, depth, and substance—precisely what marks them as non-geographical—that accounts for their appeal. Historical maps and atlases were not used to *explain* geographical problems, but rather to cultivate a shared identity by offering tangible evidence of the nation's evolution over time. The purpose was not to explore the nuances of geography, but to document the evolution of the nation as a sovereign territory.   (Schulten 2012, 12)

If Willard's maps stressed in their very design an American identity found in the geographic reach of the Union, then any prospect of a territorially divided US could only be expected to problematize them. And, indeed, as Schulten (2007) notes, Willard's textbooks and maps met with a crisis when they were set to confronting the looming Civil War. The degree to which Willard would go to protect the continuity of the Union is perhaps unsurprising "given [that] the fact of the United States was central not just to her identity as a nationalist but also to her livelihood as one of the nation's first historians" (Schulten 2007, 564).

Schulten signals Willard's rejection of civil war by noting a plan she drafted to address slavery. She proposed that enslaved persons be transported to the Northeast to work for middle-class white families, thereby avoiding armed conflict over slavery. Willard advocated for this "colonization campaign" in the 1860 edition of her *History of the United States* and in a pamphlet entitled *Via Media: A Peaceful and Permanent Settlement of the Slavery Question*, published in 1862. From her plan and her advocacy—she attended congressional sessions that addressed slavery and obtained hundreds of signatures from women in support of the plan—it is clear, Schulten argues, that Willard's notion of Manifest Destiny was threatened by the potential division in the country, especially when the "other" in war would not be Native Americans or the British, but fellow Americans (Schulten 2007, 564). Willard, consequently, found herself unable to write that history.

Because textbooks like Willard's deployed a particular narrative strategy to cultivate a sentiment of conciliation and compromise, Barry Joyce (2015) argues that they positioned Americans as passive onlookers at the divine destiny and exceptionalism of the United States.[10] One can readily agree that Willard repeatedly makes explicit and implicit appeals to divine providence in her narratives; yet, while like fellow textbook writer A. H. Grimshaw, she clearly presented

Americans as passive witnesses to the predestined disappearance of Native Americans from, and the cultivation of the institution of slavery in, the US, her narrative voice also shifts dramatically when recounting the events of the US-Mexico War in her *Abridged Histories*. There, Willard's narrative strategy is made clear by her deployment of examples of American ingenuity and military weaponry in the course of prosecuting the war. Mexicans are presented as politically unstable and vindictive. Mexico's military is depicted as unable to withstand even the audacious frontal attacks of small numbers of Americans. Even when Mexican soldiers greatly outnumber their opponents, Americans are said heroically to kill hundreds, even thousands, of Mexican troops against all odds. Also in contrast to her narrative voice in depicting the looming Civil War, in recounting the events of the US-Mexico War, Willard speaks in a different voice/ tone, one that situates the reader or student not simply as a witness, as Baym (1991) and Joyce (2015) assume, but as an active participant. Her detailed, step-by-step accounting of how the war was won brings the reader directly into the battlefield, and her work reads like missives from the front by war correspondents. Recounting a confrontation between General Scott and General Santa Anna in April 1846, for example, Willard writes:

> Gen. Scott found that the Mexican position was so commanded by the batteries of the lofty height of Cerro Gordo that approach in front was impracticable. But, aided by the skill of his engineers, Lee and Beauregard, he turned to the left, causing to be made a new road, by which,—ascending along a difficult slope, and over deep chasms, his army might reach the rear of the enemy's camp. After three days of secret labor, the road was made. On the 17th of April, the commander published a general order for the next day,—showing how the battle was to be gained,—how the fleeing were to be pursued,—and how the greatest advantage was to be reaped from the victory. All was done as commanded. About noon the steep ascent was won... At two o'clock, P.M. the enemy were put to flight,—more than a thousand having fallen. Santa Anna and a part of his army had fled, and the eager pursuit had commenced.   (Willard 1852, 367–68)

The reader, regardless of gender or age, finds him/herself, in this and dozens of examples like it, on the battlefield itself, speaking with the generals, hearing from informants, and outsmarting and shooting the "jealous" and "fiercely revengeful" Mexicans (Willard 1852, 341).

For Willard, the US-Mexico War offered a means of uniting the antebellum nation in the face of looming secession by the South over the question of slavery, as Joyce (2015, 244) suggests. Yet, it is an *active* narrative that interpellates her readers into history; she invokes American expansionism in the Southwest to distract attention from the question of slavery, which is only passingly acknowledged in her *Abridged History* of 1852. Willard's narrative thus mounts the military campaign of territorial acquisition to obfuscate internal ideological dissension; her narrative calls every American to join the fight for the common good and American destiny, at the expense of what she presents as a feckless and evil "other."

While the narrative voice changes dramatically in her depiction of the history of the US-Mexico War, some of Willard's earlier mapping and textual strategies are also in evidence in this section of her *Abridged History*. Her depictions of Native Americans as absent from the US landscape are replicated in the empty terrain of the US Southwest that she constructs, one in which European migrants could come to populate the land just as Puritans came from Europe to populate what is now the Northeast. Schulten (2012, 25) argues that Willard in recording Native American history in a preface to the edition places them outside of the historical narrative of the US, which begins with Columbus in chapter one. She further contends that the substantive chapters of Willard's textbook subsequently erase the inhabitants of the continent:

> To integrate European migrants, she emptied the interior of the tribes that had densely populated her introductory map...this removal of Native life from the map enabled Anglo-Americans to think about the land as free of obstacles and to appropriate it according to their own visions. Ironically, as contact with tribes increased, their presence on the map decreased. (Schulten 2012, 26)

Willard's post-1848 maps similarly empty the Southwest of Mexicans. Indeed, no Mexicans are ever encountered in her narrative unless they are part of the inferior Mexican military that is vanquished by the superior US troops.[11] In short, Willard simply erases Latina/o— and Spanish American—history and identities from American history, much as Native American history was excluded therefrom, all in an effort to force a coherence on a Union of peoples on the precipice of a civil war to be fought over slavery, yet another subject of US history set in the margins of Willard's narrative.

Between the Temple of Time and the Temple of Liberty

To capture America's territorial growth and to add historical meaning and significance to that growth, Willard constructed a *chronog-
rapher* [sic] she called *The Temple of Time* (see Fig. 1). The imagery of
a temple was familiar to Willard's readers, since as early as 1776
American revolutionaries deployed the concept of Columbia and
her temple as a representation of freedom against Britain. George
Washington himself referred to the United States as a Temple of
Liberty and wanted the US Capitol to be built as a replica of the
Pantheon in Rome, in order to represent American republicanism.
Thomas Jefferson similarly designed Virginia's state Capitol building
as a replica of the Pantheon and spoke of the construction of the US
Capitol as a Temple of Liberty representing the great US republican
enterprise. Yet the irony of the US Capitol being constructed by enslaved Africans was noted even by their contemporaries: James
Madison's secretary, for example, was quoted as saying that it was a
revolting sight to see "gangs of negroes" building the nation's capital
(cited in Gibbs 2011, 165). In Willard's chronographer we find the
same paradox: her American Temple of Time sought to disavow the

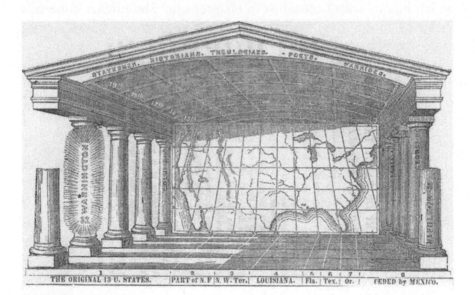

FIGURE 1. Emma Willard. *Abridged History of the United States, or Republic of
America*. New York: Barnes, 1860.

violence of slavery by making forcible US expansionism and Manifest Destiny an inevitable reality.

The American Temple of Time was created, moreover, in the late 1840s "when the Treaty of Guadalupe Hidalgo and compromise with Britain enlarged [US] territory by a third" (Schulten 2010, 34–35).[12] Willard designed her chronographer purportedly to aid, in the first place, students at Troy Female Seminary (founded by Willard in 1814, it is the first institution for women's higher education in the US) and, more generally, those who were using her textbooks throughout the US to memorize historical events and places in American history. However, even a cursory analysis of the American Temple of Time clarifies both that its very conception was possible only by tying it to the territorial acquisitions that occurred at the time of its creation, that is, the US Southwest, and that she conceived of this and her historically more expansive Universal Temple of Time, which won a medal at the 1851 World's Fair in London, as narrative tools that would announce the political and military significance of the United States on a world stage.

The concept of a temple held up by pillars is one that circulated among the Cuban compatriots in New York City, as well, specifically the editors of *La Verdad*. In an 1849 pamphlet titled *Thoughts upon the Incorporation of Cuba into the American Confederation*, which was published in *La Verdad*, Gaspar Betancourt Cisneros speaks of the Temple of Liberty in relation to Cuban annexation to the United States. As Lazo (2005, 82) suggests, "Betancourt Cisneros invoked the metaphor of the 'temple of Liberty' as a model of the future that would please slaveholders and *filibustero* separatists alike." However, Betancourt does more than this. He also wishes to please the US North and South. In the subsection titled "Cuba—A State of the Union," he writes that the island annexed to the US would be a sovereign state, "AN EMPIRE within AN EMPIRE" (emphasis his) (Betancourt Cisneros 1849, 19):

> The present inhabitants of Cuba will form its political constitution, for it belongs alone to them to do it. And they will found it on the past; conform it to present circumstances; and, with prudent foresight, regulate it to the future; harmonizing it in its structure (Republican) with that of the great edifice—the federal constitution of the United States—which has at all times a space and points of

union prepared to receive another column in that glorious temple of
Liberty.   (Betancourt Cisneros 1849, 20)

The link between Willard's American Temple of Time and her furtive
attempt to avoid any treatment of a possible or eventual Southern
secession, which in turn speaks to her colonization plan (i.e., that enslaved Africans did not have a say in their future, and certainly not
their immediate freedom), is found in the next sentence of Betancourt's
essay, where he equates slave traders with abolitionists: "How inspiring the thought that this our column will be protected and supported
by thirty or more columns which will shield it from Spain, and
England, Europe, negro-traders, or abolitionists—in a word, from
enemies within and without" (Betancourt Cisneros 1849, 20).

When he speaks of enemies within and without, it is not just Cuba
that he is addressing, but the US as well. For he equates the Union of
the States to a marriage relationship in which each individual is different, though they share a "common existence": "In A the rights of
the husband are respected. In B, the rights of the wife. In A B or both
jointly, are recognized the sovereignty of the family, and the marriage compact—the symbol of the Union" (Betancourt Cisneros
1849, 20). In his use of the marriage metaphor, Betancourt, like
Willard, thus seeks to bring a compromise to the threats of Southern
secession. He argued that the Union could remain intact, not least in
order to protect itself from European powers, as well from the threats
of slave traders to the North and abolitionists to the South; all threats
would be dispelled if both sides would live harmoniously, each allowing the other to continue in the relationship without imposing
itself on the other.

Betancourt evokes the temple metaphor in responding to an article that warned Cubans of the dangers of annexation to the US, one
that had been recently published by José Antonio Saco (1848), a dis-
ciple of Varela, who like Varela condemned annexation. As such,
Betancourt's characterization of the Temple of Liberty and the place
of slavery within it, both in Cuba *and* the US, is unsurprising. Yet it
provides another place on the Latin Continuum, demonstrating how
Cuban and US history were envisioned as mutually imbricated. The
Cubans of this era did not consider themselves as passive observers
or as potential recipients of US benevolence. They envisioned themselves as active participants in expanding democracy.

The link between *La Verdad*, where Betancourt's article is published, and Emma Willard's textbooks is found in the figure of the English-language editor of *La Verdad*, Cora Montgomery, whose real name was Jane McManus Storm Cazneau. McManus was a filibusterer who participated in the US-Mexico War as the first female US war correspondent. An avid expansionist and a land speculator in Texas, she was a student of Willard's at the Troy Female Seminary. It is this connection that most likely led to these parallel uses of language and imagery by Betancourt; it is also likely that she is the one who facilitated Tolón's translation of Willard's *Abridged History*. Willard most likely envisioned Cuba, potentially, and (parts of) Mexico, in reality, as being integral components of the US when she conceived of the Temple of Time. While she does not address the annexation of Texas in earlier publications and Cuba is only mentioned peripherally, she writes of the US-Mexico War separately in a book published in 1849 under the title *Last Leaves of American History: Comprising Histories of the Mexican War and California*.[13]

The first 100 pages of *Last Leaves* detail the annexation of Texas and the actual war, for it ends with the "Treaty of Peace" i.e., the Treaty of Guadalupe Hidalgo of 1848. The second part of the book gives a history of the Southwest from the time of Spanish discovery and settlement to the Jesuit missions. Halfway through this second section she begins to speak of the more recent migration to California by northeasterners; the *californios*, who had long lived in the region, are nonexistent in her narrative. Instead, the new immigrants from the US are the ones who, by populating the area, in fact create it. The book concludes with a discussion of the Gold Rush, noting that migrants were coming by sea and by land, the latter being a 90-day journey that could be made via Santa Fe or over the Rocky Mountains:

> It is supposed that the emigrants from the western states will exceed in number those from the eastern. Whether this is true or not, it is certain that many of our ablest and most enterprising citizens are now on the wing, of whom numbers are intending to settle in that salubrious clime...their faces be sternly set against anarchy, the scourge, and too often the destroyer of free governments. To this end, let them uphold law, found schools, observe the Sabbath, and maintain pure Christianity. (Willard 1849, 230)

In the end *Last Leaves* situates the readers so as to feel as part of the action after the US-Mexico War, this time not as part of the military but as migrants colonizing and civilizing their own country.[14]

Last Leaves is incorporated into Willard's *Abridged History* in different ways as of 1850. In the 1850 edition, Willard chooses selectively from *Last Leaves* in order to summarize the evolving westward expansion of the US. She does this by lengthening the fourth section, which had previously ended with Tyler's ascension to the presidency (the edition published before 1850 dates from 1847), this by adding a treatment of Mormonism and anti-rentism. She also includes an appendix on "American California" that narrows the California experience to the Gold Rush and immigration from the East to the West.

California becomes integral to US history when it is incorporated into the *Abridged History* in 1852, this mirroring California's annexation to the US as a state in 1850.[15] Willard concludes the text with the intersection of three historical events/moments: the Compromise of 1850, Cuban filibustering expeditions, and the creation of Liberia and the settlement campaign of the American Colonization Society (ACS), which had been excluded from the earlier publications. As is typical of her narrative, then, she again refuses to speak directly to the question of slavery in the US, in this case by isolating the issue spatially to Africa, signaling as she does that the colonization of Liberia would serve as a "safety-valve for drawing off our surplus colored population" (Willard 1852, 407). Furthermore, she also ties the issue of slavery to a Protestant missionary campaign, for in referencing the ACS, which had close ties to the anti-Catholic American Bible Society, she invokes the ambition of US global colonization through religion. She writes that the colonization of Liberia was in the main "a means of changing the present degradation of Africa into Christian civilization" (Willard 1852, 407). Simultaneously, her narrative seeks to assuage any fear of slave revolt and in doing so to diminish any concern over the question of the future of slavery in the US: citing in the concluding pages of the *Abridged History* the total population numbers in the US and noting there the presence of more than 3 million enslaved people in the country, she immediately adds that "there is a great and increasing emigration from Europe to America. In 1850, the number exceeded 800,000, and the ratio is rapidly increasing" (Willard 1852, 408).

It is in response to these narrative decisions by Willard that Tolón intervenes in his translation of her *Abridged History*, for he calls into question the validity of her history through specific textual interventions related to the text's treatment of slavery, of Latina/os (specifically Mexicans in her narrative of the Southwest), and of Catholics in the US.

Compendio de la historia de los Estados Unidos o *República de América* (1853)

Tolón's rendering of Willard's *Abridged History*, the *Compendio de la historia de los Estados Unidos o República de América* (hereafter *Compendio*), opens with Tolón's translation of Willard's author's preface ("Prefacio de la Autora"). Yet it is followed by a section written, and it seems translated, by Willard herself and titled "Al lector español" (To the Spanish reader), dated "Troy, 1851," and signed "Emma Willard." She emphasizes therein that in this Spanish-language edition of her *Abridged History*, the "últimas pájinas de esta historia han sido traducidas de un manuscrito preparado por la autora en adicion á la obra original" [*sic*] (Tolón 1853, 6) (last pages of the history have been translated from a manuscript prepared by the author in addition to the original work), meaning that her history now covers events up to the date of its publication, with mention of this fact serving to emphasize the immediacy of her account. She subsequently explains that she adds the new historical materials (which largely address the events of the US-Mexico War and the accession of California to the United States) so that the new Spanish-speaking "compatriotas," who providentially had become fellow countrymen with "nosotros los Americanos" (we Americans), i.e., US citizens, could learn about their shared history. She goes on to write that "todos deberiamos saber la historia del pais á que la en comun pertenecemos" [*sic*] (Tolón 1853, 6) (all should know the history of the country we belong to in common). Implying that the current translation may also be used by English-language speakers to learn Spanish, she notes "unos y otros hallariamos lo útil mezclado con lo deleitoso en la adquisicion de esta ó aquella de entrámbas lenguas" [*sic*] (Tolón 1853, 6) (one or the other [meaning those "compatriots" who share the same history] could find the useful mixed with the pleasing with the acquisition of both languages). She concludes, "Motivo de satisfaccion seria para la autora que su libro sirviese al mismo tiempo de provechoso medio para la consecucion de

tal objeto" [*sic*] (Tolón 1853, 6) (It would give the author much satis-
faction if the book serves at the same time as an advantageous means
for the attainment of that objective). And, indeed, Willard was correct in her assumption that anglophones might wish to use the
volume to learn Spanish, for Tolon's translation was marketed as a
textbook for teaching that language. The newspaper *New York
Evangelist*, for example, announced Tolón's translation as "The
Spanish translation of Mrs. Willard's *History of the United States*—a
fine text-book for the acquisition of that language."

Willard's Spanish-language preface next speaks directly to
Spanish-speaking Americans when she greets them as "compatriotas
mios, los que hablais la lengua castellana" (compatriots of mine,
those who speak the Spanish language), and congratulates them for
being admitted into the Union, concluding "¡Plegue al cielo que, her-
manadas las virtudes de Isabel la Católica con las de Washington,
sean los primeros en mérito los Estados que hoy son los últimos por
órden de tiempo!" (Tolón 1853, 6) (May the heavens answer our
prayers that the states that are now last [chronologically] be first in
merit, through the union of the virtues of Isabel the Catholic with
those of Washington!). With this, then, she implies that Spanish and
American virtues, represented by the figures of their founding
mother and father, respectively, will lead the last admitted states to
becoming the first in merit in the Union.

Implicit in this mention of Isabel, and with it the evocation of "Old
Catholic Spain," is reference to the Catholic mission of evangelization that her figure represented, and Willard, in evoking just this and
linking it to Washington and the American republican project,
shifted attention away from the violence of the conquest of Mexico.
This shift of symbolism was, in fact, common in the period, it being
a strategy that began immediately following the US-Mexico War, according to Lint Sagarena (2014) in *Aztlán and Arcadia: Religion,
Ethnicity and the Creation of Place*. Beginning with the writings of
Henry Dana, who penned the first description of California in 1840,
moving through the work of Elizabeth Hughes on the Franciscan
missions of California in the 1870s, and concluding with an analysis
of *californios testimonios* conducted by the agents of Hubert Howe
Bancroft in the 1890s, Lint Sagarena traces the history of the rhetoric
of US writers who supported expansionism by lauding the evangelizing mission of the Franciscan Fathers while condemning the greed
of the Mexican government that had secularized those missions, the

rhetoric thereby legitimizing a US takeover of California.[16] Regarding Elizabeth Hughes, he writes:

> Unlike the military Spanish conquest of Mexico, the Spanish conquest of California was imagined as a spiritual conquest [thus the reference to Queen Isabel in Willard] ... Just as the American "second conquest" of Mexico City was understood as having been carried out benevolently by gallant soldiers following the model of Cortés, the American conquest of California was portrayed as an echo of a Spanish Franciscan conquest—that is, as a legitimate, peaceful, and inevitable progressive transition toward greater civility, industry, and piety.   (Lint Sagarena 2014, 29)

Lint Sagarena suggests that this rhetoric simultaneously served a more sinister end. He argues that the secularization of the Spanish missions was exploited to precipitate collusion between the US Catholic Church and officials of the new State of California. Ultimately, this led to the appropriation of the vast properties and funds of the Spanish missions. (I will speak in more detail about this process in Chapter 3.) At the same time, reference to Isabel la Católica and Washington, as exemplars of the new expanded nation's past, obscured the violence of the Spanish evangelizing mission of the colonial period, as well as the American conquest of Native peoples: in seeing a common civilization shared by hispanophones and anglophones, it simultaneously obscured (by way of omission) the ongoing conquest of Southwest peoples, both Mexican and Native American, in the late 1840s and early 1850s.

Immediately following Willard's prefaces is printed Tolón's "Prefacio del Traductor" (Translator's Preface), signed "Miguel T. Tolón, New York, 1851." He begins by admitting to the great and progressive influence of the American Union on the New World, politically and economically, and explains that he completed the translation in order to make the book available to "los jóvenes en las escuelas de América" (Tolón 1853, 7) (young people in the schools of the Americas).[17]

Willard's self-translated introduction and Tolón's preface, then, when read together, may be understood to unite English and Spanish speakers in a shared cause—US expansionism coupled with Cuban annexation—which mirrored the mission of *La Verdad* in its quest to reach Spanish and English readers alike, this in its authors' endeavor to change Cuba's political standing (Lazo 2005, 75). Tolón took to translating Willard's text while simultaneously serving as the editor of *La Verdad*. And, I argue, the fact that Tolón's translation was meant (by both himself and Willard) to serve a double purpose renders it a bilingual work—it was meant to make an English-language work available to hispanophones while simultaneously serving as a tool for anglophones learning Spanish. This endeavor to reach two audiences who read two languages, moreover, was explicitly paralleled in *La Verdad*, for the English edition of that newspaper noted in its inaugural number of 1848 that:

> We have adopted the Spanish language in connection with our own [i.e., English], because one or the other is spoken by nearly all the civilized inhabitants of this New World, whose honor and interests are necessarily the nearest to an American heart. We also flatter ourselves that close communications with redeemed and tranquilized Mexico will induce such intimate attachments and family relations as will make her noble language a common property.
>
> (Quoted in Lazo 2005, 75)

As Lazo goes on to explain, "In its first issue, the paper [*La Verdad*] described Spanish and English as 'civilized' presumably in contrast to indigenous languages" (Lazo 2005, 75), thereby highlighting, in the present context, the violence of US expansionism, which finds a parallel in the violence implicit in the desire to preserve and prolong the institution of slavery via Cuban annexationism, which is all the more implicit in the reference to "civilized" languages, given the fact that African languages continued to be spoken in enslaved communities in the Caribbean in the 1840s and 1850s.

One may discern in these rhetorics, then, what must have occurred to Tolón and other annexationists of the period, i.e., the potential for an alliance between (pro-slavery) Latina/os in the US and Cubans from the island with Anglo Americans against common, "uncivilized" opponents—Native Americans and enslaved persons themselves. Yet, it was in the period in which Tolón took to translating Willard that he abandoned annexationism, because, I will argue, he came to realize that his American counterparts would not draw the boundaries of alliance as he imagined them. As was evident from their attitudes regarding the US-Mexico War and the conquest of the

Southwest, his American counterparts were disinclined to count Latin Americans as fully their equals.

While *La Verdad*, Willard's *Abridged History*, and Tolón's *Compendio* share in this erasure of indigenous languages, multiple differences may nevertheless be discerned between Tolón's translation and Willard's original: Tolón omits the leading questions at the bottom of each page and domesticates Willard's work when he translates it. Yet he simultaneously foreignizes it by including his own observations at key turns of the narrative and by excluding certain objectionable parts of Willard's history. He also includes intertextual interventions that problematize the reading of Willard's original work and its expansionist ideology. These differences signal my interpretation of Latina/o translations as historiography, a historiography that maps Latina/os in the US and their impact in constructing and questioning their place in the growing US republic.

While Tolón clearly wished to deploy this translation strategy to bring English and Spanish together, paralleling his desire for a political union between Cuba and United States, his interventions in the work bring to the readers' attention (both in English and in Spanish) the potentially unbridgeable difference between the two countries, signaling his growing suspicion of US imperialist intentions. Indeed, while it appears that Tolón is aligned with Willard's expansionist politics, the *Compendio* presents certain textual interventions that challenge the definition of a domesticating translation practice, offering something more akin with a "foreignization" (in Venuti's terms) of the source text, which demonstrates how Latina/o translations lie on the Latino Continuum.

In the *Compendio* the fundamental editorial decision by Tolón and/or the editors to omit the questions reshapes the entire work, converting Willard's textbook into a history like her longer *History of the United States*. The questions were meant to allow students to review what they had learned, and they also helped teachers to frame their lessons and assess student comprehension of the material (Joyce 2015, 71). The omission is provocative in that Tolón and Willard clearly note that the translation was meant to serve as a textbook, as well as a general history of the US. Omitting the questions ostensibly would detract from one of the central intended functions of the translation. A close reading of these questions, however, reveals why, for Tolón, there was no alternative to their omission.

When describing how Spaniards reclaimed Texas from the French in the late 1600s, for example, Willard claims that the Spaniards sought to keep the land as a deserted buffer zone that would allow them to avoid direct contact with their "Anglo-American neighbors." She further suggests that Mexicans harbored this "aversion" to Anglo-Americans up to the time of her writing, for she adds that the "aversion" led Mexicans to reject the US occupancy of Mexico City in 1847 at the end of the war. Punctuating this narrative account is the following question at the bottom of the page: "How did the Mexicans manifest aversion to Anglo-Americans, at an early day and again recently?" (Willard 1852, 333). After narrating the annexation of Texas by the US in 1845, Willard asks again, "How did the aversion of the Mexicans now manifest itself?" (Willard 1852, 340). Now, the annexation of Texas and the ensuing war were, of course, heavily criticized by Latin American countries, and if Tolón and the editors wished to sell the book more widely, they clearly would have to exclude such leading questions.

While Tolón's translation usually preserved the narrative tone of Willard's text, due to his choice of translation strategy, it nevertheless simultaneously alerted his readers that they must question its message and even its content. Tolón's translation stresses fluency: when rendering Willard, he allowed the reader to imagine no gap or difference between English and Spanish, and the two languages are presented as perfectly compatible, as mirrored languages always finding their linguistic counterparts in one another. Such fluency in translation did lead to what Venuti suggested could be expected of a "domesticating" translation practice, which, he argued, regularly "elides...discontinuities by locating a semantic unity adequate to the foreign text, stressing intelligibility, transparent communication, the use value of translation in the receiving culture" (Venuti 1995, 21). But with Tolón, situated as he was in and between multiple cultural worlds, the effects of this translation method were rather more complicated. Suffice for the moment to say that, generally, Tolón's translation seeks fluency, the results being that his Spanish-language readers were led to experience his rendering of the English-language narrative without feeling alienated by Willard's text, nor separated culturally from it, just as, overall, the anglophones who were meant to use the text to learn Spanish would find it a useful and generally faithful rendering that they could read with Willard's English-language original as a crib for Tolón's Spanish rendition.

The dual purpose of Willard's translation—as both a history book for Spanish-language readers and a text to learn Spanish for Americans—and that Tolón had both his English-language and Spanish-language readers in mind when producing the translation are best exemplified in Appleton's *Elementary Spanish Reader and Translator*, published the same year as the *Compendio*. In that work Tolón provides two introductions: one in Spanish addressed "Al lector cubano," noting that the book could be used to learn English, even though it was originally written "para los ingleses que aprenden español"; and the second is a preface in English, briefly delineating how to use the progressive exercises in the work to learn Spanish for translation purposes, particularly highlighting the use of the vocabulary list at the end of the work that would aid in learning new words. In the end the translated *Abridged History* and the *Elementary Spanish Reader and Translator* may be read as companion texts, in that together they offer a new, bilingual history of the US, one linguistically and inextricably tied to Latin America.

Two other interventions of particular note are (1) his explanatory notes at the bottom of certain pages that address content-related concerns, and (2) his inclusion of translator's notes that speak to linguistic differences between English and Spanish. Included as they are at the margins of Tolón's rendering, one can judge them to intervene in Willard's narrative even while Tolón simultaneously preserves the overall tone of her work with his fluent translation. Both, moreover, are necessary types of interventions: the former furnish historical information that may be unknown to a non-US reader; the latter aid in the translation of non-existent words in the Spanish language. Both serve as a history of the Latina/o experience, connecting Cuba, the US, and Mexico and bringing this connection into clearer relief.

In his explanation of the definition of an acre (Tolón 1853, 140), for example, today's reader might assume Tolón simply worked to harmonize diverse paradigms of measurement, much as one might today convert a measurement from the metric to the imperial system. Yet, when one contextualizes Tolón's translation historically, one sees the economic and political implications of the differing land measurements and their inclusion in his translation. In question, in particular, are the Treaty of Guadalupe Hidalgo and its impact on Mexican land grants on the northern side of the newly established border. In accordance with this treaty, Mexicans who found themselves on the US side of the border were forced legally to prove the validity of their land grants, which in turn created an opportunity for US immigrants to the region to squat on Mexican lands until the Land Grant Commission itself (established in the Land Grant Act of 1851) could verify any preexisting claims. Indeed, the Land Grant Act made squatting legal prior to the resolution of a land grant claim. Many Mexican land grant holders found themselves inundated with claims against their holdings, and they often lost their lands through having to declare bankruptcy, which in turn was caused by their having to pay heavy legal and other fees in the course of defending their claims.

Implicated, therefore, in any explanation of the differences between the measure of an acre and a *caballería* was this new practice of US immigrants, of legally confiscating Mexican-owned land in the course of moving to the newly acquired territories. If we bear contemporaneous historical events in mind, then, Tólon's explanation may be understood as educating Spanish-language readers not simply about a linguistic difference but about a legal difference that had implications for Mexican land grants throughout the newly acquired territories. Tolón writes: "*Acre* es una medida de tierra que comprende cerca de 4900 varas cuadradas; treinta y tres acres, poco mas o menos, componen un *caballería* de tierra—Nota del Traductor" (emphasis Tolón's) (Tolón 1853, 140) (Acre is a measure of land that comprises close to 4,900 square yards; thirty-three acres, more or less, comprise one *caballería* of land—Translator's Note). In this simple act of linguistic translation power is at play, the power for Spanish-readers to understand their new colonizers, and for English-language readers to inform themselves of the equivalences between the two terms. Further, by including his "Translator's Note" Tolón emphasizes that it is he and not Willard who is making the clarification.

A second example involves the Texas Rangers. Willard refers to the Rangers in the following fashion: "[Walker] had fought fifteen minutes with his company of Texas Rangers (armed with revolving pistols) with 1500 Mexican cavalry,—killed thirty [Mexicans] and escaped" (Willard 1852, 345). Tolón has to come up with a translation for the term "Texas Rangers," and what he chooses—"cazadores"—is suggestive. He writes in the translator's note found at the bottom of the page: "Creo que 'cazadores' es, en lengua castellana, el mejor equivalente de la palabra americana rangers" (Tolón 1853, 324) (I believe that "cazadores" in the Spanish language is the best equivalent for the American word rangers). The implications here are not so subtle, since the Texas Rangers were known for "hunting" Mexican nationals regardless of whether they favored annexation or not (Montejano, 1987) In addition, this rendering is particularly telling when viewed in relation to slavery and the historical concern, in Cuba, Texas, and the US, over runaway slaves. Runaway slaves escaped to Texas and Mexican territory in the antebellum period, because as of 1829 Mexico had ended slavery in its territories. The notion that the Texas Rangers are "cazadores" or hunters, then, evokes a Spanish concept of the *cazador* or *rancheador*, the individual in charge of capturing runaway slaves and bringing them back to the plantations (Rosa Corsa and González, 2004). The choice of this term is, therefore, not an innocent one, and while one might suggest Tolón simply could not come up with a better one, there is no denying his choice here implicitly speaks simultaneously to the founding of the Texas Republic, its abuses of Mexican nationals, and its relation to the enslavement of indigenous people and Africans alike. While slavery was outlawed in the Mexican territory, moreover, US immigrants brought their slaves as indentured servants in order to circumvent this law, so that the term also refers obliquely to the process of US annexation of Texas; for the issue of slavery was deeply implicated in US justifications for annexation, and with Texas admitted to the US as a slave state in 1845, enslaved people who had escaped to Texas were legally on the run.

However, another valence of meaning hidden in the term *cazadores* is this: it refers to Spanish soldiers or volunteers who fought in Cuba and the Philippines, as well as in the Spanish-American Wars of independence, both against filibustering insurgents in Cuba and revolutionaries in Latin America. Further, in a Cuban context it was the *cazadores* or volunteer militias that terrorized Cuban liberals and Afro Cubans, both enslaved and free, during the violent repression of the Escalera Conspiracy of 1843–44. If we consider how these multiple uses of the term play in this passage, we may say that Tolón equates the Texas Rangers to the hated Spanish officers who terrorized Cubans both enslaved and free, *criollo* and black, who were fighting for independence on the island.[18]

Immediately following the translator's note on the proper linguistic equivalent for Texas Rangers, there is a long explanation of the "revolving rifle" or "revolving pistol" used during the military skirmish Willard mentioned, in which a small number of Americans defeated 1,500 Mexicans. Tolón's note includes an extended description of what precisely a revolving rifle is, a description absent from Willard's account of the incident. In doing so, Tolón may be understood as self-consciously or intuitively highlighting the possible utility of the revolving rifle to Cubans in their quest for independence; and, clearly, he makes explicit for his Spanish-language readers that it is not American Manifest Destiny, as Willard stresses, that led to their victory, but instead a more advanced technology that led to the defeat of the Mexicans. Tolón adds:

> Los informes de los senadores Rush y Shields, hechos al gobierno de los Estados-Unidos en 1849–1851, demostraron que la superioridad de las tropas americanas sobre las de Méjico durante la última guerra, fue muchas veces debida a que en las primeras se hallaban provistas, en mayor o menor número, de esta especie de arma... Armados así los Americanos con la pistola jiratória, al paso que los Mejicanos carecían de ella, era de esperarse que, teniendo igual bizarría, habrían los primeros de vencer un número superior al suyo. [*sic*]
>
> (Tolón 1853, 325)

> (The reports by Senators Rush and Shields, given to the government of the United States between 1849 and 1851, demonstrated that the superiority of the American troops over Mexican troops during the last war was many times due to their being equipped, in greater or lesser numbers, with this type of weapon...the Americans armed in this way with the revolving pistol, a firearm the Mexicans did not have, it was to be expected that having such weaponry, the former would defeat a superior number of the latter.)

Tolón further added that other nations could also use Colt's revolving pistol and, as with the invention of gunpowder, one would have to think twice before going to war and risking significant loss of life. Such a technology, he noted, would engender wariness on behalf of governments; he sums up by noting that such wariness would serve "á beneficio de los intereses de la humanidad" (Tolón 1853, 325) (for the benefit of the interests of humanity). In these clarifications and additions to Willard's work, then, Tolón not only explains but, in fact, amends Willard's history: it was the technology and not any superior American nature or divinely ordained destiny that led to the Mexican defeat. Implicitly warning his Latin American readers of the skewed nature of Willard's account, he simultaneously signals the dangers of US imperialism, highlighting the unjust and brutal nature of US expansionism.

Sometimes Tolón's interventions were direct: in various places, he simply changed Willard's text in the course of translating it. For example, when Willard writes about the annexation of Texas by Congress in 1845, she justifies it as follows: "Mexico had been to the Americans an unjust and injurious neighbor" (Willard 1852, 339–40). By contrast, Tolón writes: "Méjico, bajo la influencia de preocupaciones que se sobreponían a su natural magnanimidad, era para los Americanos un vecino injusto y prejudicial" (Tolón 1853, 319) (Mexico, under the influence of preoccupations that overwhelmed their natural magnanimity, was according to the Americans an unjust and injurious neighbor). Tolón thus highlights in his translation the fact that the Americans were the ones who imagined and constructed Mexico as an unjust and injurious neighbor. That he notes Mexicans had "preoccupations" with which to deal, in turn, likely refers to their internal political struggles (between centrists and liberals) and perhaps is best taken as referring obliquely to the unjust annexation of Texas by the US to begin with, which exacerbated the same internal political disputes in Mexico. Tolón here offers a simple rephrasing of Willard's biased justification of the American annexation of Texas, then, which is but one of many interventions like it in his translation; and yet it speaks volumes as to Tolón's growing skepticism of US expansionism and annexationism and how the latter could come to pass in Cuba and the rest of Latin America. Again, then, one witnesses Tolón offering through his translation his own interpretation of history, and in doing so he engages a historiography that sought to clarify the possible futures with, in, and near the US for Latin American nations and peoples.

Tolón's interventions extend, as well, to the nature and to the place of Catholicism in the US. Willard speaks of religion as the most imperative force behind annexation, noting that American immigrants to Texas were forced to convert to Catholicism and to raise their children in that religion. That Anglo-Americans in Texas were unwilling to do this, she adds, was the driving force for independence and then annexation (Willard 1852, 335). Tolón follows Willard's text in these passages, siding with her on her erroneous interpretation of Catholicism as the cause of, first, Texan independence and, subsequently, annexation to the US. Yet, when it comes to the history of religion in the US, Tolón's narrative corrects Willard's. Willard constructs a narrative in which religious intolerance in the US had been overcome, which she contrasts with a lack of religious tolerance in Mexico and on the part of Mexicans. In the end, her narrative of the annexation of Texas labels Mexicans as "bad" Catholics in contrast to Irish and German "good" Catholics, who had overcome their differences with Protestants, which is implied by her nod to the end of all religious violence between Protestants and Catholics in her description of the Philadelphia Bible Riots of 1844. Willard acknowledged that "serious riots occurred" and noted they had to do with the jealousy of "native" American Protestants who feared that a "foreign" Roman Catholic population intended to gain control of the schools and "change the established order of instruction" (Willard 1852, 330). And she refers to the riots as "disgraceful" (Willard 1852, 330) but marks them with the past tense, moving quickly to a discussion of the suffrage party in Rhode Island.

Tolón, however, refuses to relegate the tensions between Catholics and Protestants to a period prior to 1844, as Willard wished to do. Instead, he adds one sentence that alerts Spanish-language readers that the aversion of "nativist" Protestants to "foreignized" Catholics continued to occur. He states: "Han pasado años; y sin embargo todavía prevalecen estas funestas emulaciones" (Tolón 1853, 310) (Many years have passed but these terrible occurrences still prevail). By stressing that Protestant-Catholic violence continued in the US, he thus rejected Willard's version of history, one where the violence stemming from religious differences in the US had been overcome.[19]

As is well known and as Willard sought to disavow in her historical narrative, it was, in fact, slavery and not religion that was the primary cause of the establishment of the Texas Republic and the annexation of Texas to the US. Tolón's translation signals Willard's duplicity and specifically her disavowal of the role of the question of slavery on the invasion of Mexico, since Tolón's translation is not as conciliatory as Willard's text when addressing the issue of slavery in the antebellum period. In her 1852 *Abridged History*, for example, Willard explains that the boundary between Texas and New Mexico was unclear in 1849, and that Texas sought to have New Mexico incorporated as part of its territory in order to expand slavery:

Other subjects of appalling difficulty pressed upon congress;—all, however, implicated in the one absorbing topic of slavery...while Texas was making preparations to seize this territory by force, the petition of New Mexico to be admitted into the Union was introduced...another exciting subject was a bill introduced by Senator Butler, of South Carolina, for a new law, to enable the masters of fugitive slaves to recover them from other states.

(Willard 1852, 396–97)

Following this, Willard abruptly ends the chapter and proceeds to discuss the Compromise of 1850, quoting Henry Clay and Daniel Webster at length and thereby advocating for the status quo in relation to slavery, which allowed for the coexistence of slave states with free states in the Union. Thus, while Willard does at least refer to slavery in this section, she does not actively engage the issues surrounding slavery in her text, as Joyce, Schulten, and Baym have shown.

In Tolón's Spanish rendering, however, slavery becomes a major point of discussion. First, in the text and in footnotes, Tolón augments Willard's treatment of the territorial tensions between Texas and New Mexico. He writes succinctly: "El sur apoyaba las reclamaciones de Tejas, en razón de que si triunfaban éstas, el territorio disputado aumentaría el área de la esclavitud; al paso que el norte se oponía a ellas por el mismo motivo" (Tolón 1853, 379). (The South supported the claims of Texas, reasoning that if they triumphed, the disputed territory would increase the area that permitted slavery, just as the North opposed these claims for the same reason.) This clarification does not appear in Willard. Tolón then adds in a footnote that many in Congress feared that Texas would join with Southern advocates to favor secession and civil war. When speaking of the legislation presented to Congress by South Carolina, which supported the continuation and expansion of slavery, Tolón interjects in the body of his translation that "Todos los del sur estaban unánimes en esta demanda; y se le asociaron muchos de los patriotas conservadores del norte" (Tolón 1853, 379). (All from the South were unanimous in this demand; and many of their conservative compatriots from the North joined them.) In this intervention, then, he stresses that there were Northerners who supported slavery and its expansion. Willard did not offer any of these observations or clarifications. Instead, she simply stated that slavery was the most divisive issue facing the US Congress after 1820 and noted the latitudes established that would then determine what territory could be future slave states or not (Willard 1852, 311–12).

*   *   *

When reading through Tolón's translation we can trace the origin of certain shifts in his thinking. Politically, Tolón eventually rejects annexationism and its related purpose of expanding slavery in the US and shifts toward independence for Cuba. He eventually advocates for the slow abolition of slavery versus the extension of slavery through annexation, a change made evident by his 1854 speech published in the abolitionist newspaper *El Mulato* in New York, in which he asserts as much. Tolón's translation of Willard's text, his notes, and direct interventions in the text reflect that he was critical of the US bringing in Cuba through annexation as well. Tolón could not ignore the racism and the bias, particularly against Mexicans, articulated in Willard's book, a text used in innumerable US classrooms and targeted at audiences in the newly acquired territories and in Latin America. Indeed, Tolón must have considered Mexicans as political allies, due to the colonial experience of Mexico and their struggle to establish a stable democratic government after independence. Mexico must have aroused a sense of personal loyalty as well, for this was the country that first took in Tolón's uncle when he had to flee Cuba for his anti-colonial activities. There was also a large number of Cuban exiles there (Muller, 2017).

Tolón was also wary of how Catholicism was treated in the text. He knew, through press coverage as well as through conversations with Mexican travelers to New York, of the abuses suffered by Mexicans in the newly colonized territories. As such, one could imagine he feared the same possible future for Cuba and Cubans, who were largely Catholic at the time. Why wouldn't the results of the annexation of Texas and the aftermath of the US-Mexico War presage those that could be anticipated for Cuba?

Tolon's personal history also reflects his political transformation. While in his youth he lived in a heavily slaveholding part of Cuba, where American moneyed interests were strongly represented and found support among Cubans, his later years, when he turned away from supporting American political control of Cuba, were lived out in New York, where opposing narratives were readily available to him.

Whether or not translating Willard was the precipitating cause that led to the change of position he took on Cuba's political future and whether or not it contributed to his changing views of slavery,[20] which were influenced by his youthful formation in a major slave-holding area in Cuba, what we know is that he realized there was a need for a corrective historiography, and he filled that need and composed a new kind of translation, one that offered its own history. It is a history that clearly imagined Latina/os as part of the US, as Tolón in his interventions becomes a writer of US history through his translation, as is evident in his translation strategy, his occasional rewriting of the text, and his notes instructing readers to absorb Willard with caution.

In addition, when we think about the audience for the text, one can imagine Tolón, whether self-consciously or not, grappling with the Latino Continuum. Spanish readers in the annexed territories could read the history, as Willard intended, to "know their own history", but Tolón's interventions would facilitate for them an understanding of the dangers their new political identity presented them. Anglophones reading Tolón's Spanish translation to learn that language too placed themselves onto the Latino Continuum: the fluent translation that meant to help them learn Spanish by cribbing with the English original, would, in fact, require them to edit or crib their understanding of Willard's text, and ultimately US history, with the Spanish rendering. Such readers would come to know the shared American history that Willard imagined Spanish speakers in the new territories and English speakers from the northeast held in common from a decidedly different perspective, one that gave greater voice, agency and identity as Americans to Spanish-speaking peoples. And so much could only have been expected if one accounted for the historical moment in the United States: it was a time when the very borders of the nation were in dramatic flux, with the US absorbing new territories and peoples at a nearly unprecedented rate.[21]

One thus finds a Latina/o historiography in Tolón's translation inasmuch as his rendering, however faithful it was intended to be and however much it equalized Spanish with the English medium of the source text, opened a space wherein a nearly contemporaneous narrative of US history was adapted to include historical facts and narrative themes that articulated the interests of a Cuban-born American citizen writing about Spanish-speaking peoples in the newly acquired American territories, doing so *for* those peoples, for English-speaking Americans, and for other "Spanish-speaking" Latin

Americans. The point, in short, is that the reason this translation creates a Latina/o historiography is that it is a nineteenth-century Latina/o who rendered a nineteenth-century history of the United States, one of which he was a part.

So much is not captured in the extant theory on translation. For I here find an audience that is not only often bilingual, but also located in a single nation, what Marta E. Sánchez in *A Translational Turn: Latinx Literature into the Mainstream* (2018) calls "intranational" translation, when analyzing the contemporary translation of Latinx texts from English into Spanish by major publishing houses. These contemporary translations are meant for an internal Spanish-language readership. Tolón's *Compendio*, completed with both Spanish-language and English-language readers in mind, was meant to stand ultimately as a whole. Translation in this context, then, is not meant to enrich or change or preserve the cultural world of one language, the target language, but to articulate a perspective on a single, if complex cultural world that *spans both language-worlds* and, ultimately, even extends across national boundaries to include peoples who might or might not come to be included in the nation—the United States—where its primary audience was imagined to reside. Classing his work as merely a translation, then, cannot capture the full value or potential effect of Tolón's rendering, because it did not so much import the "foreign" culture of the source language or seek to transform that of the target language as it did negotiate a complex historical and political moment in which the divisions between such cultures (and the political formations for the most part associable with them) were not only in flux, but were also not so simply distinguishable. It is not so much to translate but to negotiate this complex cultural and political world, both for himself and for his various audiences, then, that Tolón's rendering did its work: it offered not a transposition of one cultural world to another, but the negotiation of a single, if varied, cultural and political continuum. In short, it offered a historiography and not a mere translation.

Archival Formations and the Universal Sentiment

In Chapter 2, we encountered a work of translation that constituted a Latina/o historiography. In the present chapter, we again encounter a work of translation, in this instance an English-language rendering of a Spanish-language text, the key transcription of which is entitled *Rudo Ensayo*.[1] If Tolón's translation served as a form of historiography, here translation serves in the construction of the historical archive itself. The archive in question, moreover, is imbricated with a particular complexity that speaks to the nature of the formation of national, transnational, and hemispheric history. Indeed, we find *Rudo Ensayo* enmeshed in a complex web that touches the history of Spanish colonization; the history of the United States and of the Catholic Church in the United States, and the American West in particular; the history of the border in the American Southwest; and the place of Latina/os in the United States and the potential role of the Catholic Church in Cuba. That is to say, then, that a study of the translation in question and its source text illustrates the manner in which archival formation itself is constituted by, and in turn constitutes, a continuum that spans national, transnational, and hemispheric boundaries. Ultimately, the legacy of this archival document as it was constructed and situated served the purpose of its commissioner—the Catholic Church—but not entirely in the ways in which its translator would have hoped or, perhaps, would have anticipated.

To piece together this story, I proceed in multiple steps. First, I offer a précis of the contents of *Rudo Ensayo* and its Jesuit commissioning. Second, I review the complex transcription and transmission histories of the work. Here, I pay particular attention to the life of the American antiquarian, Thomas Buckingham Smith (1810–71), who published the first edition of *Rudo Ensayo* in the United States, as well as to that of his friend and collaborator in Mexico, José

The Latino Continuum and the Nineteenth-Century Americas: Literature, Translation, and Historiography.
Carmen E. Lamas, Oxford University Press (2021). © Carmen E. Lamas. DOI: 10.1093/oso/9780198871484.003.0004

Fernando Ramírez (1804–71). I also note the significance of the historical events that transpired as Smith prepared his transcription of the work, which occurred at the height of the US Civil War. Third, I review the biography and literary interests of the Latina/o translator of *Rudo Ensayo*, Eusebio Guiteras (1823–93), following which I give a detailed review of the history of the US and Cuba in his day, which sets Guiteras's intellectual and cultural interests and concerns in their proper contexts. Fifth, I offer an account of the ways in which *Rudo Ensayo* is constituted by and constitutes the Latino Continuum by way of an interpretation of the text that is guided by a reading of Guiteras's US travel diaries and a posthumous biography of Guiteras offered by the Latina Laura Guiteras, his niece (L. Guiteras 1894).

In arguing that the translator's engagement with the text, when viewed in tandem with the contribution of the translator's biography and his travel diaries, enters *Rudo Ensayo* as a document for and on the Latino Continuum, I suggest that several facets of the document in question, along with its production and the history of its circulation, must be borne in mind. In the *content* of the work, we see a picture of the Southwest that was eventually to become a part of the contiguous United States, but one thoroughly defined as a border history, where the definite limits of the state were indeterminate. The *commissioning* of the work illustrates a self-conscious effort on the part of a Catholic institution to identify a positive role and an integral place for the church in the United States, in its educational mission, which the translator, Eusebio Guiteras, identified as a proper role and possible future position for the Church in both the United States and Cuba. The *transcription history* of *Rudo Ensayo*, in turn, points to an endeavor to Americanize the document, even as it chronicles the activities of Spanish Catholics, Spanish settlers, and Spanish military forces in what was, at the time of its production, a part of the Viceroyalty of New Spain. Finally, the *transmission history* of the work calls into question the very construction of a national archive or a national literature, for it shows that a work in its legacies can boast of a transmission history as reaching that which characterizes the world novel, but with a legacy that is simultaneously made local and is reduced in its dimensions. As such, the concepts of distant reading (Moretti 2013), detached engagements (Damrosch 2003), and translation zone (Apter 2006) inform the following discussion, but not in order to argue for the place of Latina/o literature in theorizing the world novel, seeking to show it is "worthy" of inclusion. Instead, the story of *Rudo Ensayo* and its Latina/o translator(s) demonstrates the importance of the Latino Continuum as a methodological approach that makes evident the siloed readings in the field of comparative literature and subaltern studies. For a reading through deep time (Dimock 2006) that does not include the Latina/o experience as part of its analysis perpetuates the historical and aesthetic lacunae the present study seeks to fill.

To be sure, this is a complex story to relate. One must weigh the various elements that constitute the work in question—its contents and commissioning and its transcription and transmission histories (including an appreciation of the historical events that marked the historical moments in question). All this must be read in juxtaposition with the biography of the translator of *Rudo Ensayo*, Eusebio Guiteras, also taking into account both the historical context in which he worked and his wider literary and intellectual program. Doing so, however, recognizes how both Guiteras and his rendering of *Rudo Ensayo* stand on and help to form the Latino Continuum. In what follows, I will not concentrate on Guiteras's translation practice, though it does create a Latina/o history of its own. Instead, I will show how the continuum is established in and simultaneously made possible by the pedagogical approach by which Guiteras conceptualized all of his literary productions, translations included, an approach I will excavate below.

Rudo Ensayo: Transcribing the Spanish Empire and US Imperialism

The original title of *Rudo Ensayo* was *Descripción geográfica, natural y curiosa de la Provincia de Sonora por un amigo del Servicio de Dios y del Rey Nuestro Señor año 1764*. It is a work composed between 1761 and 1762, the product of a German-born Jesuit priest, Johann ("Juan") Nentvig (1713–68). Nentvig was sent in 1749 by the Jesuit Order to the Spanish territories of New Spain in areas that now are located in northern Mexico and the southwestern United States to establish Catholic missions there. *Rudo Ensayo*, meaning literally "Rough Draft," was his report to his superior delineating Jesuit evangelization activities in the region in the period of the work's composition.

The text details the missions that Nentvig had established and that he had visited or was serving, particularly in what is now northern Mexico, southern Arizona, and southern New Mexico. It discusses the life and work of the missions but includes a great deal more information than this, offering, as it does, detailed descriptions of the region's flora, fauna, climate, and landscape, as well as its peoples and their customs. Among the historical details furnished in the work are those delineating the influential role of Jesuit priests in the Spanish colonizing missions of the 1750s to the 1760s. Nentvig also details such events as the revolt of Luis de Saric in 1851; the Yaqui Wars that were ongoing into the 1860s; the faithfulness of the Opata and the infidelity of the Seris, whose members were captured and deported to Mexico City and Guatemala; and the ferociousness of the Apache—he calls them the "scourge of Sonora"—who are depicted as attacking other Native American peoples, the Spanish, and the Jesuit missionaries simultaneously.

Nentvig never left Mexico. He died in 1768, being unable to embark on a ship from Veracruz for the return journey to Rome following the expulsion of the Jesuits from the Spanish Empire in 1767. No original copy of *Rudo Ensayo* survives, and only four early transcriptions of the work remain extant, all of which date to 1762–64.[2]

First published in Mexico in 1856 as part of an effort to compile the colonial history of Mexico, *Descripción geográfica* might have been of interest only to Mexican historians if it had not been for the US-Mexico War, the US Civil War, and the Apache Wars, all of which brought the United States into intimate contact with the history of what is today the American Southwest, the geographic site of Nentvig's report. The first US publication of *Descripción geográfica* appeared in 1863 and was issued by one Thomas Buckingham Smith, who transcribed the work but changed its title to *Rudo Ensayo* or "Rough Draft," locating and dating completion of the transcription to St. Augustine, Florida, 1863. Smith refers to *Descripción geográfica* in his introduction to the work as a "Hiftorical Effay, now publifhed for the firft time" [sic] (Smith 1863, v), after dedicating the transcription to the Mexican antiquarian José Fernando Ramírez.

Ramírez, a well-known antiquarian, served as collector for and director of Mexico's National Library. He was also the director of the National Museum from 1852 until 1854, when he was forced into exile by President Antonio López de Santa Anna. He returned from his European exile in 1856 and was once again named director of the National Museum, a position he continued to hold until 1864, when he entered government service. He was again forced to leave Mexico with the fall of the French invaders that year, living with family in

Bonn—his daughter had married a German engineer—until his death. Ramírez's library was auctioned in London in 1880, and many of his priceless Mexican precolonial and colonial texts were acquired thereby by international collectors, which might explain how one of the four extant transcriptions of *Rudo Ensayo* ended up at the Huntington Library in San Marino, California (Nentvig 1762).[3]

Smith and Ramírez must have met in Mexico during Smith's time there from 1850 to 1852, when he served as secretary of legation to Mexico and chargé d'affaires for the US government. During this appointment Smith transcribed and collected Mexican colonial manuscripts for his studies and for sale to US antiquarians. Both, anyhow, were members of the American Antiquarian Society: Ramírez was named a member in 1862, and Smith was inducted the following year.[4] Friends such as Ramírez would have provided Smith with access to precolonial and colonial texts such as *Descripción geográfica* (Nentvig 1764a). Smith also traveled to Madrid as secretary of legation from 1855 to 1858, and there found one of the extant Spanish transcriptions of *Descripción geográfica* (Nentvig 1764b).

Smith's interest in those colonies of Spain that during his lifetime became a part of the United States began early in his life. While the Smith family was originally from Connecticut, his father moved south, and Smith was born in Cumberland Island, Georgia, raised in Florida, and was familiar with the Spanish language as a result of his upbringing in Florida, which had been under Spanish rule until 1819. He also resided in Mexico when he was young, when his father was US Consul to Mexico prior to his untimely death in 1825.[5]

Before publishing *Rudo Ensayo* Smith published both transcriptions and translations of important texts such as the voyages of Hernando de Soto and Alvar Núñez Cabeza de Vaca.[6] He also transcribed and published a grammar of the Heve language (the language of the Opata) in 1861 and another of the Pima language (from the Arizona and California region) in 1862, both originally produced by Spanish priests in the eighteenth century who were evangelizing these indigenous peoples during the Spanish colonial period. As Mary Lindsay Van Tine (2016, 141) notes, throughout his life, "Smith worked to uncover and incorporate the layered indigenous, colonial, and extra-national histories of a newly transcontinental United States."

The timing of the publication of these transcriptions, in particular that of *Rudo Ensayo*, is historically significant, not merely because these works functioned to bring the peoples and areas they examined under the dominion of a US *imaginaire*, but also for the contemporaneous events of history. The US Civil War under way, the Confederate Army had invaded parts of southern Arizona in 1861, when the entire region was simply identified as the Territory of New Mexico. The Confederates encountered armed resistance there from the Apaches, nuevomexicanos, and the Union army, who drove them out of southern Arizona and back to Texas. Congress subsequently converted Arizona and New Mexico into separate territories in 1862, just as war with the Apaches escalated, in order to facilitate the "pacification" of this region under Union control.[7]

The Apache Wars began in 1849. During the US-Mexico War (1846–48) different Apache groups had given the US military the right to cross their territory in order to fight against Mexico. When the US did not withdraw its troops after the Treaty of Guadalupe Hidalgo (1848) and instead settlers began to enter Apache territories, especially after gold was found in New Mexico, the Apache declared war. Consequently, since Smith published this text during a time in which paper was in short supply, because of the disruptions of the Civil War—he produced only 150 copies—we must ask ourselves if the intent of the publication served more than the peculiar interests of antiquarians like Smith and members of the American Antiquarian Society. For in his account, Nentvig makes a point of furnishing information regarding the Apache that was not simply descriptive, but also could aid in the endeavor to pacify and even eliminate them. Guiteras translates Smith's transcription of Nentvig:

> Aunque el afiento de efta cruel nacion queda fuera de los limites arriba puefto de efta Provincia, tengo por conveniente, fin embargo, tratar de ella en efte lugar para dar á nueftros lectores las noticias que he adquirido, y con ellas algunas luces, con que fe pueda difcurrir mas facilmente fobre el remedio de los daños ineftimables que caufa efte enemigo en quafi toda efta Provincia y precaber fu ultima ruina. [*sic*]   (Smith 1863, 117–8)

> Although the seat of this pitiless nation lies beyond the borders of this Province, I nevertheless think it advisable to speak of it, in this part of my work, in order to impart to my readers the information I have obtained, so that some means may be discovered whereby the immeasurable evils caused in the Province by this enemy may be stopped and its ruin prevented.[8]   (Guiteras 1894, 200)

Nentvig further details the forms of warfare the Apache deployed, noting that they had changed their tactics over time. Previously, they had mounted war only with the full moon; they subsequently chose to attack in the dark or as Nentvig explained, "finalmente han mudado en el todo fu modo de guerra: entran quando fe les antoja, con el mayor numero que les es pofible, para que por fus tierras no tengan que temer á la retirada, como antes lo folian recibir el caftigo de nueftras armas" [*sic*] (Smith 1863, 121) (they have entirely changed their mode of warfare: they come in when they choose, and in the greatest possible numbers, so as to be able to cover their retreat when pursued by our troops) (Guiteras 1894, 202). Nentvig warns against the simple use of military force, considering instead the training of Native leaders to enforce order, especially since Native peoples had begun to acquire and use firearms in lieu of the crossbow and arrow (Guiteras 1894, 239). For him, what would work to destroy the Apache was increased military numbers and persistent surveillance along the frontier:

> Por lo que toca á repremir, y humillar el orgullo del otro mui atrevido enemigo de Sonora, el *Apache*, mientras no fuere fervido el Rey Nueftro Señor de embiar algun focorro de gente con las armas que fe hallan actualmente, foy de fentir que las entradas á fus tierras, no folamente no firven para el remedio de la tierra, fino antes para mucho perjuicio...por lo qual fe vee claramente que efta guerra podran ellos mantener fiempre con ventaja, mientras fe figuiere efte modo de entradas, &ᵃ...Prefidios que, en lugar de entradas á fus tierras, fe debe en las Fronteras de un Prefidio al otro recorrer la tierra, y hallandofe huella de el enemigo que entra, feguirlo, avifando á los lugares de Efpañoles, y Pueblos de Yndios hacia donde marcha el enemigo, para que eften alerta.   (Smith 1863, 204–6)

> With regard to the restraint and subjection of the stubborn Apaches, the other and boldest enemy of Sonora, if His Majesty does not send a greater number of soldiers than we have, I think that the expeditions sent against them, far from being of use, will be harmful...The enemy, therefore, can always pursue this war with advantage if we do not adopt other methods...Instead of these expeditions into the enemy's country we ought to be constantly on the watch all along the line of the frontier, and on finding traces of the enemies follow them, sending word to the places of Spaniards and Indians, advising the direction in which the enemies advance with order to be upon the alert.   (Guiteras 1894, 262–63)

The translation further explained the military strategy Nentvig/
Smith recommends as follows:

> A mas de efto dicho, perfuaden efte modo de guerra á qualquier
> juicio defapafionado, el que dichos enemigos al entrar por la
> Provincia, hacen jornadas cortas, caminando mui defpacio, hafta que
> ven la fuya, y logran hacer algunas muertes, ó cautivar, ó algun robo
> confiderable de beftias… pero fi defde la entrada fueran feguidos, no
> lograrán hacer dichos eftragos y daños.   (Smith 1863, 207)

> An unprejudiced mind will favor this new method of waging war
> against the Apaches, considering that these Indians enter the Province
> making short journeys and going very slowly until they find a good
> opportunity to fall to, when they commit murders, take prisoners,
> steal cattle, etc.…. Were they pursued the moment they come into the
> land they could not make such havoc.   (Guiteras 1894, 264)

And finally:

> y tengo concebido que fi un folo año, afi fe continara no los habia de
> quedar ganas de volver mas por acá, y habian de entablar otro modo
> de pafarlo en fus tierras: y entonces ya algo recobrada la *Sonora*, fe
> pudiera penfar, ó en rreducirlos, ó fujetarlos por fuerza.
>
> (Smith 1863, 207)

Guiteras translates:

> I am persuaded that by pursuing this plan for a single year, the enemy
> would give up the idea of crossing the border and would try to keep
> on his own land, and perhaps then Sonora being at peace, it would be
> time to think of either conquering them or subduing them by force.
>
> (Guiteras 1894, 264)

If we take into account that the Apache declared war on the US in
1849 and that this war continued until the surrender of Geronimo in
1886—though it can be argued that the war continued until 1924,
ending only with the Native American Citizenship Act or even continuing to the present day—Smith's transcription of this text, published in 1863, reads like a manual of war and colonization. This view
is further bolstered by the fact that Nentvig describes in detail not
only the different groups and how to subjugate them, but also the
region's wealth in gold, silver, and copper. He similarly wrote of the

possibilities in agriculture that could be open to settlers, if only the Apaches could be subdued.

The translation of *Rudo Ensayo* appeared in the periodical *Records of the American Catholic Historical Society of Philadelphia* in 1894. Therein are found not only the English-language rendering of *Rudo Ensayo*, prepared by Eusebio Guiteras, but also a biography of Guiteras prepared by his niece, a Latina, Laura Guiteras (L. Guiteras 1894). Included is an introduction to the translation authored by one Lawrence F. Flick (1856–1938) (Flick 1894b), which describes *Rudo Ensayo* and explains (on his understanding) its historical signifi-cance. And, finally, the volume offers a pair of related articles con-cerning, respectively, the indigenous peoples of the West and (what is the subject matter of *Rudo Ensayo*) the American Southwest of the United States. The first of these is a California travelogue that chron-icles the history of the Franciscan missions there, offering an account of the operation of Indian schools on the West Coast by Catholic nuns and missionaries in the author's day and advocating for the same. The second article examines the history of the Papago people in the American Southwest and documents their adoption of Catholicism (Flick 1894a). Contextualizing this single volume and its multiple articles as part of the Latino Continuum allows us to as-semble a Latina/o history that merges at the intersections of these once disparate archives.

Guiteras's Biography and Literary Interests

Eusebio Guiteras, the translator of *Rudo Ensayo*, was born in 1823 in (like Tolón) Matanzas, Cuba, and lived in Philadelphia for twenty-five years, from 1869 until his death in 1893. He produced a transla-tion of Smith's 1863 transcription of *Rudo Ensayo*, which was pub-lished posthumously in 1894. It is readily evident why he would take interest in and occupy himself with this work. Guiteras was a devout Catholic, an active member of the Archdioceses of Philadelphia, and a lively participant in the intellectual and cultural life of that city. He also was a member of the Pennsylvania Historical Society and of the American Catholic Historical Society (ACHS) of Philadelphia, the same organization that published his translation; and when his translation was finally published in the *Records of the American Catholic Historical Society of Philadelphia*, the general editor

Lawrence F. Flick described it as "a labor of love by our devoted fellow member" (Flick 1894b, 109).

Being a devout Catholic, Guiteras would have taken an acute interest in the historical events chronicled in *Rudo Ensayo*, which in documenting Catholic missionary work in what became the American Southwest spoke directly to the role of members of the Jesuit Order in colonizing that region. Indeed, the work was published in the US through Catholic channels in no small part because it chronicled the story of members of that faith actively participating in securing what would become a part of the Union.[9] This was of particular concern to Guiteras around the time he prepared his translation, because Reconstruction of the US South after the Civil War had met with significant difficulties and because the Apache Wars were still a live concern even after the surrender of Geronimo in 1886.[10] That Spanish-speaking Catholic missionaries had historically played a role in "pacifying" Native peoples was of vital interest to Guiteras and to Catholics in the United States more generally, because such a history could offer a counternarrative to the resurgence of anti-Catholic nativism in the US in his day. Guiteras, like Lawrence F. Flick and other members of the ACHS, was quite concerned about the future of Catholicism in the US in the face of a resurgent nativist sentiment in the country. Guiteras would have understood that the potential for "constructive" (to nativist thinking) contributions on the part not only of Catholics but of Latina/os in particular to the effort to pacify native peoples could serve to counter new "English-only" attitudes in the US.

Furthermore, the core message of *Rudo Ensayo* would have reverberated in Guiteras's thinking about both the political future of Cuba and that of the United States. As a political exile, he was committed to a politically independent Cuba. The message of *Rudo Ensayo*, suggesting Spanish culture could pacify "less civilized peoples," could serve to reassure both Cubans and US political leaders in the United States that the island could be stable in its independence even while including a large population of recently emancipated enslaved persons. And the pacification narrative could similarly serve as a model for racial reconciliation in the post-Civil War South. Indeed, these two histories—US and Cuban—are brought together through the Catholic Church in Guiteras's translation of *Rudo Ensayo* and place Guiteras, his life, his works, and *Rudo Ensayo* on the Latino

Continuum. In order to understand this phenomenon, then, we must delve into Guiteras's biography.

Eusebio Guiteras Font (1823–93) was an educator, translator, and novelist whose first trip to the US occurred in 1842. He and his brother Antonio toured New York, Massachusetts, and eastern Canada over the course of three and half months before continuing on to Europe and the Middle East. A second visit to the US occurred in 1848 with his wife Josefa Gener, during which time he met with Henry Wadsworth Longfellow (1807–82), who was instrumental in the 1849 publication in the *North American Review* of "The Poetry of Spanish America" by William Henry Hulbert, an essay that introduced US readers to Latin American literary productions. Guiteras was instrumental in giving Longfellow Cuban writings that would later be included in the essay (Jaksic 2007, 101–2). He had two daughters while in the United States, Maria de la Piedad and Rosa. The latter was baptized by Father Félix Varela in New York. Both, however, died from childhood diseases. One of his surviving children, John Guiteras, attended the University of Pennsylvania and ultimately taught medicine there. (John is best remembered as one of the physicians who developed the yellow fever vaccine.) When Guiteras returned to Cuba, the Spanish authorities accused him of taking part in the Escalera Conspiracy of 1843–44, as a result of his public denouncement of slavery and the slave trade. He and his brother Pedro José spent six months in prison until they were proven innocent. He was also implicated in Narciso López's annexationist plot and was arrested by the Spanish colonial authorities in 1850, along with his brother Pedro José, for importing subversive materials into Cuba.

He then returned to the US for reasons of his son's health and resided in Philadelphia from 1854 to 1858, subsequently returning to Matanzas to live for an additional ten years. During his times in Cuba, he and his brother Antonio had founded the school La Empresa in Matanzas. With the outbreak of the Ten Years' War in 1868, Cuba's first organized attempt at independence, the school was closed by the colonial authorities. Guiteras then returned again to Philadelphia and never set foot in Cuba again. According to one of his biographers (his niece, a Latina, Laura Guiteras) Guiteras also lived in Charleston, South Carolina, for four years during his US residence (L. Guiteras 1894, 108). The precise timing of his stay there is uncertain; however, it is clear he chose to live there in order to be with his son, who taught at the University of Charleston for a short while, and also with his brother Pedro José, who moved to Charleston in 1889 and died there in in 1890.

Guiteras's very popular multivolume Spanish-language readers, *Libros de lectura* (Guiteras 1856, 1857, 1858, 1868), were published in Philadelphia (the first three) and Cuba (the last one), and they were used in schools throughout Latin America in the nineteenth century. They were so popular that the first volume alone had thirteen editions by 1898. These books were not only used to teach children who knew Spanish how to read, but, as in Tolón's case, to teach Spanish to English speakers in the United States as well. Guiteras was also prolific in his literary activities. Apart from his Spanish readers, he translated a French grammar, making it available to Spanish-language speakers seeking to learn French. He also corrected a Spanish translation of the Bible, having been commissioned to do so by the archbishop of Philadelphia, penned the two-part novel *Irene Albar* (which was written in Philadelphia but published in Barcelona in 1885), and left unpublished a novel entitled *Gabriel Reyes* that he had written in Philadelphia, but which was published posthumously as a serialized novel in 1903–4 in Raimundo Cabrera's Cuban iteration of *Cuba y América*.

Guiteras also composed two travel diaries. The first, *Diarios de viaje*, documents his travels with his brother Antonio to the US, Europe, and the Middle East in the 1840s. (An edited volume of the *Diarios* was finally published in its entirety in 2010 in Seville, Spain as *El pensamiento liberal cubano a través del* Diario de viaje *de Eusebio Guiteras Font*, edited by José María Aguilera Manzano and Susan Lupi.) The first section of *Diarios de viaje* is titled "Por el Norte de América y el Canadá" and details Guiteras's experiences at the beginning of his trip, including his reflections on his time in New York City, Niagara Falls, Oswego, NY, Boston, and Philadelphia, among other northeast cities. Guiteras himself published his second travel account, *Un invierno en Nueva York* (n.d.), in Barcelona, which details his experiences in New York in 1869 and includes an analysis of the US educational system while also reflecting on race relations and everyday life in post-Civil War New York. Finally, Guiteras also published the bilingual *Guía de la Cueva de Bellamar. Guide to the Caves of Bellamar* (1863) and, of course, his 1894 English translation of Juan

Nentvig's 1763 well-known account, *Rudo Ensayo*. He died in Philadelphia on December 24, 1893, exactly one day after the death of his wife Josefa Gener.

The Historical Contexts of Guiteras's Life and Works

Multiple historical events must be taken into account in order to contextualize the publication of Guiteras's translation of *Rudo Ensayo* and its place on the Latino Continuum. These are related to US history, the history of American Catholicism, and Cuba's political situation in the late nineteenth century.

From the perspective of US history, the translation of *Rudo Ensayo* was affected by the "end" of the Apache Wars and for reasons presently to be explained, the opening of Ellis Island in 1892. The continued secularization of the *misiones* in California and across the Southwest, along with the rising anti-Catholic sentiment of the 1890s (and in particular the creation of the nativist American Protective Association), were also significant. A heated debate also took place around the time of Guiteras's translation between German Catholics and so-called "American" Catholics in the US, a debate finally settled by the *Testem Benevolentiae Nostrae*, authored by Pope Leo XIII in 1899. German Catholics in the US questioned the orthodoxy of the mainly Irish leadership of the Catholic Church in America regarding their efforts to Americanize their parishioners. They argued that membership in the Catholic Church of America was declining as a result of the push by its leadership for English-language education in parochial schools and the use of English in immigrant parishes.

From the perspective of Cuban history, *Rudo Ensayo* must be contextualized within the political events on the island, as well as, and most notably, the end of slavery in 1886 and the founding of the Cuban Revolutionary Party by José Martí in New York City in 1891. By tracing these events—which occur on both sides of the (then ever-shifting) border—and contextualizing Guiteras's translation as a response to these events, both explicitly and implicitly, the significance of Guiteras's *Rudo Ensayo* and its place on the Latino Continuum produce a new understanding for classifying such Latina/o translations as Guiteras's *Rudo Ensayo* as works of world literature.

US HISTORY

The most detailed account of Guiteras's religious devotion is found in his niece Laura Guiteras's "Brief Sketch of the Life of Eusbeio Guiteras" (L. Guiteras 1894), a biography that precedes its subject's translation of *Rudo Ensayo* in the *Records*. In this "Brief Sketch," the title of which clearly parallels that of "*Rudo Ensayo*," Laura delineates, in Guiteras's own words, though now translated to English, his rededication to Catholicism, which he describes as a conversion progressively occurring in multiple parishes in Philadelphia:

> God knows His way; blessed and praised be his name; because in such a critical period of my life He remembered and was merciful to me...a natural impulse took me to the Church at the hour of Mass. Although I was not familiar with the Divine Office, nevertheless there was much that I recognized, and the *Dominus vobiscum* sounded like a mother's voice to her sleeping child. After the Gospel the priest ascended the pulpit and commenced the sermon. It was not until then I learned we were in a German Church (that of the Holy Trinity, on 6th and Spruce Sts [in what is now Old City Philadelphia]).
>   (L. Guiteras 1894, 105)

He continues:

> At last came a day in which an inexplicable emotion of the soul led me to the confessional. It was in the Church of Saint John the Evangelist [on 13th and Chestnut streets in Center City Philadelphia]. I was then thirty-four years old. I was absolutely unprepared for this solemn ceremony. The confessor seemed perplexed. The tears streamed from my eyes, and my whole soul burned with the most pure desire of reconciling itself with God. The good priest, whom I afterwards learned was an Italian missionary of the Society of Jesus, gave me absolution. What a weight was lifted from my heart! The following day I received Holy Communion.   (L. Guiteras 1894, 106)

He concludes with his confirmation in yet another church in Philadelphia:

> Shortly after my first Communion I was confirmed in the Church of Saint Patrick [it is presently located at 20th and Rittenhouse Square streets in Center City Philadelphia] by Bishop Newman. A year

afterwards, during the Lenten Season of 1859, I had the new and ineffable joy of receiving Holy Communion in my loved Church of San Carlos in Matanzas, thus making public profession of my Faith before the people who had witnessed the errors of my life.

(L. Guiteras 1894, 106)

These excerpts from Guiteras's first-hand account (though translated by his niece) signal the continuum of his faith from Philadelphia to Matanzas and back again (since he returns to Philadelphia in 1869) and speak directly to both the history of the Catholic Church in Cuba (as I will describe momentarily) and one of the great debates facing the Catholic Church in the United States at that time—how to serve newly arrived immigrant parishioners in the Catholic Church in America.[11]

In Guiteras's day, Irish Catholics headed many dioceses of the Catholic Church in the United States and occupied a large number of senior leadership posts at bishop and cardinal level. Their core aim of endeavoring to assimilate newly arrived European immigrants to US culture caused tension with German Catholics, who accused them of crudely attempting to "Americanize" the church by imposing the use of English in parish life and in parochial schools. German Catholics, by contrast, wished to retain their native language in these spaces and blamed the mainly Irish leadership for a decrease in church membership in the US, claiming that the Americanization of the US Church and the push for assimilation caused newly arrived immigrants to leave the church altogether. This debate occurred not solely in Philadelphia, but also throughout the Northeast and the Midwest. On one side of the debate were such Catholic leaders as Archbishop John Ireland (St. Paul, MN), Cardinal James Gibbons (Baltimore, MD), and Bishop John Keane (Richmond, VA), who were labeled "progressives" or "liberals" for their belief that Catholicism in the US could adjust to US culture without altering Catholic orthodoxy. They also supported the participation of the Catholic Church in the Parliament of World Religions at the Columbian Exposition in 1893 in Chicago, a decision that more conservative Catholics condemned. Furthermore, like Varela before them, they did not condemn outright public school education for Catholic children.

Countering this position were Archbishop Michael Corrigan (New York, NY) and Bernard McQuaid (Rochester, NY), who were concerned about the history of anti-Catholicism in the US and specifically the future of parochial schools (2). As Linkh summarizes:

> These conservatives saw no reason to change anything about Catholicism, even the nonessentials, and they generally favored Catholics keeping their association with Protestants to a minimum. Consequently, they saw the public school as a godless if not Protestant institution and were scandalized by Catholic participation in the World's Parliament of Religions. In short, they were opposed to any attempt to "Americanize" the Church.   (Linkh 1975, 3)

The continued membership of newly arrived immigrants was at stake for conservative Catholics. They vouched for a slow assimilation of immigrants to US culture in order to ensure their continued faith. Having priests who spoke the language of newly arrived immigrants— mainly French, Italian, and German—was of utmost importance.

This divide led to a series of public debates in Catholic newspapers and journals across the US, including the *Records of the American Catholic Historical Society*. One such debate centered around the Abbelen petition, in which a group of German priests wrote directly to Rome about their grievances, petitioning against "Americanizing" Catholics in the US. In this letter of grievance the signatories explained that Americanization was better administered slowly, over multiple generations, if it were to be accomplished without negatively affecting newly arrived Catholics. They further "warned against attempts to suppress and root out the language, the traditions, the customs, and the devotional practices of German immigrants" (Linkh 1975, 5). The (so-called) liberal Catholics countered that retaining German language and culture could be dangerous for the church in America since the church would be perceived as "composed of foreigners," and would "[exist] in America as an alien institution, and [be viewed] consequently [as] a menace to the existence of the Republic" (quoted in Linkh 1975, 5–6). The "liberal" Catholics, in fact, were not shown to be in error, since religion in the US was linked to politics in the nineteenth century (as it is today): both President William Henry Harrison and Senator Cushman Davis praised the "American" Catholics for condemning a foreignization of US Catholicism and for supporting assimilation (Linkh 1975, 9). Meanwhile, Secretary of State James Blaine spoke against the Cahensly Memorial of 1891 in which conservative Germans "demanded same-nationality parishes along with a quota system for American bishops" (Morris 1998, 97).

In 1891 Pope Leo XIII condemned the division in the American Catholic Church, and with his censure the debate seemed to have been silenced. However, a new "school controversy" unsettled this temporary stalemate. During the time of Félix Varela—in the 1840s—and much to his chagrin, the secularization of public schools in the US had been undertaken. In 1890 the State of Wisconsin passed the Bennet Law, which required that English must be taught in all schools at least sixteen weeks per year. When Archbishop John Ireland did not condemn this law, the smoldering debate in the US Catholic Church regarding language-use among newly arrived immigrants was ignited once again, in particular because Archbishop Ireland went as far as explicitly to support public school education. Like Varela before him, he hoped to find a way somehow to teach religion in public schools. Linkh elaborates:

> The school controversy was simply the most publicized of many disputes which divided liberals and conservatives in the 1890's. The liberals generally tended to be more sympathetic to civic and social reform and were ordinarily more in accord with the emerging labor movement... conservatives tended to avoid political issues of the day while liberals were more likely to take an active political role. These differences tended to divide American Catholics during the late nineteenth century and were extremely important in the Americanism controversy of the late 1890s.   (Linkh 1975, 12)

In the end, Leo XIII issued the *Testem Benevolentiae Nostrae* in 1899 in which he wrote, "We cannot approve the opinions which some comprise under the head of Americanism" (quoted in Morris 1998, 109), but also praised the work of the American Catholic Church in the United States. In fact, the *Testem Benevolentiae Nostrae* principally addressed only issues in the Catholic Church in France, which sought to use the so-called "American" case as a foundation for aligning itself with political liberalism. In the encyclical, "l'américanisme" as expounded by Father Félix Klein in France was denounced as unorthodox by the Holy See. While not addressing the American Catholic Church directly, then, this indirect denouncement of potential unorthodoxy nevertheless put an end to the debate over assimilation in the United States at the turn of the nineteenth-century and led Charles R. Morris to conclude that:

> Leo's [letter's]...only importance in America was a kind of final scorecard for a fifteen-year catfight, for by 1899, the Americanist controversies were finally over. Out of the conflict, however, the contours of a Catholic accommodation with a secular state had evolved quietly, almost inadvertently. Within a very short time, they seemed so natural, were so taken for granted, that the great controversies disappeared almost without a ripple beneath the smooth surface of the American Church.   (Morris 1998, 109)

Guiteras's narrative, then, in detailing his rededication to his faith, reflects these debates regarding the place of new immigrants in the US and, specifically, their language needs and efforts at assimilation to US culture. The place of his original reconciliation occurs at the Church of the Holy Trinity, in which, he notes, the Mass was in Latin but the sermon in German. He further reflects on his inability to understand German:

> I now found myself in a peculiar position. Uncertain and hesitating at first my lips sought expressions of love and repentance. I knew but few prayers, and had to begin to memorize some, for which the Latin I had learned at college did me good service. It was a pleasure for me to make use of the beautiful Latin tongue, which the Church has so wisely preserved, thus avoiding the frequent changes to which the modern languages are constantly subjected. Prayers, hymns, psalms, I treasured in my memory.   (L. Guiteras 1894, 105)

Then, his conversion experience migrates to different churches in Philadelphia: from the German-language parish of the Holy Trinity, he moves to St. John the Evangelist, in which an Italian priest hears his confession; and, finally, he finds himself at St. Patrick's Church, where an Irish priest leads his Confirmation. These physical and spiritual migrations in Philadelphia, then, also were presented by Guiteras as linguistic migrations, and he thus speaks to the assimilation debates of the 1880s and 1890s. Inasmuch as he refers to the "frequent changes" that modern languages experience, he indirectly advocates for the liberal position, and, as we shall see, his translation of *Rudo Ensayo* from Spanish into English on the commission of the Archdiocese of Philadelphia served to further that liberal agenda.

Fueling this "Americanization" debate was the rise of anti-Catholic nativism throughout the US. In 1887 Henry F. Bowers founded the American Protective Association (APA) in Clinton, Iowa. This secret association had a membership of up to half a million in the 1890s, comprised of members of such "patriotic" societies as the Grand Army of the Republic; the Order of United American Mechanics; the Junior Order of United American Mechanics; the Patriotic Order Sons of America; the United Order of Deputies, later called the American League; the Red, White and Blue; the United Order of Native Americans; the American Patriotic League; the Get There American Benefit Association; and the Loyal Men of American Liberty (Higham 1971, 55–61; Manfra 1996, 149–50; Bennett 2007, 170).

In a renewed call to nativism, the APA, which later itself became a short-lived political party, arose out of the political disenfranchisement of working-class Republicans and even some Democrats. As Jo Ann Manfra (1996) explains, anti-Catholicism served as a means for the APA leadership to reform politics at the local and national level. To do so, they used German-Irish ethnic tension to push forward their agenda, which included "the elimination of Irish electoral influence" (Manfra 1996, 153). According to Manfra it was not necessarily religious animosity that fueled the rise of the APA but a reaction to the collaboration between elite Republicans and the Knights of Labor, a secret labor organization largely made up of Irish members, which was founded in 1876 and was transformed into an organization opposed to capitalism after the Railway Strikes of 1877:

> Collectively, these charter members [of the APA] neither belonged to the community's economic elite nor conformed to the historical characterization of APA members as inarticulate common folk. Rather, they resembled the "middle-class" artisan and small entrepreneurial Republican reformers…whose opposition to the long-standing alliance of their party's elite with Irish Democrats evidently provoked a large number of them to become anti-Catholic activists.
>
> (Manfra 1996, 149)

With the Haymarket Massacre of 1886, the Knights of Labor began to lose their political power, while anti-immigrant sentiment rose among nativists, who blamed newly arrived immigrants from southern and eastern Europe for fueling the anarchist ideology in the US that led to labor unrest, which the nativists considered anti-American.

In John Higham's (1971) classic study of the rise of nativism in the United States, *Strangers in the Land: Patterns of American Nativism,*

1860–1925 (1955), he similarly contends that it was not necessarily anti-Catholic sentiments that fueled the rise of nativism, since most Americans believed that the country could eventually assimilate immigrants. Instead, it was the return of Old World cleavages, specifically class, that made the resurgence possible. Speaking of the Haymarket Affair of 1886 and the thousands of strikes that erupted throughout the country in the 1870s and 1880s, Higham explains the concern/matter as follows:

> The fiery nationalism of the fifties grew out of sectional cleavage; by the same centripetal principle, class cleavage could hardly fail in the eighties to produce a resurgence of nationalism. In both cases a baffled need for unity asserted itself in nativistic aggression ... Nativism, as a significant force in modern America, dates from that labor upheaval.   (Higham 1971, 53)

He further contends that while in the early nineteenth century nativism was an attack on the clergy and against the influence of the Pope, in the late nineteenth century, the immigrant became the object of attack instead of the priest:

> In an age relatively untroubled with social problems, anti-Catholics had tended to restrict their ire to the Roman hierarchy. Now they denounced immigration as a complementary national problem. Typically, they trembled at the Roman challenge to American freedom, rallied to the defense of the public school system, and urged limitations on immigration and naturalization.
>
> (Higham 1971, 60–61)

In a nod to the rise of anti-Catholic sentiment in the late nineteenth century, however, Higham does concede that the impact of Catholic voters led to nativists fears that the public school system was under threat: the election of Catholics to local school boards threatened to give Catholics an outsized say in the curriculum that would be taught in the common school (Higham 1971, 59).

Paul Kleppner (1979) in *The Third Electoral System, 1853–1925: Parties, Voters, and Political Cultures* argues that Protestant nativists had a reason to fear Catholic voters, for the "Instruction of the Bishops of the United States concerning the Public School" issued by the Vatican's Sacred Congregation of the Propaganda fueled the debate over public school instruction and educational funds. The 1875 Instruction mandated the building of Catholic schools in the US, and the clergy were instructed to command parishioners to send their children to Catholic schools (Kleppner 1979, 227). Yet the Catholic hierarchy in the US did not have the resources to fulfill this mandate and therefore the fight for public funds for parochial schools was reignited. The fight by Catholics to secularize public schools ensued (Kleppner 1979, 229–30), since the American Catholic Church was well aware that they could not raise enough funds to educate the many Catholic children that were arriving daily in the US. For this reason, they pushed to make the public school curriculum more accommodating to their Catholic parishioners. Indeed, despite a supposed separation between church and state in the public school system, most public school curricula included a compulsory reading of the Protestant Bible, mandatory temperance education, and instruction on Christian, i.e., Protestant living. For nativists, Catholic schools, coupled with the encroachments of Catholics on the public school system, embodied an attack on American ideals, since the common school was seen as a "transmitter of values, especially moral values" that functioned to convert immigrants into Americans. For them, "the problem in short was heterogeneity, cultural pluralism; and the public school was one of the problem-solving agencies" (Kleppner 1979, 229).

While Klepnner and Manfra do not refer to the place of the American West and the end of American expansionism in their studies on nativism, Higham does note the impact of the West on the rise of nativism in the late nineteenth century. First, he refers directly to the closing of the frontier, which rendered the West no longer an open space for squatters and adventurers, the region instead giving way to monopolists who came to amass vast landholdings, and with them a rise in rentism. He also alludes to the role of Catholics in Native American education in the West and its intersection with nativism:

> In the special field of Indian schools, successful lobbying by the Bureau of Catholic Indian Missions reversed the original distribution of federal funds to church-operated reservation schools, so that by the end of the decade Catholics were receiving a disproportionately large, rather than a disproportionately small, share of federal appropriations for Indian education.   (Higham 1971, 59)

The National League for the Protection of American Institutions was formed in 1889, and it revived the push for a constitutional amendment against the use of public funds for religious organizations, as

well as for the end of federal grants to the Indian mission schools
(Higham 1971, 59–60). Clearly, this proposed constitutional amendment was designed to keep public money out of the hands of
Catholics. Therefore, while Higham concludes that it was largely
matters of class that fueled the anti-immigrant sentiments of the nativism of the 1890s, he also recognizes that anti-Catholicism played a
role in American nativism of the period.

The Indian mission schools and the new restrictions on immigration that will be addressed presently are relevant when contextualizing the translation of *Rudo Ensayo* in the early 1890s, for the translation served to prove, I argue, that Catholics knew best how to
"educate" Native Americans: they had been doing so since the eighteenth century in the American Southwest.[12] The translation and
publication of *Rudo Ensayo* implicitly presented Catholics as integral
to the Republic, that is, because it suggested they (alone) were the
ones who knew how to run Indian mission schools. Catholics, that
is, were positioned in roles integral to the founding and ultimate success of the US as a nation.

We see these connections in other articles in the *Records of the
American Catholic Historical Society*, as well. These articles signal
how mission schools and the rising nativism that sought to close
them (because Catholics were beginning to run them) were on the
minds of Catholic Philadelphians such as Guiteras, for in the same
volume as the translation an extended narrative is included that describes a visit by one Edward J. Nolan to the American West in 1891.
Titled "Certain Churches in the West" and printed immediately
before Guiteras's translation, it details Nolan's travels to San Francisco
after passing through Denver and Salt Lake City (Nolan 1894). From
it we come to know that he visited Stanford University and then
moved to Monterey, subsequently travelling to Santa Barbara and
San Diego.[13] He later returned to Philadelphia via Santa Fe and
Kansas City.

The essay publishes what Nolan originally presented to the
Catholic Club of Philadelphia as a lecture titled "Impressions on the
Way" (1894, 88). In it, he spent considerable time describing the dif-
ferent church and mission edifices and structures, concluding that
"During our trip we had no opportunity of associating intimately
with either priests or people, but the edifices and the congregations
alike, for the most part, united in the assurance that the church in the
West is in no present danger of being spoiled by a superabundance of

world advantages" (Nolan 1894, 97). What is relevant about this essay is that it brings Catholic history to Nolan's present—the edifices and congregations—before turning to the past of the Catholic Church in the West, with Guiteras's translation. Specifically, Nolan goes on to devote a few pages of his essay to the Franciscan influence in California and specifically to Father Junipero Serra (1713–84), who founded missions in California in the eighteenth century. He concludes by saying, "There is no figure in the church history of the east coast, which fills anything like the same space that Father Junipero Serra does in that of the West" (Nolan 1894, 95). While I would also consider Varela, in his profound influence on US Catholicism in the Northeast, as such a figure, Nolan's essay clearly wished to guarantee the moral integrity and political utility of the Catholic Church in the West, despite its Mexican roots: Mexican secularization did not infect the churches standing in Nolan's day, he suggested, and its past was guaranteed by the virtues of priests like Junipero Serra to the degree that the western Catholic Church could be expected to be integrated into American life just as well as the Catholic Church had been integrated in the East. The placement of this article and the article's extended reflection on the role of such Franciscans as Junipero Serra in "evangelizing" and "civilizing" Native Americans, then, should be read as offering a perfect segue to the life and times of the Jesuit priest Juan Nentvig, which were to be treated by Guiteras.

That the ACHS sought to use *Rudo Ensayo* as a means to integrate Catholic and US history through the pacification of Native Americans is also made evident by the presence of the essay that follows Guiteras's translation. It was written by none other than Lawrence F. Flick, one of the founders of the ACHS and the editor of the *Records of the American Catholic Historical Society*. Titled "The Papago Indians and Their Church" (Flick 1894a), it refers to *Rudo Ensayo* itself and directly addresses the importance of Catholic missionaries for the American Republic by speaking of the evangelization and pacification of the Papago people by Jesuit missionaries like Nentvig. Examining the depictions in *Rudo Ensayo* of the Papago, who were part of the Pima nation, Flick writes, "While the Pima nation as well as some of their neighbors were undoubtedly more advanced in civilization, or possibly had retrograded less than many of the North American Indians, they were just as surely savage and were possessed of the vices of savages" (Flick 1894a, 390).

As the narrative develops, Flick narrates the beauty of the Papago church in Tucson, Arizona, and condemns the secular government of Mexico in the 1800s, which abandoned the church. He also condemns the Apache for constantly attacking the Papago once Mexican military defense was withdrawn from the friars and their congregations before the Mexican cession in 1848.

Speaking of the Gadsden Purchase of 1853, in which the Papago became a part of what would become the US states of New Mexico and Arizona, Flick describes how the bishop of Santa Fe, Jean-Baptiste Lamy, visited the Papago church and how:

> The Indians of this mission had not forgotten their religion, and upon his arrival among them, flocked about him in great joy. No sooner did the priest approach them, than some of their numbers hastened to ring the church bells to call the Indians to Church. Finding that he had come to minister to them they brought articles of church furniture from places of safe keeping, and placed them at his disposal. They listened to his instructions with the greatest attention, and gave every evidence of having retained the Faith.   (Flick 1894a, 412)

This praise for the priest Jean Baptiste Lamy captured the colonization and annexation of New Mexico not only by the US military and government but by the American Catholic Church, for Lamy actually displaced a New Mexican priest, Father José Martínez, who had been tending the Papago in Santa Fe for many years. Martínez was a key figure, who supported the US military during the US-Mexico War; yet he is absent from Flick's narrative. Instead, Father Lamy, who was French and who like Martínez became a US citizen, is memorialized there.

More relevant still is the manner in which Flick writes of the founding of Indian mission schools in the area from 1865. Describing the Papago's reaction to the founding of federally funded schools that were run by nuns, he says:

> The establishment of a [government] school among uncivilized people, who had not the faintest idea of what it meant, was by no means an easy task. As the Papagos, however, had a fair knowledge of the Christian religion, and as they had been Catholics for nearly two centuries, the sisters were aided considerably in their religious character. To start with, the Indians had a high respect for them, and this made them anxious to cooperate with them. The sisters worked hard

> to bring the young people to school, strove to learn their language, so that they might be better fitted to teach them, visited with them when they were sick, taught them how to work—especially the young women how to do housework—in short did everything possible to lead them into the ways of Christian civilization.   (Flick 1894a, 413)

This section ends with a condemnation of Protestants for advocating for and achieving the withdrawal of federal funds for Indian mission schools (Flick 1894a, 414), which signals how the publication of *Rudo Ensayo* alongside the essays addressing the role of Catholics in the churches of the American West speaks explicitly and implicitly to the concerns then facing the Catholic Church in America.

In addition to Catholic history and the rise of nativism, the dates of the translation and of the publication of *Rudo Ensayo* suggest the work was further intended to speak to the Immigration Act of 1891, in which the responsibility for monitoring immigrants entering the US was transferred from the states to the federal government. As Bennet (1988) explains in *The Party of Fear: From Nativist Movements to the New Right in American History*, 2.8 million immigrants reached the United States in the 1870s, 5.2 million more arrived in the 1880s, and 3.7 million arrived in the 1890s (Bennet 1988, 160). (Many of these immigrants were Catholic and came from Germany, Italy, and Bohemia, which shows the economic and political difficulties facing Europe at the time.) These large numbers caused alarm on many fronts. Chinese immigrants to the West were the main group to be denied immigration with the Chinese Exclusion Act of 1882 (and, one might add, variations of that Act were left in effect into the twentieth century). In the Immigration Act of 1882, coastal states were given authority to regulate immigration. The federal government simply asked states to report entry numbers for statistical purposes; they similarly sought to monitor living conditions on the ships bringing immigrants to American shores. Coastal states were otherwise free to admit immigrants as they chose. Seaboard states with ports of entry allowed unpaid charities to supervise immigrant arrivals, and no direct mandate was given to states contiguous with Canada and Mexico regarding the regulation of immigration in 1882.

Higham explains that, "the whole program [before 1891] aimed merely at an orderly reception, at helping those in temporary difficulty, and at discouraging the entry of the permanently incapacitated" (Higham 1971, 43). However, the Immigration Act of 1891, in shifting the responsibility for regulating immigration from states to the executive branch of the federal government, denied charities and states any active role in managing immigration; now only the federal government and its agents could do so, both at coastal points of entry and across the borders with Canada and Mexico. According to Higham, this Act led to the racialization of immigrants, which fueled the nativism rampant in the early twentieth century, which in turn led to further establishment of Jim Crow laws and the Immigration Act of 1924. While events of the early twentieth century and the impact that the Mexican Revolution and migration by Mexicans to the US (in order to escape the violence in Mexico) lie beyond the scope of this text, it is nevertheless important to remember how works like *Rudo Ensayo* and its translation by a Latina/o speak to immigration and nativism, especially in light of the rise of anti-immigrant sentiment in the US in the twentieth century and to the present day.

CUBAN HISTORY

Guiteras's translation also speaks to contemporaneous events in Cuba in the 1880s and 1890s. Annexationist Cubans left the Catholic Church in the first half of the nineteenth century in response to the church's alliance with the Spanish monarchy, objecting as they did particularly to the church's practice of sending Spanish-born and usually pro-Spanish priests to Cuba as a means of deterring revolution on the island. This distancing from what annexationists of the 1850s considered a pro-Spanish institution in Cuba led Félix Varela (1944), in *Cartas a Elpidio*, to question the church over this practice. This two-volume work simultaneously warned Cubans not to be seduced by the supposed separation of church and State that the United States appeared to be able to offer as a model for a prospective Cuban form of government and social organization.

This tendency of Cubans toward secularization continued with the separatist movement that fueled the Ten Years' War of 1868–78, an armed and extended island-wide insurgency against Spanish colonial rule that ended in defeat for the Cuban forces. With the Pacto del Zanjón of 1878 (the peace treaty that ended the Ten Years' War), the right to organize political parties in order to send elected representatives to the Spanish Cortes, was granted to the island. This concession led to the establishment of two major political parties in

Cuba—the Liberal (Autonomist) Party and the Partido Unión Constitucional (PUC), a pro-Spain party.

Autonomism as a political option for the island was not then new to the political scene in Cuba. After the failure of annexationism, many Cuban liberals joined the reformist ranks in the 1850s–1860s, hoping to keep Cuba within Spain's political fold while seeking political and economic reforms for the island through representation in the Spanish Cortes. The new autonomist push (1880s–1890s) for reform failed, however, due to fraud at the polls, including ballot stuffing, which led to the continued electoral success of the PUC. Yet, while autonomists were not able to further their agenda politically, the separatists continued plotting for revolution from their exile in the United States, Europe, and Latin America, as well as from the island itself. In 1895, just over a year after Guiteras's death, the final war that was fought for independence began on Cuban soil.

Earlier, during the first year of the Ten Years' War, hundreds of Cubans emigrated to the United States, most of them members of the creole petite bourgeoisie and the Cuban planter class and hailing from the region of Matanzas and Havana (Pérez 2018, 135).[14] This early migration brought Cubans to New York and other cities in the Northeast and the Atlantic seaboard who had previously traveled to the US for business and their studies and were familiar with its institutions and culture. Many of them held accounts with banks in New York, such as that of Moses Taylor, and were able to live out the war in relative comfort. However, the freezing of landholdings and embargoing of goods by the Spanish government led to the demise of both the Cuban planter class and the island's middle class. As the war continued to rage on the island and immediately after its end in 1878, a progressively greater number of Cubans came to the US, many of them from the working class.

Guiteras was one of the individuals who fled the island with the outbreak of the war. It seems that his decision arose from both personal and political considerations. On the personal front, fear for the life of his son, Juan Guiteras (who was born in 1852), was likely to have influenced his decision. His nephew, the son of his older brother Antonio Guiteras, had joined the uprising (he was later killed in battle at the age of 17), and Guiteras, who had already lost children to illness and disease, must have feared for his son's safety out of a predictable concern that he might choose to join the insurrection. And, anyhow, two of Guiteras's brothers were already in the US: both

Pedro José and Ramón were living in Bristol, Rhode Island. Pedro José had settled there as early as 1853, interrupting his time there with only two short visits to Cuba, in 1866 and 1868. He lived out the rest of his life in the United States, dying in Charleston, SC, in 1890. Ramón, in turn, settled permanently in Bristol and married into the Manchester Wardwell family, scions of the American Revolution. Like Guiteras's son Juan, Ramón's own son would ultimately enter medicine, teaching at Harvard and Columbia University.

From a political perspective, their decision to leave Cuba is not surprising given the experiences of the Guiteras family with the Spanish colonial administration. Guiteras, along with Pedro José, was imprisoned for six months in Cuba in 1850. Even before the tour taken by the brothers Antonio and Eusebio in the 1840s, Pedro José, the oldest of the Guiteras brothers, had been temporarily forbidden from disembarking at the port of Havana in 1837 on his return from a trip to Spain. He was thought to be colluding with José Antonio Saco, the avid autonomist who had critiqued the slave trade and the colonial administration and who had been expelled from the island in 1834. Pedro José had also signed a petition calling for the end of the slave trade. The then governor of the island, Miguel Tacón—the governor responsible for the Escalera Massacre of 1843–44—therefore had reason to place members of the Guiteras family under surveillance: they were part of a circle of friends from Matanzas who were known annexationists or reformists.

After the brothers were proven innocent, Guiteras stayed in Matanzas and founded the school La Empresa, together with his brother Antonio, where he taught until 1853, only then to leave Cuba once again. Biographers concur that this departure was prompted by the poor health of his son John. Subsequently returning to Matanzas, he continued teaching at La Empresa, where he taught from his readers and published a fourth from Matanzas itself in 1868, it being intended for use in secondary education. With the beginning of the armed insurrection in 1868, however, the colonial authorities closed the school, and all of his readers were banned. We may, therefore, infer that Guiteras must have feared for his life and for that of his family.

While many of the planter class and the creole petite bourgeoisie moved to New York—Guiteras belonged to the latter group—Guiteras chose Philadelphia in his period of exile. The decision is unsurprising considering that, as early as 1842, when he first visited Philadelphia, he wrote:

> Después de pasar como un mes en New York, acababa el de octubre acercándose el día de volver a mi patria querida. Entonces fue cuando visite la ciudad mas bella de los E.U., pudiendo apenas concederle 3 dias. El 26 de octubre a las nueve de la mañana salimos de New York en camino de hierro i llegamos a Filadelfia a las 3" [*sic*].
>
> (Guiteras n.d., 71)

(After spending about a month in New York City, the month of October was coming to an end bringing closer the day of my return to my beloved homeland. It was then that I visited the most beautiful city in the US, barely being able to give it 3 days. On October 26 at 9 a.m. we left New York City by train and we arrived in Philadelphia at 3 p.m.)

When in 1869 the Spanish authorities on the island embargoed the properties of all individuals who they believed supported the insurgency, Guiteras was among them. As such, he must have faced difficult economic times in the US, but he supported himself and his family by teaching Spanish. With this final return to the US—he died before being able to return to the island—Guiteras brings his Cuban and US experiences together in his translation of *Rudo Ensayo*, for the translation and its publication mirror many of his concerns regarding race in the US and in Cuba. Yet it is his travel diaries in particular that are instructive for understanding how Guiteras understood his experience in the US to be directly tied to his past in Cuba and to Cuban independence, because they illustrate how a major theme of his biography—an interest in education—in fact shaped not only his pedagogy but his overarching literary and intellectual project, his life's work.

Guiteras's Travelogue and His Engagement of *Rudo Ensayo*

While Guiteras's political views are not yet fully understood, we do see an inclination toward separatist ideas in his travel diary *Un invierno en Nueva York*.[15] This source, invaluable for understanding the experience of Latina/os in the US in the second half of the nineteenth century, was written about his personal experiences from

1869 to the mid-1880s.[16] It was most likely published in Barcelona in 1888, where Guiteras's brother Antonio was then residing.[17]

Of particular interest for the current analysis is Guiteras's reflection on the concept of education and its role in democratic institutions. For Guiteras, the notion that an individual needed to be "educated" in order to earn freedom was preposterous. He writes,

> Un error fatal ha encadenado, y encadena aún con torcidos nudos, la idea de la autonomía de los pueblos. Consiste este error en creer que un pueblo no puede gozar del bien de la libertad, si antes no se le educa convenientemente... Si se necesita real y verdaderamente de una educación preparatoria, ¿quién ha de ser el educador?
>
> (Guiteras n.d., 108–9)

> (A fatal error has chained and still chains in twisted knots the idea of autonomy for a people. This error consists in believing that a people cannot enjoy freedom if they are not educated suitably... If a people truly and honestly need a preparatory education, who will be the teacher?)

In this section of *Un invierno*, he speaks to those (in the US, Cuba, and Spain) who claimed that Cubans needed to be "taught" freedom before they could exercise it politically. Condemning this line of thinking as simply another despotic strategy to keep Cuba under Spanish colonial control, Guiteras made the following observation about recently emancipated, formerly enslaved Cubans (slavery ended in Cuba in 1886), again asking who will be able to offer instruction, if they must be taught in order to be free:

> Dice el amo de esclavos: "La libertada es peligrosa para los esclavos: no conviene darla sino después de haberlos educado para la libertad." ¿Quién ha de ser el educador? El goce de la libertad es una dignidad. ¿Cómo se educará al que tiene derecho a una dignidad, sin elevarle primero a esa dignidad? El amo no titubea en decir que niega la libertad al esclavo por el interés de este, como si la libertad fuera una máquina infernal o cosa semejante. Lo mismo dice del pueblo el déspota. En uno y otro caso el interés propio es el que habla.
>
> (Guiteras n.d., 109)

> (The master says of slaves: "Freedom is dangerous for slaves: it is not suitable to give it before educating them for freedom." Who is to be the teacher? The exercise of freedom is a dignity. How do you educate someone who has a right to dignity, without first making him

equivalent to that dignity? The master does not hesitate in saying that he denies freedom to the slave for the slave's best interest, as if freedom were an infernal machine or something similar to this. The same says the despot of the people. In one or the other case it is self-interest that is speaking.)

It is important here to recall what was noted earlier, namely, that members of the Guiteras family were friends of the exiled and ardent autonomist José Antonio Saco. For, despite these personal connections, Guiteras's commentary on education and freedom, especially in relation to recently emancipated Afro Cubans, here stands more in line with the thinking of the Spanish autonomist Rafael María Labra. A co-founder of the Spanish Abolitionist Society, which was founded in 1865, Labra had called for immediate abolition without compensation to slaveholders, while autonomists who supported Saco's vision believed in gradual emancipation with indemnification.[18]

Statements like those by Guiteras recorded above help to place the translation of *Rudo Ensayo* in Guiteras's historical moment. Slavery had ended on the island by the time of the production of his translation, and while autonomists in Cuba no longer used the threat of Cuba becoming a black Republic akin to that of Haiti to discourage Cubans from organizing a new uprising, they did maintain that it was necessary to keep the island under Spanish colonial rule, since under that system they could better educate previously enslaved people in order to teach them how to become citizens. Guiteras must be understood as speaking directly to these issues with statements like that cited above.

Additional observations made by Guiteras in *Un invierno* similarly offer insight into his views of Cuba's political future. When speaking of the US Civil War and its effect on the US, for example, he writes of the continuing importance of race:

Ya han pasado algunos años, y el sentimiento de rencor agitado por las armas no se ha extinguido de todo punto, que mala mezcla hace la sangre para cimentar la unión. Lo prueban las seguridades mismas que a cada paso se dan de una y otra parte para estrechar la fraternidad que debe existir entre los estados que forman la confederación americana. El negro ha ganado. Hoy es libre. Tiene derechos políticos. Es ciudadano. La gran anomalía de los Estado Unidos de América ha cesado de ser objeto de discordia para su pueblo y de escarnio para las extrañas naciones.   (Guiteras n.d., 22)

(Already some years have passed, but the feeling of rancor agitated by war has not been completely extinguished, what a bad mixture the shedding of blood makes for cementing a union. This is proven by the many assurances of fraternity that are given at every step to strengthen the fraternity that should already exist between the states that form the confederation that is América. The black man has won. Today he is free. He has political rights. He is a citizen. The great anomaly of the United States of America has ceased to be an object of discord for its people and of ridicule by foreign nations.)

Yet Guiteras is quick to highlight the fact that in order to ensure this liberty, legal measures had to be enacted; for it was necessary to amend the US Constitution to force compliance with the new rights granted to black citizens. Like Varela before him, then, Guiteras speaks of a blatant contrast between the conferral of a legal freedom in the US and a lived experience that in reality was characterized by continued harassment and oppression. He writes:

Empero, la emancipación y la enmienda de la Constitución, que en tan breve espacio hicieron tamaño trueque en la condición de los negros, no podían dar a éstos posición en la sociedad; porque las leyes no tienen fuero sobre las simpatías y antipatías del corazón humano.   (Guiteras n.d., 23)

(Emancipation and the constitutional amendment that was made in such a short period of time made an immense barter on the condition of black individuals in society, but it could not give them a position in society; because laws have no power over the sympathies and antipathies of the human heart.)

The "barter" to which Guiteras refers, then, is a constitutionally mandated freedom for those who were formerly enslaved, which was traded—that is to say substituted—for the work of changing the cultural and social views and values of those who supported slavery prior to the Civil War. In other words, while race relations *de jure* might have changed, de facto they had not, i.e., with the legal enactment of equality, the majority settled into complacency, not seeking to further eradicate racism in the many forms— whether individual or institutional—it could and did take after the Civil War.

Guiteras further identifies two particular obstacles facing African American citizens of the United States, which mere legal measures could not sufficiently address: their previous enslaved state and poverty. He pinpoints these two obstacles to demonstrate how European immigrants to the United States were able to overcome obstacles such as poverty: "Gracias a barberos, sastres, zapateros y demás manipulantes de las jerarquías sociales, tiende las alas como brillante mariposa, sin que, en la apariencia, se le descubra el pelo de la dehesa" (Guiteras n.d., 23) (It is thanks to barbers, tailors, shoemakers, and other manipulators of social hierarchies, [that] the most brilliant butterflies extend their wings, without, at least in appearance, the grass being discovered in their hair [meaning their peasant origins]). Those who had been recently emancipated did not have that opportunity, and this, in turn, he suggested, reflects the vanity and racism of white citizens. He writes, "Al pobre negro desde lejos se le conoce que es negro, y que viene de negro. Y nos envanecemos con nuestra civilización, cuando una ligera modificación de la piel nos hace caer en la más extraña de las inconsecuencias" (Guiteras n.d., 23) (The poor black man is recognized as black from afar and that he comes from a legacy of slavery. And we pride ourselves with our civilization, when in fact a slight modification of the skin makes us fall into the most odd of consequences).[19]

Guiteras goes on to note explicitly that while Mexico and South America have indigenous populations, the Caribbean and the US South have African populations. His goal is to suggest that those recently emancipated in Cuba are best identified as laborers, positioned in society in a place analogous to that of the proletariat (a term he uses) who are arriving in the US from Europe in the northern states. They are equal. The latter are not a threat to the US, however; and, by extension, he suggests, Afro Cubans should not be taken to pose a threat to the US (in the form of a body politic that might establish an independent Cuba along the lines of the—to certain US sensibilities—threatening model of Haiti's black Republic) or to the future of Cuba. Rather, he argues, emancipated Afro Cubans, like Catholic Irish immigrants, would continue to offer benefit to the future of the nation, no longer as enslaved workers but as active participants in the building of the nation:

De la misma manera que en la isla de Cuba el dueño de un grande ingenio de hacer azúcar deja al negro las rudas faenas, sin tomar ninguna parte en ellas, el americano de los Estados Unidos, poseedor de una fábrica de tejidos o una fundición, pasa la vida descansadamente o viajando por Europa, mientras los irlandeses hacen todo el trabajo.   (Guiteras 1885, 38)

(In the same manner that in the island of Cuba the owner of a great sugar plantation leaves to the black man the rough labor of the plantation without taking any part in those labors himself, the American of the United States, owner of a textile factory or a foundry, spends his life in rest or traveling through Europe while the Irish do all of the work.)

Ultimately, Guiteras's goal was to condemn the differential treatment of the two groups, this being the direct result of an inherent racism at the heart of US culture. He even extends this criticism to suggest that the US possesses and has cultivated no catalyst by which to coalesce the states into a true nation:

Las admirables instituciones que la Gran Bretaña estableció, o, mejor dicho, dejo establecer, en sus colonias de la América del Norte, y que confirmó la guerra de independencia, por las cuales las colonias se convirtieron en nación; las instituciones republicanas, digo, permiten la vida y el movimiento a los más opuestos elementos de población. Pero ellas no son bastantes a formar y cimentar, a lo menos en corto tiempo, una verdadera cohesión, una cohesión que se afirme en algo más que los intereses materiales. Constituyen la nación una unión de estados, no una unión de pueblos.   (Guiteras n.d., 40–41)

(The admirable institutions that Great Britain established, or better said, permitted to be established, in its North American colonies, and were affirmed with the war of independence, by which the colonies were converted into a nation; the republican institutions, I say, allow the life and movement to the most diverse elements of the people. But these are not enough to form or cement, at least in a short period of time, a true cohesion, a cohesion that is affirmed on something more than material interest. The US is a nation constituted by a union of states, not a union of people.)

The different groups that make up the US, Guiteras stresses, "viven y se mueven juntos, unidos por el interés de la propia conservación; pero sola y únicamente por ese interés" (Guiteras n.d., 40) (live and move together, united by the interest of self-preservation; but solely and only because of that interest).

Education, Guiteras concludes, is indispensable to the effort to transform the US from a legally bound union of states into a nation, and he bemoans that its institutions rested nearly exclusively in the hands of Protestants who controlled the school boards (Guiteras n.d., 52), which forced Catholics to establish and pay for non-governmental, parochial schools while having simultaneously to finance the public schools through taxation—a double financial burden for the predominantly working-class parishioners (Guiteras n.d., 53). He also laments the fact that school attendance was not obligatory in his day, noting, as he does, that various US states refused to institute obligatory training in reading and writing (Guiteras n.d., 54). Finally, he speaks directly to the important role he envisions for Catholicism as a transmitter, through education, of civic values. This he does by condemning Protestantism for "su fatal noción de la interpretación individual de las Escrituras" (Guiteras n.d., 148) (its fatal notion of the individual interpretation of the Scriptures), which led to the establishment of innumerable denominations—a criticism he supports by quoting a Protestant minister, Reverend Ferdinand Ewer (1826–83), who criticizes his parishioners for their religious infidelity, lack of respect for the elderly, parents, and the authorities, and lack of dedication to the poor (Guiteras n.d., 152–53). Ewer is quoted as concluding:

Las dos bases fundamentales del protestantismo, son: primera, la Biblia y solo la Biblia para los cristianos; segunda, cada individuo es prácticamente intérprete infalible de la Biblia. ¿Cuál ha sido la consecuencia? Que el protestantismo no ha fomentado la humildad, sino la arrogancia.   (Guiteras n.d., 153)

(The two fundamental bases for Protestantism are: first, the Bible and only the Bible for Christians; second, each individual is practically an infallible interpreter of the Bible. What have been the consequences? That Protestantism has fomented arrogance instead of humility.)

Guiteras immediately concludes:

La Iglesia católica apostólica romana, libre en los Estados Unidos, con su clero sano y vigoroso por la libertad, ve los males que el orador protestante deplora; y lucha como en los tiempos apostólicos. Dios bendice la lucha, haciendo que se aumenten sus hijos de una manera prodigiosa, y viva en ellos la fe mas fervorosa.   (Guiteras n.d., 153–54)

(The Apostolic Roman Catholic Church, free in the United States, its clergy made healthy and vigorous by freedom, sees these evils that the Protestant orator deplores; and fights as in apostolic times. God blesses the fight, making his children increase prodigiously and making the most fervent faith alive in them.)[20]

From *Un invierno* we see that Guiteras believed that true national cohesion, one that is not led by self-interest, could only be accomplished with and through the guidance of a mature religious institution like Catholicism. But not the Catholicism then still prevalent in Europe and being exported to Cuba. Instead, he advocated for a Catholicism similar to what was then being practiced in the US, where the Catholic Church had to find a way to survive and grow in the context of a secular government that legally separated church and state.

If Guiteras sought to avoid the excesses of European Catholicism, which often sided opportunistically with those in political power, he similarly condemned Protestantism for its excesses, implying it was not the proper form of religion to ensure a separation of church and state. Indeed, for Guiteras, Protestantism had proven itself to be detrimental to the well-being of the republic: it led the US to lack cohesion; the diversity of biblical interpretations licensed by Protestantism had led, in Guiteras's view, to too great a splintering of Christianity into diverse Protestant denominations and had converted Americans thereby into citizens who acted only in their splintered self-interests and, similarly, only for the sake of individual material advancement.

Bearing these histories and contexts in mind, then, we may understand the translation and publication of *Rudo Ensayo* as articulating not just Guiteras's view of the proper role for the Catholic Church in the Indian mission schools in the US and in US history more generally, but also in Cuba's political future. Since Cuba's indigenous population was eliminated through disease and abuse by the seventeenth century, it must be the place for emancipated Afro Cubans that Guiteras ponders when completing his translation. For him, just as the Catholic Church in the US still intervened in "civilizing" Native Americans, so too could they intervene to "civilize" emancipated Afro Cubans. By translating a piece that spoke of the pacification of Native Americans in New Spain by compassionate, yet also morally and spiritually dedicated priests (at least by Guiteras's account), Guiteras's *Rudo Ensayo* may thus be read as suggesting that

Catholicism as modeled by the Catholic Church in America could offer a means to ensure true independence in Cuba. Who was to educate black Cubans? Catholic priests, who, at least in the US, were agents of assimilation, and continued pacification. Yet it was more than even simply this. For, through the title of his biography, "Brief Sketch of the Life of Eusebio Guiteras," published as it was *immediately* preceding his translation, Guiteras was in a sense identified with Juan Nentvig himself (though posthumously so, given that, as already noted, his translation of *Rudo Ensayo*, Nentvig's "Brief Sketch," was published posthumously). On this interpretation, he himself stands as the answer to his own rhetorical question in *Un invierno*, "Who will be the teacher?"

José María Aguilera Manzano has explained, already, that Guiteras conceived of his diaries from the 1840s not simply as travel accounts but as manuals, since Guiteras believed that "descripción animada" (Aguilera Manzano 2010, 37) (animated description) of his travels would better serve to impart his experiences to readers, who were, in fact, his students at La Empresa. His goal was to provide a "Cuban" point of view, a Cuban perspective, on universal history—he traveled to the US, Europe, and the Middle East, including Jerusalem, and his diary incorporates the history of these places along with personal reflections about his experience encountering these places for the first time. Aguilera Manzano argues that Guiteras wanted his Cuban reader in a sense *to experience* what he had seen, so that the visual and textual could come together not simply to provide historical information, but to furnish nothing less than a Cuban vision of those spaces and that history (Aguilera Manzano 2010, 37). This in turn was meant to bring the author as teacher together with the reader and, ultimately, to lead to the construction of a Cuban consciousness that would provide a Cuban perspective into the conceptualization of history, and most importantly, the conceptualizing of a Cuban nation on terms accented by just such a universalizing reach. He brings the visual and the textual together, Aguilera Manzano notes, through "cuadro[s]" or sketches, both visual and descriptive, of what he, as a Cuban traveler, experienced (Aguilera Manzano 2010, 37).

Aguilera Manzano does not elaborate on what he means by "cuadros" or sketches—he could simply be referring to the short, descriptive vignettes that populate the diaries of the 1840s. On the other hand, the *cuadros de costumbres* was a popular genre in Spain, Cuba,

Mexico, and Latin America during the 1830s–1860s.[21] Guiteras, in fact, had written two *novelas costumbristas—Irene Albar* (1885) and *Gabriel Reyes* (posthumously published in 1903–4). If we read *Un invierno en Nueva York* as participating in this generic practice, then the work in itself must be understood as being nothing less than a manual for its readers, one that creates a certain concept of society and more importantly educates the future citizens of a future independent Cuban nation. In this light, the role of the author and narrator (they are one and the same in Guiteras's text) is particularly important: the author-narrator is the "teacher" who educates his reader on the creation of an equitable and democratic society.

We may recall a pointed comment exemplifying this understanding of the text as a manual that Guiteras makes in *Un invierno* after visiting the Tombs in New York City. Bemoaning that those who are rich are able to post bail, while those who are accused of the same crime—public drunkenness—and who are poor are unable to pay for it and must therefore await trial in prison, he ironically questions the so-called notion of equality in the US:

> Pobreza y servidumbre parecen palabras sinónimas. Siempre ha de haber amos y esclavos. Pero si ésta parece una necesidad en el cuerpo social, por más que se halle constituido en república democrática, el alma no puede menos de regocijarse al contemplar la hoja de papel en que se halla escrita la Constitución de un pueblo libre. "Nosotros, el Pueblo del Estado de Nueva York, agradecidos al Todopoderoso por nuestra libertad, para asegurar las bendiciones de ésta, queremos establecer, y establecemos, esta Constitución." El principio de que todos los hombres son iguales, puede ser una chimera; pero no hay duda que la base es la libertad.   (Guiteras n.d., 108)

> (Poverty and servitude appear to be synonymous words. There must always be masters and slaves. But if this appears to be a necessity in the social body, even though it was constituted in a democratic republic, the soul can do no less than rejoice in contemplating the piece of paper on which the constitution of a free people is written: "We, the people of the State of New York, grateful to the all-powerful for our liberty, in order to ensure his blessings, wish to establish, and do establish, this constitution." The principle that all men are equal could be a chimera; but there is no doubt that its base is freedom.)

In this difficult but instructive passage, Guiteras deploys what is a common narrative technique of his prose, whereby he turns a question around on all sides, alternatively offering contrasting assessments of a given political or other concept or event in the United States, plainly questioning the matter to hand in a pedagogical mode, such that his readers could learn to do so for themselves. With such passages he may be said to converse with the reader, then, presenting multiple sides of the given social manifestation or practice, so that the reader may learn *how* to think about what he (i.e., Guiteras) has seen. The readers may be trained, that is, to interpret history from a Cuban or, I would add, a Latina/o perspective to become the genius who sees just as the teacher does.

In the example just offered, at issue was the very inconsistency he saw in the US between *de jure* rights and de facto lived realities, the latter hardly living up to the promise of the former. But the pedagogy of his travelogue, its intended role as a *manual* embodying a pedagogy, extended to a host of concerns and social issues and, more than even this, issuing a reaching intellectual vision of literature itself and its relationship with its (national and global) readers. Indeed, Guiteras understands *Un invierno* as providing more than merely a manual that can bring the reader and the writer together in thought (or, rather, mode of thinking): written more than forty years after his first travel narratives, *Un invierno* goes further than they did by offering a full-blown theory of world literature. For Guiteras, in offering his observations on US culture, politics, religion, and customs, explicitly argues that literary works—including not only creative works of various genres but also works of history proper—have a decisive role to play in the betterment of society.

In a chapter titled "Como se pasa la prima noche" (Guiteras n.d., 76) (How Opening Night Occurs) he begins his discussion of world literature through an analysis of drama, which he refers to as one of "las lenguas de la literatura" (Guiteras n.d., 79) (the languages of literature), analyzing in particular its role in creating a national consciousness through the example of Shakespeare's dramas and their impact on the "lengua, la literatura y aun sobre el carácter de la raza anglosajona" (Guiteras n.d., 78) (language, literature and even the character of the Anglo-Saxon race). He argues that these types of works "arraiga en la grandes verdades de la vida" (Guiteras n.d., 78) (take root in the great truths of life.) Indeed, in his view, dramatists like Shakespeare have a "filosofía [que] es la del pueblo" (Guiteras n.d., 78) (philosophy that is of the people) and can have "una

influencia real sobre el pueblo" (Guiteras n.d., 78) (a real influence
on the people). In other words, great works can and do impact not only
the individual spectator but also the masses and the nation. He notes:

> Shakespeare podría presentare como una prueba de que el teatro
> ejerce una influencia real sobre el pueblo. Moliere se halla quizás en
> el mismo caso; pero ¡qué diferencia entre uno y otro! ¡qué diferencia
> entre el espíritu libre del inglés y el caprichoso servilismo del francés!
> Del teatro de Shakespeare salimos llenos de simpatía hacia nuestros
> semejantes; del de Moliere burlándonos de ellos y de nosotros mismos.
>
> (Guiteras n.d., 78)

(Shakespeare could be presented as proof that theater can exercise a
real influence on the people. Molière may offer a similar case; but,
what a difference between the one and the other! What a difference
between the free spirit of the Englishman and the servile caprice of
the Frenchman! From Shakespeare's theater we come out full of sym-
pathy toward those who are like us; from Molière's making fun of
them and of ourselves.)

More importantly, the genius of someone like Shakespeare or Molière
resides, in Guiteras's view, not simply in their talent but in the fact
that they were also actors who studied their audiences: "Fueron
ambos actores; y desde las tablas estudiaron a sus espectadores"
(Guiteras 1885, 79) (They were both actors, and from the stage they
studied their spectators). And it is this relationship between the
dramatist/actor and spectator/audience that transforms national literature into world literature and ultimately offers a means to better
society: "¿Imprimieron ellos un carácter con la fuerza de su ingenio
o le recibieron?" (Guiteras n.d., 79) (Did they [Shakespeare and
Molière] stamp their characters with the strength of their genius or
did they receive it from their audiences?), Guiteras asks rhetorically.
He answers in the elliptical mode typical of his pedagogy: "Resuelvan
otros la cuestión; pero hay que tener presente que en Inglaterra pre-
cedió á Shakespeare, Chaucer, y Rabelais a Moliere en Francia"
(Guiteras n.d., 79) (Let others resolve the issue; but we must be aware
that in England Shakespeare was preceded by Chaucer, and Rabelais
preceded Molière in France). The paragraph abruptly ends here.

Guiteras's answer to his own question is undoubtedly enigmatic. In
fact, he appears to offer a *non sequitur*. His reply, however, in fact exemplifies the Socratic nature of his pedagogical approach. First, he
presents his readers with a dilemma: Do literary authors create

characters through the power of their individual genius in that they have exceptional gifts that others do not possess; or are they simply good observers who serve as vehicles for the expression of the national and, ultimately, universal sentiments of the people around them in that they are (merely) a part of a communal experience of which their works are simply receptacles for depicting the human spirit? The former implies genius is individual, the latter that real genius emerges communally in the relationship between the people and the dramatist. While Guiteras refuses to answer the question, instead shifting the responsibility to some unknown "other" ("Let others resolve the issue"), he simultaneously invites his readers to develop their own answers rather than simply await *the* answer from *the* teacher.

And yet Guiteras also does not abandon his students completely. He provides a tool by which they may begin to think about the issue: the establishment and development of a national literature is proffered as a starting point; Shakespeare and Molière had predecessors whom they read and studied, Chaucer and Rabelais, respectively. True knowledge, in other words, may come from studying those authors who depicted real people and their circumstances, which they could do because they could identify with them and were in fact inspired by them. This "reading" of the genius in the people (by "great" literary geniuses) is precisely what effected the creation of the national literatures of England and France, Guiteras suggests. By implicit analogy, then, we may understand Guiteras here as inviting his Cuban/Latina/o reader to do the same. He wants Cubans—he dedicates the book to his son John—to understand that a national Cuban consciousness is inherent in themselves; it can and would emerge from the Cuban populace itself. That inward movement of a particular Cuban awareness could then exteriorize in the form of a more universal sentiment, one that could serve to teach humanity about love, and social and racial equity. Just as there is no need to "learn" how to be independent—dignity is a universal right already and always possessed by Cubans of all races, in his view—a national literature, by logical extension, is already present in the genius of the Cuban people; Cubans simply need to give it expression in order to make it universal.

Guiteras, moreover, does not limit his observations to drama. For him, "Es el drama una de las lenguas de la literatura, y como ésta tiene por objeto la transmisión de ideas, parece que el que tenga más ideas, que es el hombre de grande ingenio, ha de transmitirlas á los

que tienen menos" (Guiteras n.d., 79) (Drama is [only] one of the
languages of literature, since drama has as its object the transmission
of ideas, it appears that he who has more ideas, who is the man of
great genius, has to transmit them to those who have less). Yet, for
Guiteras, it is merely a matter of appearances that the genius trans-
mits knowledge unidirectionally to a more ignorant audience; for he
immediately expands his understanding of drama, and his understanding of literature, as follows:

> Cualquiera que sea el grado de civilización de la sociedad, en ella han
> de ser necesariamente maestros el poeta con sus poemas ó sus dramas,
> el orador con sus discursos, el historiador con sus anales, el hombre
> científico con sus cálculos ó experimentos. Sucede también que hay
> ideas, ó nociones, ú opiniones que se ciernen, por decirlos así, en la
> sociedad, y tanto el sabio como el ignorante, sin darse cuenta de ellos,
> las aspiran; y aquí entonces la excelencia magistral de los ingenios
> privilegiados, los cuales adivinan el sentimiento universal y son los
> primeros á darle forma.   (Guiteras n.d., 79–80)

> (Whatever the level of civilization of society, the poet with his
> poems; the orator with his discourses, the historian with his annals,
> the man of science with his calculations and experiments, all will
> necessarily be teachers. It also occurs that there are ideas or notions
> or opinions that hover or loom, to say it in that fashion, in society,
> and as much the wise as the ignorant, without noticing, aspire to
> them; and here is where the magisterial excellence of privileged
> genius enters. They discern the universal sentiment and are the first
> to give it form.)

For Guiteras, the poet, historian, and scientist learn from those who
are around them and reflect their knowledge back to their readers/
students: the role of literature, or history in the case of *Rudo Ensayo*,
and the concurrent act of translation, is thus understood as trans-
mitting "the universal sentiment" and giving it form.

Similarly, *Un invierno* itself may be counted as a contribution of
Guiteras to (world) literature; it was a medium for him to give form
to a Cuban national consciousness that was also a part of the universal sentiment.[22] His diary seeks in its very structure and pedagogical
approach to integrate Cuban readers, the Cuban people *tout court*,
into the world. If contemporary readers of Guiteras's *Un invierno*
had any doubts as to whether he places himself in the position of
teacher and author (and an informed one at that, since he learned

from Shakespeare), we must only read the sentences that follow his discussion of the role of literature (including history and science) that was cited above. He writes:

> Yo he ido al teatro cuando artistas como Booth interpretaban las obras de Shakespeare; y, desprendiéndome completamente de la escena, he hecho de los espectadores mis actores. Dos, tres, cuatro mil personas llenaban palcos, lunetas y bancos. El lujo del vestido y las monadas de unas, indican la gente que llaman fashionable; la atención pensativa se veía retratada en la mirada del crítico inteligente, Allá por las localidades altas, que son en realidad las bajas, acerté a descubrir la cabeza calva y rostro sereno del mulato que, en la casa de huéspedes, me servía la mesa y me limpiaba los zapatos. Todos escuchaban atentamente. La risa y las palmadas eran seguramente á veces arrancadas por el esfuerzo artístico del actor; pero con mayor frecuencia las provocaban la imagen florida, el agudo gracejo, el pensamiento sublime del gran poeta, cuyo cuerpo, hace siglos, yace en el polvo [*sic*].   (Guiteras n.d., 80)

> (I have gone to the theater when artists like [Edwin] Booth interpreted the works of Shakespeare; and, detaching myself completely from the scene, I have made actors out of the spectators. Two, three, four thousand people filled boxes, orchestra seats, and benches. The luxurious dress and the amusing behavior of some indicated those people who are called fashionable; the pensive attention was portrayed in the look of the intelligent critic. There in the highest places, which are in reality the lowest, I was able to discover the bald head and serene countenance of a mulatto, who, in the boarding house, served me at dinner and cleaned my shoes. All listened attentively. Laughter and applause were surely sometimes elicited suddenly by the artistic effort of the actor; but with more frequency they were provoked by the florid image of the sharp storyteller, by the sublime thoughts of the great poet, whose body has lain in the dust for many centuries.)

In converting the spectators around him into actors—he is the dramatist who observes them and learns from them—Guiteras transformed himself into author and teacher, and, he suggests, his reader must likewise follow suit.

＊　＊　＊

In its role as a manual or textbook, then, *Un invierno* presents the relationship between teacher and reader as a communal one in which

Guiteras positions himself (and the historian) in the role of the priest who may be giving the homily, but who is in fact a servant of the people, since it is within the parishioners that true faith abides. The priest's role is simply to create a space for the parishioners to experience this faith communally, which explains why Guiteras had such a difficult time accepting the individualistic nature of Protestantism, just as it explains why he condemned the (in his view) deleterious effect such individualism had on contemporaneous democratic institutions. In doing so, Guiteras identifies the Catholic Church in America as the means par excellence for establishing a social and racial harmony that is constrained neither by national borders (US-Mexico or US-Cuba) or national traits (US material interest or US and Cuban racism), but is intimately united with a universal human sentiment, one that denies politically and racially and economically motivated—and facetious—distinctions between Afro Cubans and working-class Irish Americans, or the like. This is the way, I propose, that we must read *Rudo Ensayo* today and the way *Rudo Ensayo* was meant by Guiteras to be read in the mid-1890s; it explains why his niece would title his biography a "Brief Sketch," paralleling—indeed, repeating—the title of *Rudo Ensayo*: she wants us to understand that Guiteras intended his translation to be *both* a manual or textbook *and* a literary work that was to have a transformative effect on society, a historiographic work with a transcription and translation history that spans continents and could "exercise a real influence on the people" (L. Guiteras 1894, 78), including Cubans in Cuba, Latina/os in the US, and even American nativists, who would need great coaxing to see the proper role of the Catholic Church in American history.

Here, then, the Latino Continuum finds representation not merely in the biography of a Cuban who spent nearly half his life in the United States, but also in the work he elected to translate and in the translation. The original text, written by a German about events of the eighteenth century that took place in New Spain, was transcribed in Madrid by an American, who published it in the US in order to help to incorporate Arizona into the Union and into the US *imaginaire* just after the Confederate Army had forcibly claimed part of the territory for the South. It detailed the activities of the Catholic Church in a part of the world that was, at the time of the narrative of the work, a Spanish territory but which was acceded to the United States. Its treatment of native peoples offered a model, primarily, not for integrating them but rather black Cubans and those recently emancipated in the United States into their respective states, when the Church in Cuba was being abandoned by those who supported a political distancing of Cuba from Spain and when the Church in the US was a minority institution under attack by (mostly Protestant) nativists.

In contextualizing *Rudo Ensayo* in the context of Guiteras's life and that of the Catholic Church in the West and Southwest, then, as the *Records of the American Catholic Historical Society of Philadelphia* (under Flick's editorship) did, Guiteras's rendering of that work offers more than a translation of an historical document that could identify a role for the Catholic Church in the United States, which surely is what the ACHS leadership would have wanted. It also served in its translation to *create* an archive that—developed and implicitly shaped as it was by Guiteras's thoroughly developed intellectual program, which saw literature in a pedagogical light—imagined an emerging sentiment. Yes, it was one developed out of a Cuban national consciousness *and* a human and universal sentiment simultaneously, one that could speak to the futures of the republics in Cuba and the United States alike, but through the Latina/o experience, and, perhaps most significantly, across the racial boundaries that had marred each in their complex and mutually imbricated hemispheric and global histories that lie on the Latino Continuum.

The Black *Lector*

FORGING A RADICAL REVOLUTION

While Chapter 3 analyzed Eusebio Guiteras's articulation of the future of the Cuban nation and the place of Afro Cubans in that future, expressed ambivalently through his translation of *Rudo Ensayo* and his deep engagement with US Catholicism, this chapter directly explores the place of black Cubans in Cuba and in the US during the late 1880s and 1890s directly, as articulated through the life and works of Martín Morúa Delgado (1856–1910), the son of a previously enslaved woman. The first black reader or *lector* in cigar factories in Havana, New York, and Key West, Morúa labored incessantly for workers' rights on both sides of the Florida Straits. Reading Morúa's life and works from the Latino Continuum allows us to recover the political significance of this figure for literary and historical studies.[1] Specifically, we immediately notice that he dialogues directly with José Martí—the founder of the Cuban Revolutionary Party in New York City and the well-known author of the essay "Nuestra América." Most significantly, juxtaposing Morúa's and Martí's literary works and translation choices allows us to understand more fully why Morúa was at odds with Martí regarding Cuba's future and the role that Afro Latina/os had played and would continue to play in Cuba and in the Americas. While the translation of Helen Hunt Jackson's *Ramona* (1884) by Martí in 1887 and the publication of Martí's novel *Amistad funesta* in 1885 speak specifically to US expansionism, its effect on Native American populations, and the role of the Latin American intellectual in the face of that expansionism, they did not necessarily engage Cuba's most pertinent question at the time—the role of black Cubans in the upcoming wars of independence and in the future Cuban Republic, both being planned in the US and Cuba in the 1880s and in the first half of the

The Latino Continuum and the Nineteenth-Century Americas: Literature, Translation, and Historiography.
Carmen E. Lamas, Oxford University Press (2021). © Carmen E. Lamas. DOI: 10.1093/oso/9780198871484.003.0005

1890s. In that exclusion, there was also an omission of the role and place of Afro Latin Americans and Afro Latina/os in the hemisphere more broadly. Morúa, who interacted with Martí, whether in person in New York or through the press, was well aware of this absence, as I will demonstrate, since he uses his two novels, *Sofía* (1891) and *La familia Unzúazu* (1901), to question the political intentions and social prejudices of Americanized Cubans like Martí. Moreover, Morúa translated James Redpath's (1863) *Toussaint L'Ouverture: A Biography and Autobiography*. This translation choice, which differs significantly from Martí's choice of *Ramona*, further articulates the diverging visions for the place of Afro-diasporic histories—and futures—in Cuba, the United States, and Latin America, as espoused by these important turn-of-the-century thinkers.

José Martí: "Nuestra América" and the Latino Continuum

José Martí (1853–95), his life and works, fall squarely on the Latino Continuum, so much so that the "ritual invocation of Martí" by US Americanists, as Kirsten Silva Gruesz (1998, 397) once pithily put it, threatens even now to overshadow the early period and formation of the Latino Continuum that this book recovers. Nevertheless, Martí's life and works can help to further illuminate the conceptual significance of the continuum and its bearing on the hemispheric literature of the Americas. In particular, his best-known and frequently cited essay, "Nuestra America" (1891), exemplifies the multifaceted experience of individuals living in and moving between different countries through their life and works.[2]

Martí was born in Havana, Cuba to *peninsulares* (Spanish-born individuals) who supported Spanish control of Cuba. At the age of 17, he was arrested for sedition against the Spanish government and was sentenced to serve six years' hard labor but only served from 1869 to 1871. The intervention of family friends led to his being exiled to Madrid (1871–74), where he finished the remainder of his sentence and studied to be an attorney. He subsequently travelled to Mexico and Guatemala, finally arriving in the US in 1880. He spent eight months in Venezuela immediately thereafter before returning to New York City in 1881, residing there until his death in Cuba in 1895, with intermittent travels to the Caribbean and Central America.

As is evident from Martí's life and writings, specifically translation in this case, Martí falls on the Latino Continuum, his works published extensively throughout Latin America, the Caribbean, Europe, and the US. Because of his role as the founder of the Cuban Revolutionary Party, which organized and led the fight against Spain during Cuba's last attempt at independence (1895–98), he is an important historical figure for Cuba and for Latin America more broadly. Martí died in battle on May 26, 1895 in eastern Cuba in one of the first skirmishes in Cuba's third and final attempt at independence. Because of his political organizing, his prolific literary and journalistic writing career, and his vision for a Cuba "with all and for the good of all"—as he put it in his November 26, 1891 (and now infamous) speech of the same title to tobacco workers in Tampa—his early death in battle led to his designation as a martyr for the Cuban cause, as well as the Apostle of Cuban Independence, as his contemporaries and biographers termed him. But he was also known as "El Maestro" because of his work with La Liga, a night school for Afro Latina/os in New York City.[3]

During his time in New York, Martí labored tirelessly for Cuban independence, articulating its rationale, especially in his newspaper, *Patria*, which he edited with Rafael Serra (1858–1909) and Sotero Figueroa (1851–1923), Afro Latino intellectuals from Cuba and Puerto Rico, respectively.[4] He also wrote his well-known collections of poetry, *Ismaelillo* (1882) and *Versos sencillos* (1891), both of which he published in New York. These works have led contemporary scholars to consider him an early figure in *modernismo* along with Manuel Gutiérrez Nájera (1859–95) from Mexico.[5] While in New York, he edited *La Edad de Oro* (1889), a children's magazine meant to educate children about civic life; he translated English-language articles, sending these to multiple Latin American newspapers; and he penned over 250 articles about American life, sending them to such newspapers as *La Nación* in Buenos Aires, *El Partido Liberal* in Mexico City and *La Opinión* in Caracas, Venezuela. These vignettes covered such events as the completion of the Brooklyn Bridge (1883), the Haymarket Massacre (1886), and the Charleston Earthquake (1886). As part of his translation practice he rendered and published Helen Hunt Jackson's *Ramona* (1884) in 1887, as well as the then popular mystery novel *Called Back* (1883) by Hugh Conway, whose real name was Frederick John Fargus (1847–85), an English novelist.

He completed this translation for Appleton & Co. and titled it *Misterio* (1886).

Translation was a regular practice for Martí and many Latina/os of the nineteenth century.[6] As early as 1875, Martí translated Victor Hugo's *Mes Fils* (1874). It is in the prologue to this translation that he begins to elaborate his vision of translation as *impensar* or *transpensar*, a form of "trans-thinking." Demonstrating his theory, he writes:

> Victor Hugo no escribe en francés: no puede traducírsele en español. Victor Hugo escribe en Victor Hugo...cuando hay una inteligencia que va más allá de los idiomas, yo me voy tras ella, y bebo de ella, y si para traducirla he de afrancesarme, me olvido, me domino, la amo y me afranceso.   (Martí 1963, 24: 16)
>
> (Victor Hugo does not write in French; he cannot be translated into Spanish. Victor Hugo writes in Victor Hugo...when there is an intelligence that goes beyond both languages, I follow it, I drink from it, and if to translate it I have to become French-like, I forget, I control myself, I love it, and I Frenchify myself.)

As the early creation of *transpensar* and *impensar* suggests, Martí was engaged in the theory of translation as well as its practice, and he understood its meaning as extending far beyond the unproblematic carrying over of content into a different tongue. For example, in the prologue to *Misterio* (1886) he explained:

> Traducir no es, a su juicio, mostrarse a sí propio a costa del autor, sino poner en palabra de la lengua nativa al autor entero, sin dejar ver en un solo instante la persona propia.   (Martí 1963, 24: 40)
>
> (Translation is not, according to his [the translator's] judgment, to reveal oneself at the expense of the author, but to put into words the native language of the entire author, without allowing the reader to see in any instance the actual person [the translator].)

This emphasis on the process of translation, one in which the translator literally becomes one with the author, moves beyond a straightforward linguistic mimesis. In his reflections on G. De Zéndegui's translation of H. Hojorth Boyensen's poem "Evolution," he wrote:

> Traducir es tanto como crear; y casi puede decirse que solo puede traducir bien aquel que posee condiciones semejantes, cuando no

iguales a las del autor interpretado, porque el que traduce ha de salir
de sí y ponerse donde el autor se puso, para dar a cada palabra el alma
y fuego que la harán durable.

                                    (Quoted in Arencibia Rodríguez 2000, 136)

(Translation is much like creating; and one can almost say that only
he who possesses similar, when not the same conditions, as the interpreted author can translate well. Because he who translates must
leave himself and place himself where the author placed himself, in
order to give each word the soul and fire that will make the text
long-lasting.)[7]

Translation in Martí's view required a cognitive shifting with the
translator, an emergent ability not merely to speak but to think across
languages, and thus an ability to think across disparate, often incom-
mensurate worlds. They are worlds where the translator is invisible
but also forever present. In this instance of trans-thinking, Martí
places the work of translation on a continuum between the original
and the final product, with the translator and author, like the original
and the translated text, at either endpoint. The creative process of
translation is hidden from view as a new text emerges that mirrors
the "soul and fire" of the original.

Laura Lomas's (2009) highly-acclaimed book *Translating
Empire: José Martí, Migrant Latino Subjects, and American
Modernities* speaks directly to this creative translation process
through what she terms Martí's "border writing" (Lomas 2009,
222) and his use of "infiltrative translation" (Lomas 2009, 231).
Lomas bases her observations on Martí's critique of US expan-
sionism through his works that engaged the US border regions.
Lomas writes:

The past of indigenous displacement in the borderlands of Florida
and Oklahoma illustrates for Martí's readers a possible future of in-
vading Anglos, against which he hopes his readers will join him in
plotting...infiltrative translation was for Martí a means to prevent
preemptive invasions and to ensure his Americas' survival.

                                                        (Lomas 2009, 231)

The term "infiltrative" comes from Martí's hand, from a letter he
wrote to his friend Manuel Mercado in Mexico in which he describes
his fears pertaining to the A. K. Cutting case, which in 1886 almost

caused a second invasion of Mexico by the US. In the letter, dated August 2, 1886, Martí had written about:

> la necesidad de infiltrar en la frontera un elemento numeroso de gentes de buen consejo y cautela, y abrir sobre la masa de este país una campaña infatigable de lo que pudiera llamarse "explicación de México",—para que conociéndolo y respetándolo más la masa, lo estime como lo estiman ya los que lo conocen y respetan.
>
> (Martí 1963, 20: 97)

(The need to infiltrate into the border a numerous element of people with wise advice and counsel, and to open to the masses of this country [the US] an indefatigable campaign of what could be called "an explanation of Mexico"—so that knowing and respecting this country [Mexico], the [US] masses will esteem the country as those who already know and respect Mexico esteem it.)

Consequently, Lomas (2009, 236) explains: "The infiltrative translator discreetly enters Anglo-American cultural settings, studies the rhetoric of imperialism, and then translates it for readers in the lands that would be most affected by it. Infiltrative translation unmasks the imperial ambitions that the rhetoric of democracy and equality sometimes obscures from view." Like Tolón before him in his translation of Willard's *Abridged History*, and as Lomas so clearly articulates, Martí envisions translation not simply as a professional practice or an aesthetic venture, but as a political and anti-imperialist act. As such, Susan Gillman (2012) argued that Martí's translation of *Ramona* was a form of social protest in the vein of Harriet Beecher Stowe.

Scholarship on Martí's writings has concentrated on his political essays and journalism, and more recently, his "Escenas americanas" or chronicles of life in the US.[8] I propose, however, that reading Martí from the Latino Continuum forces us to turn to his translation practice, in particular *Ramona* and its relation to his serialized novel *Amistad funesta* (1885). For Martí, translation was a political act, as I will show. Since *Amistad funesta* speaks to the place of the Latin American intellectual in modernity and nation-building, it is, in this manner, likewise related to politics. Martí, though a prolific author—the most recent edition of his complete works stands currently at twenty-eight volumes (Havana, Cuba: Centro de Estudios Martianos)—authored only one novel, the aforementioned *Amistad funesta*, during his highly productive career. It appeared in installments in *El Latino Americano* in 1885, a Latino-run newspaper in New York City.

And it is from *Amistad funesta*, read in its relation to his translated *Ramona*, that we begin to understand why such an important figure for racial integration in Cuba as Martín Morúa Delgado would question Martí's intentions and would lump him in with other New York Cubans of the 1880s as wasting away from the ideological "marasmo que nuevamente se iba apoderando de los cubanos en el extranjero" (*El Pueblo* (Key West) April 16, 1887) (paralysis that was once again taking over the Cubans who lived abroad).

"Nuestra novela" versus "esta noveluca"

Scholarship focusing solely on Martí's translation of *Ramona* is still relatively limited compared to work concentrating on his poetry and journalism,[9] even though Martí clearly argued for the importance of *Ramona* for the future of Latin America. In the introduction to his translation he wrote, "Como Ticknor[10] escribió la historia de la literatura española, Helen Hunt Jackson, con más fuego y conocimiento, ha escrito quizás en *Ramona* nuestra novela" (Martí 1963, 24: 204) (As Ticknor wrote the history of Spanish literature, Helen Hunt Jackson, with more fire and knowledge, has probably written in *Ramona* our novel). He then ties the novel's advocacy for indigenous communities in the US to advocacy for these communities in Latin America: "El primoroso gusto de su autora afamada, de Helen Hunt Jackson, le permitió escribir una obra de piedad, una obra que en nuestros países de América pudiera ser de verdadera resurrección" (Martí 1963, 24: 203) (The exquisite inclination of the famed author, of Helen Hunt Jackson, allowed her to write a work of compassion, a work that in our countries of America could serve as a true resurrection). Martí, convinced of the importance of the work, paid for the book's publication himself, envisioning it as one of a series that would be distributed in Latin America (Pampín 2012, 63–65). Not only did he imagine that Spanish-speaking readers would purchase the novel, ensuring economic success in Latin America to match what it had achieved in the US, but he also saw it as a means to effect political change, since *Ramona* was, as he said, *nuestra* (ours) (see Martí 1963, 24: 205).[11] These assertions and this publication enterprise have led literary scholars to pronounce the importance of

Martí's translation of *Ramona* for capturing his vision of a united Latin America that could stand against the imperialism of the US (Arencibia Rodríguez 1998; Rodríguez Morell 1995–1996; Vallejo 2013). And it is in the overt oppression of Native Americans in the novel that Martí hoped to warn Latin Americans of the fearful neighbor to the north. However, the link between *Ramona* and *Amistad funesta* (1885) has more to tell us about Martí's vision regarding the place of Native Americans in the hemisphere.[12]

As with his translation, Martí had strong opinions about his literary production in the novel form. Specifically, while *Ramona* was "nuestra novela," he dismissed his own novel as inconsequential. In the proposed introduction to a second edition of *Amistad funesta*, which he planned to retitle *Lucía Jerez* and which he never finished because he died in combat in Cuba in 1895, Martí explained his disdain for his own work: "Quien ha escrito esta noveluca jamás había escrito otra antes, lo que de sobra conocerá el lector sin necesidad de este proemio, ni escribirá probablemente más después" (Martí 1963, 18:191) (The person who wrote this "noveluca" (bad novel) had previously never written one, which the reader will know well without the need for this introduction; nor will he probably write more later). He then asks his readers for forgiveness, stating that he is publishing the novel in book form to honor the request of others and not from his personal desire: "Se publica en libro, porque así lo desean los que sin duda no lo han leído. El autor, avergonzado, pide excusa. Ya él sabe bien por dónde va, profunda como un bisturí y útil como un médico, la novela moderna" (Martí 1963, 18: 192). (It is published as a book because this is what is desired by those who without a doubt have never read it. The author, embarrassed, asks for forgiveness. He knows how the modern novel is going, deep like a cut from a scalpel and useful as a doctor.)

To this criticism of the contemporary novel, and specifically the rise of naturalism, he adds his appraisal of the genre: "El género no le place, sin embargo, porque hay mucho que fingir en él, y los goces de la creación artística no compensan el dolor de moverse en una ficción prolongada; con diálogos que nunca se han oído, entre personas que no han vivido jamás" (Martí 1963, 18: 192). (The genre is not pleasing, however, since there is much to feign in it, and the joys of artistic creation do not compensate for the grief of moving within a prolonged fiction; with dialogues that have never been heard, and between people who have never lived.) He concludes by emphasizing that he believes his novel is "inútil" (useless), and he calls the novelistic enterprise on his part a great fault and even a sin: "una grandísima culpa. Pequé Señor, pequé, sean humanitarios, pero perdónenmelo. Señor, no lo haré más" (Martí 1963, 18:192). (A great offense. I sinned, Lord, I sinned. Be humanitarian, but forgive me this novel. Lord, I will never do it again.) And he did not, since he did not produce another novel during his short lifetime. Yet this *noveluca* is inextricably tied to *Ramona* through the figures of the indigenous characters in the work.

Amistad funesta/Lucía Jerez has a simple plot line. The namesake of the novel, Lucía Jerez, is a young woman with two cousins, Ana and Adela. Lucía is engaged to marry Juan, a young man of abundant means, who is an attorney. He symbolizes the Latin American intellectual and statesman, or what Angel Rama (1984) aptly called the *letrados* or men of letters, the cultural and political elite who built and led the nation in the nineteenth century. Juan is devoted to Lucía, but he also takes financial responsibility for the orphaned Sol del Valle and her mother. The young woman is beautiful and intelligent, and Lucía becomes unnecessarily jealous of her, thinking that Juan is deeply in love with her even though neither Juan nor Sol has given her any reason to doubt his devotion for Lucía. Obsessed with destroying Sol and quashing Juan's supposed love for her, in the last scene of the novel, Lucía kills Sol in a fit of jealousy and rage.

That *Amistad funesta/Lucía Jerez* contains a few cameos of indigenous individuals who are not important for the plot, yet appear as part of the setting for the work is the focus of some Martí scholars on the novel. The purpose of their analysis is not necessarily to understand the place of "indigeneity" in Martí—as scholars have done with his translation of *Ramona*—but to discuss the role of the intellectual at the turn of the nineteenth century, in that Martí the writer, or *modernismo* the literary movement, serves as the driving force of their studies, not what Martí's depictions of indigenous people might tell us of Martí's own racial conceptualizations regarding Latin America (Morales 1994; Pellón 2007). Overall these figures are interpreted as serving the development of the figure of the Latin American intellectual at the turn of the century. They do so, appearing in two roles: inaudibly serving the Latin American *criollo* elite and landholders by making their visit to the country house possible, or audibly serving as victims who have reached out to Juan, the *criollo* attorney, so he can defend their land claims. Indeed, these characters appear as props that serve only to make possible the main theme of the novel, the role of the Latin American *letrado* in the face of modernity and US economic and political imperialism.

Another scholarly focus on the novel examines how it articulates Martí's vision of "Nuestra América." In "El espacio americano en la novela de José Martí" Núñez Rodríguez (2003, 57) argues for the literary significance of *Amistad funesta/Lucía Jerez* not necessarily because of its identification as a narrative that captures the social and historical reality of the Latin American intellectual and Latin America more broadly as it faced modernization, but from the geographic significance of the plot's setting. He reminds readers that:

> Estéticamente no le aportaría más a su argumento situar la acción en uno u otro lugar, que el autor no quiso precisar, mas bien universalizar, o mejor, continentalizar...más allá de especificaciones, prefiero considerar que es el espacio—único y multiple—de Nuestra América lo que está reflejado en *Amistad funesta*.   (Núñez Rodríguez 2003, 55–56)

> (Aesthetically it would not contribute to his argument to situate the action in one place or another that the author did not want to specify, but instead to universalize, or better, *continentalizar* (make continental)...beyond specifications, I prefer to consider that it is a space—unique and multiple—of Our America that is reflected in *Amistad funesta*.)

The unnamed "espacio americano" as structurally integral for articulating Martí's vision of Our America is further emphasized by Núñez Rodríguez when he establishes a link between the spatial and the change in title of the novel from *Amistad Funesta* to *Lucía Jerez*. He writes:

> Este título estaría en consonancia con las características de la novela latinoamericana que se estaba haciendo en el continente en aquel momento, por ejemplo: *Amalia* (1851), de José Mármol; *María* (1867), de Jorge Isaac; y en Cuba, *Cecilia Valdés* (1882), de Cirilo Villaverde, entre otras. Sin lugar a dudas, Martí, conocía el desarrollo novelístico de finales del siglo XIX. No fue casual que...posteriormente [hiciera] una traducción de la novela de la escritora norteamericana Helen Hunt Jackson a la que titula *Ramona*.   (Núñez Rodríguez 1997, 12)

> (This title would be in accordance with the characteristics of the Latin American novel that was being written in the continent at that moment, for example: *Amalia* (1851) by José Mármol; *María* (1867) by

Jorge Isaac; and in Cuba, *Cecilia Valdés* (1882) by Cirilo Villaverde, among others. Without doubt, Martí knew of the developments of the form of the novel at the end of the nineteenth century. It was not by chance that…later he would make a translation of a novel by the North American writer Helen Hunt Jackson that is titled *Ramona*.)

For Núñez Rodríguez this reading of the name change transformed *Amistad funesta/Lucía Jerez* and *Ramona* into a foundational fiction of Latin America, as Doris Sommer (1991) aptly called these allegorical works in her book of the same title.

It is precisely this symbolic renaming that links *Amistad funesta/Lucía Jerez* and the translation of *Ramona*, but one established through the characterization of the indigenous characters in the texts. This link points to Native Americans as founding metaphors for the future of the Americas, both in their physical embodiment in the texts and in the geographic spaces the novel and translation occupy. Their presence parallels their appearance in "Nuestra America," where Martí reminds his fellow Latin American intellectuals and leaders that they must learn about the history of the region and populace they govern in order to withstand US imperialism: "Los gobernadores en las repúblicas de indios, aprenden indio" (Martí 1963, 6: 21) (Those who govern in republics with Native Americans learn their language). These "indios" are ultimately depicted as passive; they must be saved, either through Juan Jerez's intervention or through Martí's translation, in which he "saves" Alessandro's story in order to educate his Spanish-reading audience about US imperialism. The same occurs in "Nuestra America," in which Martí warns Latin American intellectuals that they must take into account the indigenous masses; otherwise, they will rise up against the liberal ruling class: "La masa inculta es perezosa, y tímida en las cosas de la inteligencia, y quiere que la gobiernen bien; pero si el gobierno le lastima, se lo sacude y gobierna ella" (Martí 1963, 6:17) (The uneducated masses are lazy, and timid regarding intelligent things, and they want to be governed well; but if the government hurts them, they get rid of it, and they will rule).

Robert McKee Irwin (2003) has taken scholars to task precisely through the "espacio americano" that *Ramona* constructs and the characterization of indigenous people found in both the original and in Martí's translation, specifically targeting the notion that Martí's translation of *Ramona* makes the novel truly "*nuestra*" (ours). To do so, he argues that Martí's "tropes of racial harmony" in "Nuestra America" do not align with what was happening in Latin America when he translated *Ramona*, and this in turn parallels American studies' own "reductive understanding"of the borderlands, where the translated novel took place (McKee Irwin 2003, 540):

> It [*Ramona*] was not for Mexicans of the northwestern borderlands. In the late nineteenth century, Mexicans of the northwestern border-lands not only were at odds with imperialist interventions of their northern neighbors but also were engaged in their own projects of colonization in Mexican territories controlled by as yet unconquered, unassimilated indigenous groups.   (McKee Irwin 2003, 540)

McKee Irwin demonstrates how the indigenous characters in *Ramona* and therefore in the translation disappear from the reality of the borderlands. In addition, the contemporary field of American studies replicates the imperialistic politics to which Martí sought to alert his fellow Latin Americans, but through an "intellectual impe-rialism" (McKee Irwin 2003, 540). As such, he argues for a rereading of *Ramona*—on both sides of the border—in order to correct the lacuna that American *and* Latin American studies have of the region, and thereby to correct the misinformation that arises from that absence.

The challenge arises, McKee Irwin rightly asserts, because of the identity of the main character Ramona, who is a *mestiza*—she is the daughter of a Scottish man and a Native American woman—who is assumed (erroneously) to be a *californio* since she is raised by a *cali-fornio* family. This mestiza identification exceeds the black-white binary framework that traditionally frames studies of US history and American literature. Additionally, it does not meet the "white and non-white" fluidity that might allow for a readable "racial or national allegory" (McKee Irwin 2003, 542) in Latin America. Proof of this impossibility appears in the reaction to the novel in the US, which focused on the romantic elements of the plot and the revivalism of Spanish colonial mission culture as Edenic, along with its mission architecture, downplaying the revolutionary impulse of the work. Citing Sommer's (1991) *Foundational Fictions: The National Romances of Latin America*, McKee Irwin explains that in Latin America the doomed romance between two star-crossed lovers from different classes or castes is typical and integral to the national romance that creates the nation in the nineteenth century. In the nineteenth-century US, by contrast, racial mixing was not permissible (McKee Irwin 2003, 543) as a founding narrative romance. At the same time, however, *Ramona* does not fit snugly into Martí's—and by extension Latin America's—myth of racial harmony, because "Ramona's *mestizaje* is quite different from that of the Mexican national literary tradition" (McKee Irwin 2003, 552), a tradition that seeks to whiten the indigenous elements in its midst through racial and cultural assimilation. Ramona enacts the opposite. She marries Alessandro, a Native American man, and moves down the Latin American caste ladder, a move in which "Ramona gives up her *criolla* identity and assumes an indigenous one" (McKee Irwin 2003, 552). Consequently, *Ramona* diverges from both the Latin American integration novel, one that is propelled by whitening, and the US American founding novel, which cannot tolerate racial mixing. To put the matter differently, *Ramona* is a border novel, and this, in and of itself, creates a new possibility for thinking through the nation (McKee Irwin 2003, 544), one that recognizes "the importance of the Mexican borderlands...in forming a postnational vision of race and intercultural relations in the Americas" (McKee Irwin 2003, 540).[13]

McKee Irwin further demonstrates that Martí, like Jackson, only approaches Native Americans from a US context in order to stress the danger of US expansionism. This limitation does not allow for the many possibilities that arise in the historical reality of the borderlands (McKee Irwin 2003, 549). For example, from a Mexican perspective, McKee Irwin shows that nineteenth-century Mexico sought to whiten its Indian and mestizo populations, since Mexican policies toward indigenous people were brutal and racist (McKee Irwin 2003, 550), as exemplified by the violent Yaqui Wars in the second-half of the nineteenth century. This violence problematizes any notion of a racially harmonious Mexican state.[14] At the same time, we must consider what was occurring in northwestern Mexico at the time of Martí's translation: the exclusion of the Seris, Pima, Opata, and Yaqui from Mexican historiography by constructing Mexican history and contemporaneous reality through the praise of ancient Aztec civilization. I would add the exclusion of the Apache as well. María Josefina Saldaña-Portillo (2016) addresses this erasure of Native Americans from the borderlands in *Indian Given: Racial Geographies across Mexico and the United States*.

In light of these contexts, Martí's translation appears to contribute powerfully to a paternalistic vision of indigenous Americans, one in which the *indios* "are the conquered race, who belong in *nuestra* America but are not quite capable of making themselves part of it" (McKee Irwin 2003, 555). This vision emerges because "Martí's scheme of unification involved both an elimination of racial prejudices and hierarchies on the part of *criollos* and an assimilation into national culture on the part of indigenous groups" (McKee Irwin 2003, 556), the former being impossible and the latter simultaneously demanding an end to indigenous culture. While McKee Irwin does not include *Amistad funesta/Lucía Jerez* in his analysis, his arguments can be extended to this novel, since, as I will show, Martí only speaks peripherally of the land issues and continued colonization of indigenous communities in the Americas in order to discuss the role of the Latin American elite in the hemisphere.

What I find most useful about McKee Irwin's essay is his observation that Martí's need to garner support for Cuban independence throughout the Americas may have caused him not to acknowledge what was actually happening in northwestern Mexico in the 1880s. Of course, contemporary scholars have more to answer for than Martí, for their subsequent studies of *Ramona* are inherently limited by "a tradition of monolingual study and closed national dialogue that only recognizes those Mexicans who cross or have crossed into US territory and who communicate in English" (McKee Irwin 2003, 561).[15] He likewise calls out Latin Americanists for their own blindness toward northern Mexico and the border, concluding that "the Mexican borderlands become a source only of regional culture in the context of the national, but never the transnational" (McKee Irwin 2003, 567). The borderlands' potential for a truly hemispheric vision for the future of Latin America in the face of US imperialism was thus lost to history then and now. As McKee Irwin argues, Martí's translation and contemporary critical analysis alike enact an erasure of the actual agency of indigenous people on both sides of the US-Mexico border, since Martí's own emphasis on the role of the Latin American intellectual in addressing social and racial problems disavows the very cultural and political possibility inherent in these communities to effect true political change.

While McKee Irwin calls for a deeper understanding of the borderlands in any analysis of Martí's translation of *Ramona,* especially by taking into account Martí's deep involvement in Cuban independence, Schulman (2005) extends this insight by elaborating how Cuba is present in both Martí's translation and novel, even though it is never mentioned outright. In Schulman's view, it is necessary to tie the writing of *Amistad funesta/Lucía Jerez* to the emotional distress Martí experienced when he distanced himself from the Cuban military leaders Máximo Gómez and Antonio Maceo in 1884 (Schulman 2005, x). For Schulman, accepting this periodization and this experience transforms *Amistad funesta/Lucía Jerez* into a novel about Cuba and about Martí's vision for achieving Cuba's independence, even though the novel is set in an unnamed Latin American country with indigenous characters. Schulman writes:

> Si insistimos en esta nota autobiográfica y en la indeclinable posición ética de Martí respecto a la liberación de su patria, proyecto al cual desde su juventud hizo la decisión de dedicar su vida, es porque la ideología revolucionaria de Martí, junto con sus ideas sobre la modernización socioeconómica finisecular, se insertan en la voz de los personajes (principalmente en la de Juan Jerez) y en la del narrador de su novela.   (Schulman 2005, x)

> (If we insist on this autobiographic note and in Martí's ineludible ethical position respecting the liberation of his homeland, a project to which since his youth he made the decision to dedicate his life, it is because Martí's revolutionary ideology, along with his ideas on turn-of-the-century socioeconomic modernization, is inserted in the voice of the characters (principally in Juan Jerez) and in the narrator of his novel.)

Ultimately, Schulman argues for the importance of Martí's novel and links it to his translation of *Ramona*, because these works must be read as "trans/textos" or:

> creaciones de otros escritores, las cuales, mediante el proceso de la traducción se trans/forman y se insertan en el arte literario martiano, más que nada por los conceptos morales que el cubano descubrió en ellas, y por su carácter de literatura combativa, la que Martí prefería y deseaba cultivar.   (Schulman 2005, xvi)

> (Creations by other writers, which through the process of translation are trans/formed and are inserted in Martí's literary art, more than anything because of the moral concepts the Cuban [Martí] discovered in them and for their character as literature of combat, which Martí preferred and wished to cultivate.)

He concludes:

> Estamos persuadidos que es posible conjeturar que las trans/textual-
> izaciones elaboradas después de *Amistad funesta/Lucía Jerez* le hayan
> sugerido al escritor revolucionario que la novela tenía la posibilidad
> de levantar el espíritu público y ser un instrumento poderoso de
> transformación social.   (Schulman 2005, xvii)
>
> (We are persuaded that it is possible to conjecture that the trans/tex-
> tualizations elaborated after *Amistad funesta/Lucía Jerez* suggested to
> the revolutionary writer that the novel had the possibility to lift the
> public spirit and to be a powerful instrument of social transformation.)

Following Schulman, a rereading of *Amistad funesta/Lucía Jerez*
reveals a text not rejected by Martí because of its generic form—the
novel—but rather remade by his experience with translating such
novels as *Ramona*: it is a transformed text in which he creates an
alternative reality, one that depicts the "conflictivo y entristecido
mundo de la modernidad" (Schulman 2005, xxiii) (conflictive and
saddened [grieving] world of modernity), a vision originating with
and framed by his rupture with the Cuban generals Máximo Gómez
and Antonio Maceo.

If we extend Schulman's hypothesis [that it is the rupture in the
1880s with the Cuban revolutionary leadership that leads Martí to
re-evaluate the novel form as a "literatura combativa" (literature of
combat)] to the ideological rupture between José Martí and Martín
Morúa Delgado, we can, first, better understand the distancing
between Martí and Morúa, two important Cuban revolutionary
figures, and, second, decipher Morúa's vision for Cuba, one based
on the foundational roles Afro Cubans had played in its past and
would play in its future. For just as "Martí's mission takes for granted
the conquest of indigenous America and the colonization of their
lands"[16] (McKee Irwin 2003, 559–60), Martí's translation choice
takes for granted the history of African enslavement on both sides of
the Florida Straits and the US-Mexico border. Indeed, Martí's selec-
tion of *Ramona* as an exemplar of the Latin American experience
elides Afro Cubans, Afro Latina/os, Afro Latin Americans, and
African Americans from "Our America," reducing the diaspora to a
reference to drinking "vino de plátanos" (banana wine) in "Nuestra
América" (Martí 1963, 6:17). Martí's broken relationship with the
Afro Cuban leader Antonio Maceo and the Dominican Máximo
Gómez is spread across the pages of both his novel and his translation.

The Afro Cuban *lector* and novelist Martín Morúa Delgado was quite aware that indigenous communities had been exterminated in Cuba and the Caribbean by the 1880s and 1890s due to enslavement, suicide, disease, and colonization during the late fifteenth, sixteenth, and seventeenth centuries. And he well understood the ideological implications of appropriating a lost indigenous history to serve as the foundation for Caribbean cultural identity, and for Cuba in particular. In poetry, the rise of the Siboneista poets of the 1860s and 1870s, such as Juan Nápoles Fajardo (1829–62) and José Fornaris (1827–90), marked a literary attempt to racially remake Cuban history through the figure of "el indio." And Morúa also knew that just as the Siboneistas sought to elegize indigenous figures as a means of erasing the large presence of black Cubans on the island and the participation of black Cubans not only in the Ten Years' War, but in Cuban and Latin American history, Martí too aimed to bypass the problem of Afro *Cubanidad* in his *Amistad funesta/Lucía Jerez* and in his particular translational choice of *Ramona* as "our" novel, the novel of Latin America. Kevin Meehan and Paul B. Miller have questioned Martí's depiction of the black experience in "Nuestra América" and in Martí's writings more generally in "Martí, Schomburg y la cuestión racial en las Américas" (Meehan and Miller 2006). Delineating some of the difficulties in comparing Martí and Du Bois, and citing passages from "Nuestra América" to support their claim, they explain that in Martí's marginalization of blackness in the essay and in his concurrent emphasize on the "mestizo," i.e., European and indigenous ancestry of "Our America," blackness is not simply marginalized but absented (Meehan and Miller 2006, 73).[17] For Martí, when we read Morúa's writings more critically, Africans and those of African descent could not be presented as foundational figures for establishing the future Cuban nation or for Latin America.

Taking on Martí and Cuban literary history more broadly, Morúa not only addressed the glaring racial denial in Martí's novel and translation choice, and, before him, the Siboneistas, but also forged a path of radical black dissent in his creative works and his translation practice. For, instead of a novel like *Ramona*, he chose to translate James Redpath's (1863) rendition of John R. Beard's (1853) *The Life of Toussaint L'Ouverture*, calling it *Biografía del Libertador Toussaint L'Ouverture por John Beard. Vida de Toussaint L'Ouverture (Autobiografía)*. In addition, in writing *Sofía* (1891) and *La familia Unzúazu* (1901), Morúa further questioned the role and intentions of the Latin American intellectual in fighting US cultural and economic imperialism—as Martí is said to have done in *Amistad funesta/Lucía Jerez* by scholars of *modernismo*. This more complex interpretation of Morúa and his writings becomes possible only if we place Morúa on the Latino Continuum, if we take into account the almost ten years that he lived in the US, and his travel between Key West and New York, to the Caribbean, and to Central America. In rereading his life and works from this perspective, we find that Morúa provides a corrective to the manner in which history was being written at the time and offers a parallel vision for the Americas. While never deny- ing the suffering and the settler colonial war against the indigenous people of Latin America and the US, he suggests that it is a black revolutionary leader like Toussaint L'Ouverture[18] who is needed in order to gain Cuban independence and ultimately to establish the nation and, more broadly, a hemisphere that is free of US hegemony. For it is in his translation of Redpath's text that he presents the *collective black* in the Americas as an alternative, erased, but crucial presence to stand against US imperialism. In this translation choice and in his novels and journalism, Morúa does not simply warn of US interference in Cuba and by extension Latin American affairs.[19] He warns his readers, Afro Cubans, Afro Latina/os, and Afro Latin Americans that the very economic and political imperialism that the US would exert on the continent would come from within Latin America itself, from compromised individuals who sought only their self-interest. So, while like Martí, Morúa emphasizes a hemispheric approach for leading the Americas, by focusing on such an impor- tant figure as Louverture, Morúa includes Haiti in the Americas, even though Haití was excluded from the Pan American Congress of 1890. His translation and writings about Haiti also signal the impor- tance of the black intellectual in this process of uniting the Americas. Ultimately, he positions the model of a radical black leadership and the black experience as the foundation for such a vision across the Americas.

Martín Morúa Delgado and the Black *Lector*

Born in Matanzas, Cuba in 1856 to a formerly enslaved woman and a Spanish immigrant, Martín Morúa Delgado was arrested in 1880 for anti-colonial activities and subsequently escaped to Key West on

January 19, 1881. Supporting Máximo Gómez and Antonio Maceo in their continued quest for Cuban independence,[20] Morúa also traveled to New York, Philadelphia, and New Orleans, finally settling in Key West. His revolutionary activities also took him to Jamaica, Mexico, and Panama in the course of advocating for Cuban independence, before his subsequent return to Cuba in 1890, where he remained for six years.

While Morúa advocated independence during his time in the US, in a letter dated January 22, 1894, he expressed support for the Partido Liberal Autonomista on the grounds that they advocated universal suffrage, which would benefit black Cubans. He also argued that remaining under Spanish rule offered the best political course for avoiding bloodshed.[21] (Like his contemporaries, Morúa was quite aware that Afro Cubans would fill the majority of the ranks in any armed revolt against Spain.) His political affiliation, moreover, was driven by social concerns: at one political rally, Morúa indicated that he had joined the Autonomist Party because it had opened its doors to the popular classes, asking for immediate full emancipation for all *patrocinados* in 1882. Additionally, in the pamphlet *Martin Morúa Delgado, ¿Quién fue?…*, Nicolás Guillén (1984) explains that Morúa may have favored autonomism because he found intellectual and financial support from such autonomists as Raimundo Cabrera (1852–1923), who published *Sofía* in Havana. (Morúa dedicated the novel to him.) Cabrera was also key in having Morúa initiated into the epitome of Cuban high culture, the Real Sociedad Económica Amigos del País in 1895 (Guillén 1984, 17). By 1896, however, Morúa, back in the United States while the third and final war for independence raged on the island, supported Cuban sovereignty once again. Following US military intervention in 1898, Morúa became a famed and also detested politician. He voted for the Platt Amendment (1901), which placed Cuba under US protectorship, frustrating the independence efforts of Cuban revolutionaries. According to his contemporary, Julián González (1902, 53–5), Morúa voted for the amendment in order to ensure some form of independence from the US, fearing that, otherwise, the US military would never leave the island due to the intransigence of President William McKinley. He also climbed the ranks of the Cuban government under the auspices of the Liberal Party—a party accused of garnering black support but then failing to deliver on the campaign promises that secured it.

Contemporary scholars and some of Morúa's own contemporaries have agreed that his support for the legislation that banned the formation of political parties based on race directly led to the Race War of 1912.[22] More than 3,000 Afro Cubans, mostly women and children, were killed during the summer massacre, and while Morúa died before this horrific event transpired, his advocacy for the legislation in question is considered key to causing the violence.[23] Yet even Morúa's critics concede that his vision for a raceless society emerged in the 1870s—when he published integrationist articles in his Cuban edition of *El Pueblo* in 1879. He was also at odds with such prominent separatists as the black intellectual and revolutionary Juan Gualberto Gómez. In the 1890s, Morúa refused to support Gualberto Gómez's Directorio Central de las de Sociedades de la Raza de Color de Cuba, an organization for black Cubans that sought to enforce black equality. It was also the political arm of the Cuban Revolutionary Party in Cuba. In a series of articles published in his short-lived newspaper, *La Nueva Era* (1892), Morúa argued that race was a social category to be dispensed with: black Cubans, he asserted, could not organize separately from whites if they wished to see an end to racism on the island. He condemned any group that organized itself on the basis of race for replicating the "difference" advocated by the colonial system and ex-slave holders (Morúa Delgado 1957, 3: 232–33).

Morúa also had a run-in with José Martí in 1887, who, also then in exile in the United States, responded to an anonymous letter, now lost but published in the US edition of *El Pueblo*, a newspaper founded and edited by Morúa in Key West. Martí suggested that the publication of the letter, titled the "Carta de Nueva York," constituted "un acto de malivalencia increíble" (Martí, 1963, 1: 206) (an incredibly malevolent act), for it characterized the speakers at a meeting addressing Cuba's political future that took place in New York as "bufones indignos de expresar su pensamiento sobre los problemas santos de la patria" (Martí 1963, 1: 207) (buffoons unworthy of expressing their opinions regarding the sacred problems of the homeland) and further questioned their very integrity. At the meeting were not only Martí and Enrique Trujillo, a well-known publisher and also an enemy of Martí, but also Tomás Estrada Palma, another prominent, white Cuban exiled for an extended period of time in the United States who would later become Cuba's first president. Moreover, Trujillo offered a bitter description of the episode in his *Apuntes históricos*, where he describes *El Pueblo* as a "periódico violento y exaltado, que sin criterio sano y juicioso editaba el señor Martín Morúa Delgado" (Trujillo 1896, 26) (violent and excitable newspaper that without sound and judicious judgment, Señor Martín Morúa

Delgado edited). He further reported that: "En la carta se acusaba al señor Martí de haberse declarado autonomista o haber vertido conceptos contrarios á la Revolución" (Trujillo 1896, 26) (In the letter Señor Martí was accused of declaring himself an autonomist and of having supported concepts contrary to the Revolution).

Morúa's disenchantment with exile politics dates back to the failed Sánchez-Varona and Maceo-Gómez expeditions of 1884–86, insurrectionist attempts by exiles to bring arms and men to Cuba to start another revolution. In these attempts Cuban exile communities, mainly tobacco workers, raised money to buy arms. Unfortunately, many times the expeditions failed. In addition, the New York leadership did not support the initiatives. Specifically, after meeting Máximo Gómez and Antonio Maceo on October 1, 1884, Martí wrote a letter to Gómez dated October 20, 1884 in which he distanced himself from Gómez and Maceo, noting that a new approach needed to be taken when it came to Cuban independence because "un pueblo no se funda, General, como se manda un campamento" (Martí 1963, 1:177). (A nation is not founded, General, as one rules a military camp.) He adds:

¿Qué somos, General?: ¿los servidores heroicos y modestos de una idea que nos calienta el corazón, los amigos leales de un pueblo desventurado, o los caudillos valientes y afortunados que con el látigo en la mano y la espuela en el tacón se disponen a llevar la guerra a un pueblo para enseñorearse después de él?   (Martí 1963, 1:178)

(What are we, General? The heroic and modest servants of an idea that warms our hearts, the loyal friends of an unfortunate people, or the brave and fortunate caudillos that with the whip in their hands and the spur on their heel choose to take war to a people in order to take possession of them?)

It is not surprising, then, that in 1886 Morúa, who supported the expeditions, wrote to Máximo Gómez, one of the military leaders of the independence movement in exile, in an effort to distance himself from exiled political leaders over concerns that they had also failed to act in the best interests of the majority of Cuban immigrants in the United States. Instead, Morúa suggested, the participation of the predominantly working class and mostly black immigrants had been "coartada," i.e., inhibited, limited, or restricted, since they were relegated to subsidizing military ventures (Morúa Delgado 1957, 5: 174).

The use of the word "coartar" evokes a specific historical context for Morúa, recalling that enslaved Cubans were given the opportunity to "coartar" or slowly purchase their own freedom. Since the leadership (both civil and military) refused to recognize the political demands of this large section of the exile community, Morúa proposed a "cura radical, pues la enfermedad es grave" (Morúa Delgado 1957, 5: 174) (radical cure, for the illness is grave) for the Cuban leadership in exile: fire all of them, along with their subordinates, and start from scratch (Morúa Delgado 1957, 5: 174–75).[24]

Strategically, as José Martí argued, a revolution in Cuba could not be started from abroad without a political platform that could be supported by a popular rebellion on the island (Poyo, 1989, 67–69). Socially, however, conflicts arising from class differences and issues related to race divided the exile leadership from its constituents. Wealthy white Cubans owned many of the cigar factories in which exiled workers labored. That the exiled leadership did not support their demands for fair pay and better work conditions reflected the separation between the two groups. Furthermore, since in 1880 about a fifth of the émigrés were black Cubans, of whom two-thirds were cigar workers (Poyo, 1989, 81), the unwillingness to meet the demands of strikers—various strikes took place in Florida and New York in the 1880s—was inextricably linked to race. Morúa, who was the first black reader/*lector* in cigar factories in Key West and New York, was actively involved in unionizing efforts (Stebbins, 2007).

Now, it is prima facie evident that the major themes and concerns that I have here identified in Morúa's biography are addressed in his novels, as we shall see, a fact that of itself invites us to read his fiction in light of them. The trans-American and political trajectory of Morúa's own publishing career further authorizes such a reading: *Sofía* was written in the 1880s while Morúa was in exile in the United States, though it was not published until 1891, after his return to Havana. *La familia Unzúazu*, in turn, was written in Cuba in the early 1890s, and Morúa tried unsuccessfully to publish it in the United States in 1896, subsequently putting it into print in Havana in 1901. In addition, two years after his return to Cuba in 1890 and following nearly a decade of forced exile in the United States, Morúa published a scathing review of Cirilo Villaverde's now infamous novel *Cecilia Valdés* (1882). His extensive 1892 critique, titled *Las novelas del Sr. Villaverde* (henceforth *Novelas*), condemns the novel for its inaccurate depiction of race relations on the island,[25] suggesting that it reflects the author's nearly total indifference to the real-life concerns of black Cubans. The critique perhaps turns most acerbic when he suggests that "no obstante de iniciar un plausible período de mejoramiento literario, ostenta en su fondo un marcadísimo apego a las más detestables vejeces de una época de maldición" (Morúa Delgado 1892, 40) (even though it is plausible [*Cecilia Valdés*] initiated a period of literary improvement, at its base it holds a marked attachment to the most detestable, antiquated ills of a cursed epoch), for Morúa was particularly troubled by Villaverde's romanticized depiction of race relations in Cuba of the early 1830s, which was witness to the most oppressive and violent phase of slavery on the island.

His too was a forced exile, but Morúa condescendingly refers to Villaverde as "el digno expatriado" (Morúa Delgado 1892, 24) (the dignified expatriate) and ironically suggests that his misconceptions of race relations in Cuba are "tanto más perniciosa cuanto que la confirma desde el extranjero, después de residir *treinta y tres años* en un esfera libre" (emphasis in original) (Morúa Delgado 1892, 39) (even more pernicious since he makes this claim from abroad, after having lived for thirty-three years in a free country). The sarcasm bites with Morúa's description of the post-bellum United States as a "free country," especially, after living nearly ten years as an Afro Cuban in Key West, New Orleans, Philadelphia, and New York. He feared that the more rigid US attitude toward race, made evident by the failure of Reconstruction, would serve to reinforce old divisions that would sabotage the post-racial future he advocated, a future in which race did not exist as a marker of difference.

That Morúa's novel *Sofía* (1891) is a purposeful rewriting of *Cecilia Valdés* (Luis 1990, 141), moreover, and that it is followed by *La familia Unzúazu* (1901) as its sequel beg us to critically reconsider these, his only two novels, in a trans-American light and to recover these works for Latinx studies by acknowledging their place on the Latino Continuum, particularly since Morúa dedicates *Novelas* to another long-term Cuban exile, Enrique Trujillo, who was both the founder and editor of *El Porvenir* (1890–96), the longest running Cuban newspaper in New York of that era. He writes:

> Al erudito y graviprofundo crítico literario, al riguroso catoniano moralista, al periodista insigne, al orador verbilocuente, al patriota intérrimo, al—en fin—ilustradísimo, correctísimo, etcetera, etcetera, "littérateur," Sr. D. Enrique Trujillo, director insustituible del muy

popular, muy magnífico y muy periódico "El Porvenir" de New York, dedica este deficiente estudio, —como débil prueba de la admiración muy alta y respetuosidad muy humilde que a su elevado criterio e incomparable discernimiento le profesa, EL AUTOR.

(Morúa Delgado 1892, n.p.)

(To the erudite and gravely profound literary critic, the rigorous Catonian moralist, to the distinguished journalist, the verbosely eloquent orator, the patriot of the greatest integrity, the—in the end— most erudite, most correct, etcetera, etcetera 'littérateur,' Sr. Enrique Trujillo, irreplaceable director of the very popular, most magnificent and very newspapery 'El Porvenir' of New York, I dedicate this deficient study—as weak proof of the very high admiration and very humble respect that to his elevated standards and incomparable discernment I profess for him. (The AUTHOR)

Morúa's sardonic dedication channels his disdain for the racist attitudes toward black Cubans exhibited by privileged white exiles like Trujillo and, implicitly, Villaverde and Martí: while Trujillo, like Morúa, opposed the annexation of Cuba by the United States, he also cited, in 1887, the influx of black Americans under US tutelage to the island as one of the reasons for opposing statehood (Poyo 1989, 86). Trujillo was also a proponent of whitening Cuba through increased white immigration and banning black immigration to the island, and he promoted the return of black Cubans to Africa. Such political views, so plainly reprehensible to Morúa, reflected the capacity for elite white exiles to advocate for racially motivated political policies for Cuba while simultaneously intimating that racism was no longer a problem on the island, a paradoxical attitude that, for Morúa, could only have been cultivated in the context of the Northern post-slavery racial dynamics that emphasized a segregated distance between the races.

More than *Novelas* and its sardonic dedication, however, Morúa's life and writings as situated on the Latino Continuum beg a new reading of his novels. Taking stock of the transnational and trans-American nature of Morúa's life and fiction, we cannot enjoy the happy ending Luis (1990, 160) finds in the texts, in which "the expected union between Eladislao and Magdalena [two Americanized-Cubans], in so far as they represent the most benevolent characters in the novel...reflect[s] an optimistic outcome of historical events". For Morúa did not share such an optimistic view of Cuba's future, as a detailed reading of his novels will illustrate. And while contemporary critics have described Eladislao as "a noble figure" (Horrego Estuch 1957, 89), as the "image of the ideal white Cuban" (Labrador Rodríguez 1993, 333), as the "articulation of the erasure of class and racial differences" (Williams 1994, 197), and even as a representation of José Martí (Kutzinski 1993, 133; Handley 2000, 81), scholars to date have failed to notice that Morúa's novels offer ardent critiques of US race relations through his characterizations of white Americanized Cubans who are modeled on the likes of Villaverde, Trujillo, and even Martí, and who, as Morúa sensed, would wield a disproportionate and distortive influence on Cuba's political and social future (see Lamas 2008 for a detailed discussion of the term "Americanized-criollos"). In addition, that Morúa purposely titled his novel *Sofía* signals the practice at the time of constructing works that were meant to allegorize the nation-building enterprise by giving them proper names. As with Martí's titular shifting from *Amistad funesta* to the proper name *Lucía Jerez*, Morúa too created an analogy between the novel and his own alternative vision of Cuban history and its probable future. Yet, instead of the indigenous person or the white intellectual as the foundation for a new nation, Morúa argues that it is accepting the valiant history of enslaved people and their contribution to Cuban independence that will constitute a truly free Cuba and true equality for those who were previously enslaved both on the island and across the Americas.

Attention to contemporaneous political events at the time Morúa was writing the novels places this central theme of his literary works in full relief and unveils a further dimension to his critique, particularly given that the author was the first black reader or *lector* to work in cigar factories in Key West and New York. (He subsequently served as a *lector* in Havana.) Readers or *lectores* sat at the front of cigar factories and read aloud to workers while they labored. In the 1880s and 1890s, they were paid by the workers themselves, many of whom were Afro Latina/o (Poyo 1989, 81), and they regularly sought both to educate and to politicize their listeners by reading from newspapers and pamphlets that kept them apprised of current events, and from novels by authors such as Victor Hugo that decried social injustices.[26] That Morúa likely read his own novels to tobacco workers therefore demands that we understand them not (or not merely) in terms of what they communicate to a white Cuban readership, but in terms of how they address a black one, many of which were to be found in the United States. For, Morúa conceived of literature—and his own writings in particular—not merely as works of imaginative and aesthetic expression but as instruments that were to be used to educate and empower black readers/listeners, or what I refer to as black *lectores*. For Morúa was fully committed to the idea that literary works made a political impact on their readers, an idea shared by contemporaneous African American writers, as Robert Stepto (1986) has argued.

I propose, then, to engage a three-tiered approach to reading Morúa's novels, one that brings together the trio of interwoven meanings of the term *lector/lectores*, represented by Morúa's roles as a reader of texts in cigar factories on both sides of the Florida Straits; as one who "read" the state of US race relations and anticipated its potentially damaging influences for Cuba; and, finally, as one who believed firmly that his fictional writing, as well as that of a host of other Cuban and non-Cuban authors, should be "read"—heard and interpreted—by the black communal *lectores*—readers and listeners—who engaged his texts collectively in the cigar factories or elsewhere. In so doing, I propose to offer a corrective to a prominent scholarly misreading of Morúa's novels: as a black *lector* of US racial relations and politics, Morúa rewrites *Cecilia Valdés* not to educate white readers, as Richard Jackson (1979, 48) argued, but to empower and politicize black *lectores*. Specifically, through his two novels Morúa wished to warn his audience of the trans-American and transnational nature of the racism Afro Cubans would face. It was no longer colonial racism that they needed to combat; now, they would also have to battle an Anglo-American conception of race that structured the national-imperial US political formation to the north.

Yet I propose we take this analysis one step further, concluding that contemporary scholars must continue to recover writers like Morúa for American, Latinx, and Latin American studies, since, when we take into account his experience as a Latino in the United States, his concerns are not only for the future of Cuba but for the Cubans who had emigrated to the United States at the time of his writing, many of whom stayed in the United States. He is also concerned about the African diaspora throughout Latin America, as I will show in Chapter 5. By extension, to reread Morúa's novels in light of contemporaneous political and social realities provides a rare glimpse into the little-studied trans-American experience of Afro Cubans and the impact they had on the post-Reconstruction US. For while we may not have written testimony of the lives and political activities of these nineteenth-century *lectores*, we have distinct traces of their concerns in these writings.

The task, then, is to explore the "histotextuality" in Morúa writings, a term coined by Gabrielle Foreman that refers to historical and cultural markers in the writings of many turn-of-the-century black novelists, markers that black readers would have recognized and decoded. By identifying such markers, which served to interpellate black readers into a specific discourse about race, today's readers can comprehend the socially and politically transformative nature of Morúa's writings, much as Foreman (1997, 329) did for Frances Harper. For Morúa, like other black writers of his time, believed that fiction was politics, and for it to be effective, it had to lead to a change in public consciousness and to constructive social action.[27]

Morúa's *Sofía* (1891) and *La familia Unzúazu* (1901)

Sofía (1891) is the first installment of a proposed trilogy titled "Cosas de mi tierra" (Aspects of my Homeland) (Morúa Delgado 1891, xiii). This first novel is about a white *criolla*, the daughter of two Spaniards, who is mistaken for a slave. Repeatedly raped by her half-brother Federico Unzúazu, Sofía dies from a beating received from Acebaldo Nudoso, her owner and brother-in-law, after his discovery of her pregnancy. As she lies on her deathbed after losing her unborn son, her half-sister Magdalena Unzúazu tells Sofía she is an Unzúazu and not a slave. This news devastates Sofía, since she dies after she realizes that she had been a slave her entire life, and that Federico, her rapist, was her brother. While this series of events is the central narrative of the novel, when one takes into account Morúa's biography and US experience, the critique of white, Americanized Cuban characters such as Eladislao Gonzaga, Magdalena Unzúazu, and the Alminto family emerges parallel to Sofía's storyline.

América Alminto, her younger sister Albina (the name already alerts the reader to this family's racial genealogy), and her mother Amalia emigrate to New York at the outbreak of the Ten Years' War.[28] América's father is killed in the fighting, and the Spanish government confiscates the family's landholdings. Albina marries a wealthy North American businessman, which leads to a sweeping change in the family's economic situation (Morúa Delgado 1891, 95). América marries Eladislao Gonzaga, whose patriotism is firmly associated with his wealth, as well: early in the novel, Morúa mentions that "Con la pérdida de su fortuna aumentábase su ardor patriótico"

(Morúa Delgado 1891, 93) (his political ardor increased with the loss of his fortune). After he marries América, he accepts a position at the firm of Albina's North American father-in-law, signaling his ties to US business interests.[29] América and Eladislao subsequently return to the island to claim the Alminto fortune, at which point the reader realizes that Eladislao has learned a subtle and pernicious form of racism from his Northern experience. Sofía, who is wandering the streets of Belmiranda (the fictitious setting that mirrors the city of Matanzas) seeking a new owner, asks Eladislao and América for help after the Unzúazu family, discovering her pregnancy, has dismissed her, giving her a mere three days (the time sanctioned by law) to find a new owner or face being relegated to hard labor in their sugar mill. Eladislao appears to treat Sofía kindly but emphasizes the social and racial division between them by addressing her with the informal "tú." One might miss the social implications of this form of speech, but Morúa's narrator refuses to let the reader get away with such na-ivety when he comments condescendingly, "Estos modernos libre-pensadores no se dan cuenta de su contradicción, como no se la daba Eladislao al tutear a Sofía...¿Habríala tuteado si ignorase su pobre estado social?" (Morúa Delgado 1891, 155). (These modern freethink-ers are not aware of their contradiction, just as Eladislao did not notice when he used the informal tú with Sofia... Would he have used the informal tú if he ignored her poor social state?) The "con-tradiction," the narrator indicates, lies with the fact that Eladislao's suffering under US racial prejudice should have led him to cultivate empathy. Instead, he embodies for Morúa the same racist attitude of Northerners in the United States: they appear to support racial equality but treat blacks as inferiors. (Eladislao arrived penniless in New York City, having lost all of his wealth in Cuba and having been forced to work in a clothing store, which marked his economic and social decline and racialization as a Latin American immigrant in New York [Morúa Delgado 1891, 93].)

Morúa stresses the negative impact of the conciliatory, yet conde-scending nature of Northern rhetoric by further developing the two US-influenced characters whose destinies revolve around Eladislao, just as Cuba's destiny could potentially be one of dependence on the United States: América, his wife, and Magdalena, his mistress. For example, he stresses that spending five years in the United States changed Magdalena, since there she comes to believe that, although slaves need to be educated, they must be kept separate from whites, something we are told she learns from her time in a Quaker school in Philadelphia (Morúa Delgado 1891, 51). The narrator ironically explains this contradiction, as he tries to work through the many reasons a separate but equal ideology could be deemed acceptable in the post-Reconstruction society of the Northeast that Morúa had personally experienced:

> Pero, por una aberración de las costumbres, o por el hábito secular de las razas del norte, encerradas en sí mismas, y acaso también por un exquisitismo estético, tenido en cuenta su grado superior de civilización, y quizás por todas estas proposiciones reunidas, tenían *los amigos* [sic] de la hermandad neoanglicana una extremada aversión al cruza-mineto de las razas humanas. Claro es, pues, que esta aversión había de crecer tratándose de individuos entre los cuales el contraste exterior es tan notable como el que ofrecen a la más simple vista el negro y el blanco.   (Morúa Delgado 1891, 51)

> (But, because of an aberration in customs, or because of the secular habit of the races of the north, trapped within themselves, and maybe also because of an exquisite aestheticism, taking into account their higher grade of civilization, and maybe because of all of these propositions put together, the *Friends* [sic] from the neo-Anglican brotherhood had an extreme aversion to the crossing of human races. It is clear, then, that this aversion would grow when dealing with individuals in whom the exterior contrast is so notable as what is offered to the most simple view between the black and the white.)

By noting that Magdalena learned her US form of racism at a Friends school, Morúa records a significant histotextual marker that calls to mind not only the separate-but-equal approach of Quakerism toward race, but also the fact that Tomás Estrada Palma converted to Quakerism in the United States and founded and ran the Instituto Estrada Palma, a Friends school in Central Valley, New York.[30] Villaverde and his wife Emilia Casanovas likewise started and ran a school in New Jersey.

Not coincidentally, back in the United States, Morúa asked Estrada Palma, the president of the Partido Revolucionario Cubano after Martí's death in battle, for PRC funds in 1896 to support the publication of *Sofía*'s sequel, *La familia Unzúazu*. In his response, Estrada Palma conceded the importance of the work—he suggested it effectively and persuasively paints the political and social effects of colonialism on Cuban society—but then rejected Morúa's request to publish the book, because, he said, the raging war on the island had depleted PRC funds (quoted in Mesa Rodríguez 1956, 29). This rejection may have been fueled by Estrada Palma's overt racism—when he was president of the Cuban Republic, he did not invite Morúa's wife and daughters to a state dinner because they were black (Fuente 2001, 62–63). It also signals the division between New York exiles and tobacco workers in Florida: after Martí's untimely death in 1895, Estrada Palma, who replaced him as the head of the PRC, subordinated efforts to address race issues and workers' rights, changing the socially transformative mission of the organization by replacing it with an effort to recruit US support for the war (Guerra 2005, 62–77).

Morúa's critiques of Americanized Cubans such as Estrada Palma also must have stemmed from the latter's collaboration with John McCook, a New York corporate lawyer, and Samuel Janney, a partner at a Wall Street banking firm, to float bonds to purchase Cuba from Spain (Fletcher 1998, 334–35; Offner 2001, 63–64; Guerra 2005, 85–86). With the Quaker reference, then, Morúa can be understood yet again as associating Estrada Palma with the greedy, immoral, and racist Americanized Cubans of his novels. It is also likely that Estrada Palma identified himself in the character of Eladislao in the novel.

Depicted as indifferent to both the injustices of slavery and the larger question of its fundamental immorality, Magdalena, Eladislao's mistress, invariably ignores the plight of Sofia, her childhood playmate and personal slave, in particular in the face of Sofia's mistreatment by Magdalena's sister's husband, Acebaldo. She also ignores the cruelty Sofía experiences at the hands of her half-brother Federico, who, as already noted, rapes Sofía repeatedly. All of these instances of looking pointedly away reflect the studied distance she learned to cultivate when it came to matters of race while in the Friends school in the United States. This directly signals the contradiction at the heart of US race relations in the following manner:

> Imbuido, en fin, el cuáquero en sus severas doctrinas religiosas, no se considera con derecho para esclavizar al hombre porque éste sea negro o rojo, antes bien le conserva y le defiende su estado natural, libre—aunque por otras razones no le admite en el estrecho recogimiento de su comunión sino que se sacrifica por tenerle apartado, a la mayor distancia posible.   (Morúa Delgado 1891, 51)

> (Imbued, in the end, with his strict religious doctrines, the Quaker does not feel the right to enslave a man because he is black or red, in

fact, he maintains and defends his natural state, free—even though
for other reasons, he does not admit him into the strict seclusion of
his communion, instead sacrificing himself to ensure him separate, at
the greatest distance possible.)

Morúa's novels intimate the dangers of placing Cuba under the leadership of Americanized Cubans most clearly in their narration of the
events surrounding the life of América, Eladislao's wife. At first her
name appears to symbolize a pan-Americanism that would bring together different elements of the hemisphere (perhaps along the lines
of what Martí envisioned): in *Sofía*, she is compared to an Irish maid
who sings "canciones vivarachas de las gentes del sur de la Unión"
(Morúa Delgado 1891, 63) (lively songs of the people from the American
South), intermingled with Cuban ones. In addition, when read in
light of what was happening in the United States at the time of the
composition of the novel, the irony of this amalgamation cannot
escape the reader.

While one might imagine that Morúa wished to evoke the long
history of oppression of Irish immigrants in the United States—the
Know Nothing Party or American Party was organized to combat
Irish Catholicism and to support US nativism in the 1840s and 1850s,
for example—one must remember that many Irish people in the
United States aligned themselves with the pro-slavery Democratic
Party. Irish men also rioted in New York City in 1863 when conscripted
into the Union army, a reflection of the fact that the question of slavery was not among their greatest concerns (Rodgers 2007, 43). Most
poignantly, the reference to Irish people speaks to the violence
against black people by Irish rioters during those riots (Roediger 1991).
Mention of Irish people further evokes their ambivalent position
toward abolition in the United States.[31] In addition, and as shown in
Chapter 3, anti-Catholicism continued to exist in the 1880s and
1890s. Ultimately, América does not in any way associate herself with
the particular historical realities of Afro-diasporic people in the
hemisphere. Instead, she romanticizes the very real fight for freedom
of African Americans in the Civil War and Afro Cubans in both the
Ten Years' War (1868–1878) and the Guerra Chiquita (1879–1880).

Morúa captures this dissociation and complete ignorance by highlighting the violence that feeds this romanticization in one poignant
scene: as Sofía dies, Magdalena (who is Eladislao's mistress) whispers
"es mía," or "she is mine," referring to Eladislao's soul or "alma," but

América thinks she speaks of the dying Sofía (Morúa Delgado 1891, 253). Touched by this devotion between a master and her slave, she believes Magdalena mourns Sofía's passing, when, in fact, she weeps because she has finally met América and envies her marriage to Eladislao (Morúa Delgado 1891, 252–53). Any illusions about América's pan-American name are dispelled here by her total failure to understand the plight of enslaved people in Cuba, the United States, or the Americas: she idealizes the relationship between slave and master.

These female characters allow Morúa to stage his critique of Northern attitudes to race, and he does so, in part, to criticize the sentimental romance and the use of melodrama that was deployed by writers in the North during this time period; for he saw it as a genre that sidelined racism in the United States, disempowering black people in the process. As multiple critics have noted (Silber 1997; Gillman 2003; Luis-Brown 2008), abolitionist rhetoric in the North adopted a conciliatory tone following the Civil War, one that produced the sentimental romances of the 1880s and 1890s. Such romances regularly featured the marriage of a Northern male to a Southern belle, offering a narrative thereby that was meant to heal the divide between North and South. In addition, as Nina Silber's study shows, the sentimental romance served to smooth over problems related to the labor unrest that ravaged the United States during that period, which in turn was caused, in particular, by the immigration of what were then considered ethnic minorities, such as the Irish, from Europe (Silber 1997, 128). For Silber, the focus on marriage and family in these texts parallels the abstraction of the economic situation of those who were previously enslaved throughout the South, as it also embodies the North's need to situate new ethnic groups, such as Irish people, in urban settings. Consequently, Silber argues, those who were previously enslaved were erased from the process of Reconstruction altogether, as was the violence suffered by them at the hands of Southern "gentlemen" (Silber 1997, 109, 156).

Sofía, which, as noted, was written in the United States, uses the same narrative structure as these Northern, post-Civil War melodramas, but Morúa deploys it not to replicate the genre, but rather to destabilize it. The Northern exile Eladislao eventually finds his way to the Cuban *criolla* Magdalena, so that the overall narrative frame is one of a Northern gentleman eventually winning his land-rich Southern lady. Their union leads them to ownership of the plantation, and the reader can easily recognize a concomitant erasure of the agency of the black characters of the novel, at least if one adopts the couple's point of view. The romance also solidifies the place for a Northern, Americanized view of race in Cuba, one to which both Magdalena (from her schooling) and Eladislao (from his exile) implicitly subscribe. This assimilation of Northern mores can perhaps be seen as a sort of analog to the assimilation of (Irish and other European) immigrants to the North that the sentimental romance was meant to accommodate, but the resulting equilibrium in *Sofía* is decidedly dystopic: the violence of US racism, found in the very subtlety and insidiousness of its so-called separate but equal stance toward race relations, promises the creation of a permanent black underclass due to its distinctly hierarchical nature.

In other words, the national romance is an illicit affair that produces an illegitimate (bastard) child (Magdalena gives birth to a baby girl), with the characters purposefully forgetting the close associations of the ruling elite (Magdalena) and the black underclass (Sofía), because US attitudes toward race promise the rise of a new ownership class in Cuba—capitalist Northerners like Eladislao—who would further complicate the already damaging effects of Spanish colonialism on race relations, further inhibiting the racelessness for which Morúa advocated. In the end, then, the romance narrated in *Sofía* leaves its intended audience with little to be sentimental about; what remains is a decided foreboding regarding the impending invasion of US attitudes to race. While Silber examines the harmonizing project of these sentimental and melodramatic works on late nineteenth-century US culture, Morúa as a black writer inverts the entire marriage plot in *La familia Unzúazu*, Morúa's sequel to *Sofía*. He does so to critique the US concepts of race that, for Morúa, ultimately produced such politically inert literary products as the sentimental romance and melodrama itself. Consequently, *La familia Unzúazu* contains multiple histotextual references that were meant to be read by black *lectores*, such as the burning of sugar cane fields by enslaved workers as well as by black insurgents who wished to deprive the plantation owners of their profits. It also provides a different vision for Cuba, one founded on the model of black leadership and the black experience. The events surrounding one María de Jesús offer a histotextual reference of particular note, one meriting detailed attention because it illustrates precisely how Morúa encouraged black readers to forge a place for themselves in Cuba's future.

In *La familia Unzúazu*, Eladislao must recruit the help of Magdalena's personal slave, María de Jesús, in order to facilitate his affair with Magdalena. While Vera Kutzinski (1993, 133) read Morúa's female characters as epitomizing the author's patriarchal construction of black women, I argue that Morúa repeatedly shows his black readers that María de Jesús's interventions are proactive and shaped by her particular knowledge of the ground on which she operates.[32] Consider, first, that Eladislao is forced to pay for her freedom in order to hide his affair from his wife. Doing so, however, haunts him throughout the text, a narrative element that would have encouraged black readers to question the "benefactor role" of the Americanized Cubans.[33] For Morúa, such duplicitous individuals were also comparable to their counterparts in the North, since many ex-abolitionists did nothing to end racism once the Civil War ended.

Elsewhere, Eladislao tries to meet up with María de Jesús at the Parque de la Marina, a place where white Cuban men historically sought concubines and where Afro Cuban women hoped to win white lovers in order to better their legal and/or economic position—the very type of scene on which Villaverde's Cuban classic was structurally built. To a black *lector* familiar with such racialized and sexualized spaces, however, this scene would signal Eladislao's moral depravity and his desire to seduce María de Jesús. And a sexual tension indeed pervades their interactions in the text, at least from Eladislao's point of view (Morúa Delgado 1901, 144). María de Jesús, however, refuses to meet him at the Parque and, further, while agreeing to deliver Eladislao's letters to Magdalena, she refuses to transport her letters to him. Instead, María de Jesús insists on writing the letters that will update Eladislao on Magdalena's well-being. Thus, María de Jesús not only circumvents his amorous advances but also uses her literacy and her own authorial powers to control the flow of information between the lovers. When Eladislao presses her as to why she will not serve as a direct intermediary between the two parties, she simply says her reason was her "secret" (Morúa Delgado 1901, 144). While the "secret" is never revealed, Michael Craton (1997, 229) highlights the link between secrecy and slave revolt. In the context of Morúa's novel and the post-slavery historical moment, the secret, therefore, may be taken to refer to black insurgents plotting revolution. Morúa explicitly says as much in the article "Ensayo político," (Morúa Delgado 1957, 3: 45-109) which I will discuss in Chapter 5. And in the novel itself, Fidelio, an Afro Cuban character introduced in *La familia Unzúazu*, is imprisoned for meeting with insurgents recently arrived from Key West who are recruiting for the Guerra Chiquita.

It is beyond the scope of this text to discuss in detail the potentially revolutionary roles of two Afro Cuban characters who appear in *Sofía* and *La familia Unzúazu*: Fidelio and Liberato. These characters would most likely have been the protagonists for the third install-ment of "Cosas de mi tierra," which was never written. Liberato, who is owned by the Unzúazu family, rapes Ana María while she is dream-ing about making love to Eladislao. He flees and then is coerced by Federico into extracting monies from Ana María and Magdalena—Federico pretends he has been kidnapped by bandits. Liberato takes advantage of his *alzado* (escaped) status and with the help of Nicanor Moreno (a fellow, though white, *náñigo*) threatens to set fire to the sugar cane harvest if he is not paid a monthly ransom for not doing so. Morúa highlights that Liberato was taught this type of exploita-tion by his very owners. Yet this reference to monthly ransoms also addresses the controversial practice by some insurrectionists of rais-ing funds for the revolution through monthly ransoms.[34] It further references a longtime practice of slave insurrections in which fire was set to sugar plantations as a form of protest. Conversely, Fidelio is taken into their confidence by Eladislao and Alvarado. After lis-tening to their ambivalent discussions regarding race relations on the island—they fear black Cubans—he decides to start a newspaper because "En él se concentraban las dos razas opuestas: la negra y la blanca, la oprimida y la opresora. ¿Quién con más legítimos títulos ni más autorizada ejecutoría podría constituirse en paladín de la equ-idad proclamando la ley de amor y de concordia?" (Morúa Delgado 1901, 305–306). (In him were concentrated the two opposing races: black and white, the oppressed and the oppressor. Who with more legitimate titles or more just authority could be the defender of equality proclaiming the law of love and harmony?) Provocatively, Morúa's biography is closely aligned with Fidelio's. That the third in-stallment was never written speaks directly to the impossibility or at best the necessary deferment of being able to imagine Cuba's future as based on the black experience after US intervention on the island.

Further, Eladislao's surprise that María de Jesús could write (Morúa Delgado 1901, 178–79) serves as notice to black Cubans regarding his limited perception of their abilities and capabilities. More conspicu-ously still the narrator tells the reader: "María de Jesús escribía en agresivas letras como puñetazos" (Morúa Delgado 1901, 179) (María de Jesús wrote in aggressive letters, like stabbings). These stabbings are significant, since Acebaldo (Magdalena's sister's sadistic husband) is stabbed and murdered as he leaves the house of his mulatta mistress, Domitilia, and Federico (Magdalena's brother) suffers the same fate in the arms of his mulatta paramour, Clarissa. (These stabbings also invokes the violence of slave insurrections and suggest that María's writing and the machete are tied together, making a place for female agency, both written and military, in a revolutionary uprising.) While associating Eladislao with "un libertino que había arruinado a su esposa arrebatándole a montones el dinero...para libertar a una mulata y mantenerla como objeto de lujo y de placer" (Morúa Delgado 1901, 183) (a libertine who had ruined his wife, taking large amounts of her money...to free a mulatta in order to maintain her as an object of luxury and pleasure), the narrator emphasizes that the similarity Eladislao regrets sharing with the libertine is not his infidelity, but rather being forced to pay for a loyal slave's freedom.[35]

As such, when Eladislao's best friend and confidant, the family physician *doctor* Alvarado, finds Eladislao deep in thought and apparently troubled, he asks him what is wrong, speculating it could not involve money. He knows that his wife América had been given an advance of 10,000 pesos on her confiscated properties (Morúa Delgado 1901, 185), which not incidentally is the same amount Sofía would have inherited from Acebaldo, her brother-in-law, if she had survived (Morúa Delgado 1891, 87). Yet Eladislao, who was indeed stewing over having to pay the manumission, deceives Alvarado by saying that he worries for Magdalena, who is sick and needs help. Publicly, then, he identifies Magdalena's well-being as what bothers him. Privately, he mourns the financial cost of the manumission in total indifference to the fact that a human being was freed by his purchase. The plot is reduced to a question of money, and Morúa thus warns his black *lectores* of the true motives behind the supposed benevolence of powerful Americanized Cubans like Eladislao toward Afro Cubans.

Since América dies in the next and final chapter of the novel, and the unborn male heir of the Alminto family perishes with her, Morúa suggests that Eladislao will likewise "pocket" some of the monies, just as he was forced to use the 10,000 pesos previously returned to América in order to reluctantly pay for María de Jesús's freedom (Morúa Delgado 1901, 182–83). Furthermore, Eladislao had temporarily managed the Unzúazu estate after the death of Acebaldo, an estate that included sugar mills and slaves. That he profited from helping the slave-owning Unzúazus and that now he is marrying Magdalena and will manage the Unzúazu landholdings once again make Eladislao the new head of the slave-owning and previously slave-trafficking dynasty (Kutzinski 1993, 133).

Morúa's narrative ultimately suggests that Americanized Cubans like Eladislao would herald US control of the Cuban sugar industry by US companies through their complicity, echoing what Dr. Alvarado fears would happen to Cuba if a plan originally concocted by Acebaldo to convert the Unzúazu sugar mills to a *colono* system were put into effect: small farmers would be forced to sell their sugar cane to a powerful central processor (Morúa Delgado 1901, 299). Alvarado fears that Cuba would move from African to white slavery under such a system, a system that became the status quo after US political intervention and subsequent economic control of the island as of 1898. This simultaneously signals the pernicious nature of Alvarado's racial self-interest—he is afraid of white slavery but has no problem with the real enslavement of the black Cubans around him. And while his fears regarding the US proved prescient, it was still black Cubans who suffered most under both colonial and US imperial formations. When presented with Acebaldo's plan, Alvarado exclaims:

Pues todo su plan viene á reducirse á un nuevo jénero de servidum-bre que podría llamarse la esclavitud blanca; porque esos colonos que usted dice enriquecer con su sistema, no serían otra cosa que forzo-sos patrocinados, sujetos al capricho de aquellos centros de explo-tación arbitraria, según el caracter más o menos desconsiderado de los propietarios. Ahora, como gran negocio, ¡no digo yo si lo es! Y si después de fomentar en la isla media centena de "molinos en grande escala", como usted dice, se uniesen los propietarios y organizasen una asociación que les constituyera en Liga Azucarera, se comple-taría el monopolio de la producción y la industria más rica del país, y... ya tendrían con ello dignos sucesores los esclavistas de los buenos tiempos coloniales! [*sic*]   (Morúa Delgado 1901, 299)

(Well, all of your plan is reduced to a new type of servitude that could be called white slavery; because those tenants farmers who you say will be enriched by your system would be nothing else but forced *patrocinados*, tied to the whim of those centers of arbitrary enrichment, according to the more or less inconsiderate character of the proprietors. Now, as a great business, I say it certainly is! And if after they promote on the island half a hundred "large-scale mills," as you say, the owners get together and organize an association that would constitute them into a Sugar League, the monopoly of the production and the richest industry of the country would be completed, and…you would have with it the dignified successors to the slavers of the good old colonial times!)

In marrying Magdalena and eliminating América, Morúa indicates that as the new Acebaldo—as noted, Acebaldo had concocted the *colono* plan to begin with—Eladislao is the very embodiment of a neocolonial relationship that would be established by Americanized Cubans with the United States, which would ultimately doom the new Cuban Republic. As such, he represents merely another manifestation in the chain of oppression and exploitation, fueled by the greed that perpetuated African slavery in Cuba and the United States and would now recreate economic slavery for all on the island. As a black *lector* and labor activist, Morúa beckons Afro Cubans on both sides of the Florida Straits to become aware of the pernicious role of Americanized Cubans and to act in order to influence the nation-building project, which was developing without them. In the end, then, Morúa incites his black *lectores* to "read" the situation on the ground as it really is, and then take matters into their own hands, whether with pen or machete.

* * *

Taking into account Morúa's experience in the post-Reconstruction US and his experience as a black *lector* in cigar factories on both sides of the Florida Straits, it becomes evident that trans-American concerns pervade his novels. Indeed, they provide the key that reveals the revolutionary dimensions of his fiction. For careful attention to the three levels of readers and reading that a close examination of Morúa's novels demands reveals the inextricable ties of his fiction both to contemporaneous political and social concerns and to the fortunes of the mostly working-class and/or black *lectores* who read or heard his novels in Cuba and the United States. That this is so forecloses on the possibility of understanding Morúa's novels as simply exposing the racist colonial attitudes of a white readership, as Jackson (1979) has argued with respect to *Cecilia Valdés*. For, through his novels, Morúa examines black characters such as María de Jesús, showing them to be active agents, intimating thereby that the black writer or the black reader/listener/*lector* is himself or herself an actor in history, not a mere prop for teaching a white audience of the need to overcome their own overt and implicit forms of racism.

Morúa's histotextual mode of writing also opens a new perspective for American and Latinx studies, because his concerns are not only for the future of Cuba but for the Cubans who had emigrated to the United States at the time of his writing, and the impact they would have on the post-Reconstruction era. For while we may not have written testimony of the lives and political activities of these *lectores*, we have distinct traces of their concerns in these writings. This is so because Morúa's work recognizes and presupposes the very agency of his black readership, both in Cuba and in the United States. The proactive, black characters of his novels are themselves histotextual markers, not imagined possibilities. That many among Morúa's readership never returned to Cuba but stayed in the United States further suggests that he and authors like him who have traditionally been classified as Latin American writers should now be recovered and incorporated into the canon of American and Latinx studies,[36] even if they ultimately returned to their home countries or wrote predominantly in Spanish. These authors can offer an expanded view of the lived experience and the particular views and modes of knowledge production of Latina/os in the United States in the nineteenth century, begging us thereby to cross, recross, and ultimately renegotiate the still existent boundaries between Latin American, Latinx, and American studies.

In addition, when we pair Morúa's novels with his 1883 translation of James Redpath's (1863) *Toussaint L'Ouverture: A Biography and Autobiography*, we begin to decipher his vision for an independent Cuba and the place of black Cubans within it, those who were previously enslaved incorporated as an integral part of the hemisphere, just as Martí had done with indigenous people in Latin America in his translation of *Ramona*. To frame this link I turn to Daut's (2015) *Tropics of Haiti. Race and the Literary History of the Haitian Revolution in the Atlantic World, 1789–1865*, in which she argues that:

> Reading together for the first time several of the many passages from *The Life of Toussaint L'Ouverture* that Brown adapted to an antebellum

U.S. context in the 1853 version of *Clotel*, as well as his mingling of
Clotel with "St. Domingo," suggest that ideas about Haiti and ideas
about "race" were often *one and the same thing* in his literary imagination. That is to say that to talk about Haiti in the antebellum U.S. was,
for Brown, to talk about "race," and in many ways to talk about "race"
for him was to talk about Haiti. It is the twinning of these ideas that
ultimately reveals the way in which the material practices of power
that led to the development and institutionalization of what we are
calling the trope of the "colored historian." (Italics mine)

(Daut 2015, 494)[37]

This twinning also happens in Morúa, but in his case through his
translation he seeks a new way of thinking about leadership in particular, since he does not see Afro Cubans, Afro Latina/os, and Afro
Latin Americans as simply part of the nation, and by extension the
hemisphere, but locates them at its very foundation. And doing so
implicitly but unequivocally, he emended Martí's vision for the hemisphere, which for Morúa shamefully excluded any deep sensitivity to
race. For, through his translation and journalism, in which he addresses the figure of Toussaint L'Ouverture repeatedly, he expounds
a foundational blackness for the nation and the hemisphere, not as
a fiction, but as historical reality. That the final part of the trilogy
"Cosas de mi tierra" was never written, in which the figure of Fidelio,
a black budding journalist, would have been used to present Morúa's
vision for the future of the Cuban nation and the place of Afro Cubans
and Afro Latina/os in it speaks to the impossibility of writing a novel
in which blackness was at the very heart of political independence in
Cuba and one in which freedom from US imperial rule in the Americas
could occur. This impossibility rested not only upon the colonial Cuban
production of race but also the pernicious race relations learned in
the US by Americanized Cubans who would come to rule the island.
He further feared, and not unfoundedly, that this US-based vision for
race relations would be brought to Cuba through legislative means if
annexation were to occur.

In Chapter 5, I will study Morúa's translation of James Redpath's
Toussaint L'Ouverture: A Biography and Autobiography, since like his
novels, it speaks directly to Morúa's vision for the place of the African
diaspora in Cuba, the US, and the Americas more broadly. As I will
show in Chapter 5, diverging from Martí's vision, which placed the

indigenous experience and legacy at the heart of a hemispheric resistance to US expansionism and its concurrent imperialism, it was the black experience in the Americas that Morúa believed could also serve as the foundation for conceptualizing a truly politically free and socially transformed hemisphere that could even be used to redeem the US from its deeply racist and violent national origins. In other words, Morúa constructs an Afro Latina/o continuum in which Cuban racial integration, not merely including but framed by the black experience, could be brought to the US.

{ 5 }

Morúa's Continuum

REDEEMING THE AMERICAS

Martín Morúa Delgado's vision for Cuba's future and his concern for Afro Cubans on both sides of the Florida Straits extend beyond the island to the Americas and are found not simply in his literary production but in his translation practice. His translation of James Redpath's (1863) rendition of John R. Beard's (1853) *The Life of Toussaint L'Ouverture: The Negro Patriot of Hayti*, completed in the early 1880s just as Morúa's disenchantment with the politics of Cubans in exile began, reflects his belief that the written word had the power to wield a hemispheric influence and could serve to support political transformation in Cuba and by extension the Americas. Toussaint L'Ouverture[1] and this translation were at the center of this vision, for Morúa would reference the Haitian liberator throughout his literary and journalistic career, thereby expounding his belief that a leader modeled on L'Ouverture would bring true political independence to Cuba, inaugurating social change across the hemisphere. As I argue in this chapter, it is through this figure and the translation that Morúa conceived an alternative vision for Cuba and for the Americas, one that did not involve the leadership of the US-compromised Americanized Cubans and Latin Americans he so feared. His vision called for a black leader who would fill the moral void created by the likes of Tomás Estrada Palma, Enrique Trujillo, and José Martí. It was a pan-American vision that spoke to the place of Afro Latin Americans and Afro Latina/os as the new foundation of a truly politically and socially free hemisphere, redeemed of its racial prejudices and biases.

The Latino Continuum and the Nineteenth-Century Americas: Literature, Translation, and Historiography.
Carmen E. Lamas, Oxford University Press (2021). © Carmen E. Lamas. DOI: 10.1093/oso/9780198871484.003.0006

Morúa's Continuum (Take 1): Translating Haiti and Cuba

While John R. Beard's (1853) and James Redpath's (1863) biographies of the life of Toussaint Louverture are well known, Morúa's transla- tion has not been studied to date. Morúa translated James Redpath's *Toussaint L'Ouverture: A Biography and Autobiography* between 1882 and 1883 during his stay in New York City. He had traveled with the Cuban general Flor Crombet from Key West to New York in order to raise funds for a new military insurrection on the island. Crombet, along with Antonio Maceo, had taken part in the Guerra Chiquita or Little War (1879–80), rejecting the terms of the Pacto del Zanjón which ended the Ten Years' War. Mostly Afro-Cuban insurrectionists continued fighting for Cuban independence, the main point of con- tention being that slavery had not been abolished on the island with the surrender of Cuban forces. Morúa was implicated in this rebel- lion and was imprisoned before he could join the revolutionaries on the battlefield. Now in the US, Morúa's concerns and answers for the future of Cuba and the Americas are present in his translation choice and the translation itself, since Morúa makes a series of interventions in the text that move beyond Redpath's rendition to reflect Morúa's own perspective regarding Cuban independence and the founda- tional role enslaved people and freedmen and freedwomen played and should continue to play in the hemisphere.[2]

In 1853, the Unitarian minister, John Relly Beard (1800–76) published in London a biography of Toussaint Louverture and therefore a history of the Haitian Revolution with the title *The Life of Toussaint L'Ouverture: The Negro Patriot of Hayti*. James Redpath (1833–91), like Beard, was both a journalist an abolitionist. He reprinted Beard's work as *Toussaint L'Ouverture: A Biography and Autobiography* (1863), and published it in his series "Books for the Times," which included works by such authors as the US abolitionist and fugitive ex-slave William Wells Brown. As Redpath had done with Beard's original biography, Morúa makes multiple interventions in Redpath's reprint of Beard's work to forward his political agenda. Morúa envisioned that his translation would be published as a 500-page book that would be distributed throughout the Americas (Horrego Estuch 1957, 122). Parts of the trans- lation were published in *La Revista Popular* (in Key West, 1889); it was also published in Havana in *La Nueva Era* in 1892 (Horrego Estuch 1957, 85, 122). Because of Morúa's work as a reader in cigar factories, it is likely that he read from his translation to tobacco workers. These publications render Morúa's translation a trans-American text, both in its crossing of the Florida Straits and because it served as the foundation for Morúa's vision of the importance of the black experience in the Americas, both north and south of the US borders, closely following Lazo's (2020, 242) clarification in *Letters from Filadelfia: Early Latino Literature and the Trans-American Elite* that "Latino literature in the nineteenth century is inherently trans-American and not just 'American' in the hemispheric sense because it involves the crossing of texts and people among various countries." Morúa's writings also abide by what Sara E. Johnson (2012) in *The Fear of French Negroes: Transcolonial Collaboration in the Revolutionary Americas* has termed the transcolonial, a geopolitical and methodological concept that further deepens how we might read Morúa's translation, his life and his other works whose "intercolonial contact zones…provide a counternarrative to the linguistically and disciplinarily isolated fields of American and Caribbean studies that still tend to compartmentalize the region according to categories such as francophone, hispanophone, anglophone, and Dutch-speaking territories" (Johnson 2012, 3). By bringing together these two conceptualizations of early Latina/o literature and the literature of the Haitian Revolution, respectively, Morua's literary productions, and his translation practice in particular, signal the existence of the black experience as integral to and constituting the Latino Continuum and our understanding of race in the Americas.[3]

Morúa's interventions in the Redpath/Beard translation are varied.[4] To begin with, he includes exclamation points in order to ensure that his readers take a moment to understand the importance of certain passages, such as when Redpath notes that "Toussaint was a negro" (Redpath 1863, 41). Morúa exclaims "¡Toussaint era un negro!" (Morúa Delgado 1957, 4.1: 46), signaling the significance of L'Ouverture's blackness as important for leading the revolution and for universal history more broadly. Specifically, we must read these exclamation points—which occur throughout the translation—not merely as markers of significance, but as emotional and purposeful effusions that call nineteenth-century black readers in particular into a collective experience of racial triumph. They may also be read as prompts for other *lectores* in cigar factories or cultural and educational gatherings at social and political clubs. Prompting these *lectores* on "how" to enunciate and stress important moments in the text, he politicizes the *lector* and listener. As with his novels, he brings together the oral tradition and the written word to instigate revolution.

In other instances in the translation he directly counters contemporaneous and late nineteenth-century historiography of the Haitian Revolution, as well as accounts circulating in both the Spanish press and the loyalist press in Cuba and New York, by emphatically stressing that Frenchmen and freedmen were *also* responsible for violence that occurred during the revolution, and not merely enslaved people, as sensational and fundamentally white supremacist accounts had insisted (Morúa Delgado 1957, 4.1: 138).[5] These dominant narratives touted the certain possibility of a race war and the acts of violence that would be committed by those who were previously enslaved on their previous owners if independence occurred on the island, an assertion that Morúa denounced as unfounded and simply untrue. Morúa also reincorporated into the main text passages by Beard that had been merely footnoted by Redpath, as is the case when Redpath footnotes a long passage by Abbé Raynal in which Raynal depicts Europeans as morally bankrupt and condemns them for their enslavement of Africans.[6] Including this pronouncement in the body proper, Morúa ensures that his readers will have a first-hand account, written by a European, that calls into question dominant theories of European superiority, offering a new framework for understanding slavery and racial oppression. Moreover, it is in this footnote that Raynal called for a new leader to rise up and defend the oppressed. In undertaking the translation, Morúa adds his own version of the sentence using "Toussaint leyó; y de aquel instante surgió el restaurador de la libertad de los negros" (Morúa Delgado 1957, 4.1: 54) (Toussaint read; and in that very instant emerged the restorer of the liberty of black men) for Redpath's/Beard's "Toussaint read; and became the leader of the negros" (Redpath 1863, 41). Morúa's use of "surgió" (rose up, arose, emerged) instead of the more passive "became" addresses his *lectores* directly, inviting them to rise up and take part in bringing equality for all across the Americas.

Although we know that Louverture was indisputably literate (Pierrot, 2019), historians and biographers in the nineteenth century had debated the extent and precise forms of Toussaint's literacy. Morúa's unequivocal pronouncement offered his readers a scene of literary reception as direct political action that parallels the much later imaginative creation of this moment in C. L. R. James's (1963) *The Black Jacobins*. Indeed, this sentence signals the emerging nature of a radical literary-political vision, for, through this intervention, Morúa speaks directly to both his future readers and listeners as if they, like

L'Ouverture, will read themselves into history, rising up to claim a new insurrectionist movement, one not simply military (as in the Cuban case) but also social in nature, capable of spanning across the diasporic Americas with the force of enlivened political imagination.

This intervention by Morúa reflects Deborah Jenson's (2012) analysis of narratives of unbecoming enslaved and becoming a brigand (in the case of Haiti). Specifically, Jenson argues that while the slave narrative is a particular US genre, for the Caribbean other genres— such as political essays or newspaper articles—must be read as forms of the slave narrative. These works might not speak directly to life under enslavement, but they must be taken as literary slave narratives in their own right, since, for example, "The words of Toussaint Louverture and Jean Jacques Dessalines are literary in the degree to which they harnessed poetics to persuade large audiences, represent the stakes of freedom and domination, and engage in political construction of themselves and their constituencies" (Jenson 2012, 9). Morúa does the same with his novels and translation of Redpath/Beard, especially when we take into account his practice as a *lector* in cigar factories and the purpose behind his translation, which he envisioned as a print book that would be widely circulated.

If we consider Morúa's historical moment, one of his most powerful interventions is to align Haiti's history with Cuba's. Redpath, following Beard, writes that slave insurrections would be avoided if other countries, specifically the US, would follow the example of Haiti (at that historical moment Haiti was still the French colony of Saint-Domingue), which through its constitution, written by L'Ouverture, emancipated all those who were enslaved and instituted free trade. Morúa pauses at this assertion to add his own supportive commentary:

> ¡Cuánta verdad en las apreciaciones! ¡Cuánto acierto y conciencia en sus abrumadores fallos! ¿Deberemos agregar por nuestra parte una sentencia más, dedicándola a nuestro país y a sus opresores? No creemos que sea necesario. Este libro cuadra a Cuba como ningún otro, y solo eso nos ha decidido a traducirlo.—N. del T.
>
> (Morúa Delgado 1957, 5.1: 182)

> (These appraisals are so true! How much correctness and awareness in their overwhelming failures! Should we add for our part one more sentence, dedicating it to our country and its oppressors? We do not believe that it is necessary. This book frames Cuba like no other, and only this has made us decide to translate it.—Translator's Note.)

Morúa thus here praises Redpath's/Beard's assessment of Haiti's constitution and its positive effect as well as Redpath's/Beard's condemnation of United States slaveholders for their refusal to educate those who were enslaved, and for their outright juridical obstruction of black literacy—which, as Morúa saw it, thereby curtailed the emergence of a hero like L'Ouverture in that country.

In equating the political circumstances of Cuba and Haiti, Morúa provides his own solution for the former, in which complete legal and political emancipation for those who were enslaved presents a viable course of action; it is one in which education is key for complete integration, both political and social, and one in which slave uprisings must be interpreted as political acts. This solution is not only rhetorical. For while Cuban slavery was abolished, in name, in 1880, the *patronato* system was still in effect while Morúa was carrying out this translation.[7] Here again, Morúa's translational effort suggests his investment in laying bare the ongoing forms of chattel slavery in Cuba, and in addressing the political consciousness of those Cubans still enslaved on the island.

It is important to note that the word *sentencia* in Spanish means "judgment," "declaration," "maxim," or "precept." But it might also mean a grammatical "sentence" (a Spanglish term, since *oración* would be the correct way to translate "sentence") that is added to Beard/Redpath, since in alluding to "fallos" or failures Morúa is extending Redpath's/Beard's condemnation of the US to Cuba. He may also be read as correcting Redpath/Beard for not including slaveholding Cuba in their abolitionist program. Redpath/Beard had written: "Give that advantage [education] to the myriads of blacks that now vegetate and pine in slavery in the United States, and other practical philosophers will appear among them to vindicate the race by wise laws as well as philanthropy and heroism" (Redpath 1863, 141). And Morúa translated: "Dad estas ventajas a los millares de negros, que hoy (1) vegetan y sufren silenciosamente bajo las cadenas de la esclavitud en los Estados Unidos, y surgirán de entre ellos otros filósofos prácticos para vindicar la raza por sus sabias leyes, así como por su filantropía y su heroísmo" (Morúa Delgado 1957, 4.2: 181). (Morúa further footnotes this sentence by noting that the author had written it in 1852, placing a historical marker for his readers that both contextualizes Redpath's/Beard's original text but also indirectly criticizes the exclusion of Cuba.)

I reference Morúa's possible conflation of English and Spanish words, since it once again places Morúa on a linguistic continuum between the US and Cuba and Latin America. It is revelatory to note that in a blatantly racist essay "La población de color en Cuba," Rafael Merchán (1894), a fellow exile and contemporary of Morúa, criticized Morúa for erroneously using certain Spanish words in *Sofía*, noting that Moruá "inventa palabras inútiles" (creates useless words), such as *obtenimiento* (from *obtener*) for *obtención* (the proper way to say "obtaining" in Spanish) or *planear* (from *plan*) for *idear* ("to design") or *proyectar* ("to plan"). Merchán presents these linguistic errors as proof of Morúa's failure as a writer and his inability to accurately interpret race relations in Cuba (Merchán 1894, 492). In this instance, language becomes a yardstick for authenticity, veracity, and authority, especially since immediately following a condemnation of Morúa's use of *palabras inútiles*, Merchán criticizes Morúa for his use of provincialisms. He claims that even though they are accurate, in this instance, they are not comprehensible by non-Cubans, and, therefore, Morúa's novel fails aesthetically. Morúa is then caught between an incorrect use of Spanish and a use of Cuban provincialisms that are unreadable to other Latin Americans. He is both an outsider and too much of an insider. Basically, Merchán places him nowhere. He does not belong, and his presence as an authority on Cuba, Latin America, and the black experience is effectively erased. Yet these linguistic examples place him squarely on the Latino Continuum.

In agreeing with Redpath/Beard about the particular manner in which the US withheld education from those who were enslaved, Morúa speaks indirectly of his own experience in the post-Reconstruction South as well. This experience is made evident in his use of Spanglish terms and in his *sentencia* regarding the failures of the US and the exclusion of Cuba from the political imaginary of abolitionists. His translation serves as a warning of what could happen in Cuba if a US-style post-emancipation approach to social change came to the island, further converting Morúa's translation into a hemispheric call to action, a call for *lectores* to understand their place in history and forge a new, free Cuba, and a hemisphere free of US neocolonialism. As I will show next, Morúa enacts this call by countering Spanish and US accounts in which the fear of a so-called "race war," purportedly catalyzed by the possibility of independence, was fomented to stymic international support for revolution in Cuba, and thereby to secure disparate forms of white supremacy throughout the hemisphere, whether in US or Spanish interests.[8]

Morúa's writings—literary, journalistic, and political—can be read fruitfully as in dialogue with Cedric Robinson's (1983) *Black Marxism: The Making of the Black Radical Tradition* and Saidiya Hartman's (1997) *Scenes of Subjection: Terror, Slavery and Self-Making in Nineteenth-Century America*. Like Robinson's, Morúa's writing is consistent with the theorization of a black radical tradition emerging from below, but, for Morúa, with L'Ouverture as a model for *all* in the African diaspora. Morúa's focus on labor and his labor activism likewise parallels Robinson's analysis of capitalism and its impact on enslavement and the post-emancipation experiences of those who were previously enslaved. Aligning with Hartman's theorization of the burden of emancipation, Morúa's novels address specifically the questionable future for black Cubans under the governance of Americanized *criollos* and their US-influenced visions of post-emancipation and post-independence race relations. An extended discussion regarding the place of Morúa within US Black Studies is much needed. Yet, as I hope this chapter demonstrates, Morúa was deeply engaged in articulating the philosophy of the black political experience and even, one could argue, its potential impossibility—he never wrote the third installment of "Cosas de mi tierra."

Morúa's Continuum (Take 2): "Ensayo político" (1883) to "Factores sociales" (1892)

Morúa's interest in L'Ouverture moved beyond his translation, shaping his vision of the hemisphere throughout his career and his journalism. One of his early allusions to L'Ouverture occurs in a series of articles he published in *El Separatista* in New York City in 1883 (as he was simultaneously translating Redpath/Beard). The newspaper was originally under the direction of Cirilo Pouble and then Ramón Rubiera de Armas. As is well known, Rubiera broke with Martí because of the latter's failure to support military expeditions to the island in the 1880s, and Martí made it a point to distance himself publicly from the paper, writing a letter dated September 6, 1883, to José Antonio Cuyas, the Spanish correspondent in New York for the *Diario de la Marina*, the pro-Spanish newspaper in Havana. The *Diario* had published an allegation that Martí was a contributor to the newspaper. Martí clarified that he was not a contributor, stating instead that "Las diferencias políticas no dan derecho, entre hombres corteses y leales, a la inversión, o admisión indiscreta, y publicación voluntaria, de noticias falsas...no afirme en lo sucesivo respecto de mí aquello que, en lo que hace a mi conexión con un periódico nuevo en esta ciudad, es inexacto" (Martí 1963, 20: 427). (Political differences do not give the right, between courteous and honest men, to the inversion, or indiscreet admission, and voluntary publication, of false information... in the future do not affirm about me, in that you make a connection between me and a new newspaper in this city, that which is inexact.) In this context, then, Morua's choice to publish in *El Separatista* was a provocative one, and it was here that he framed his critique of how Spain was fomenting the fear of a race war and manipulating the history of Santo Domingo to stymie an independence movement in Cuba.[9] The series of articles is aptly named "Ensayo político: Cuba y la raza de color" (Political Essay: Cuba and the Colored Race).

Morúa begins "Ensayo político" with a clarification that one of the purposes of the article series is to show how knowing the history of enslaved Africans in the New World is important for understanding history more broadly:

> Quisiéramos que nuestros hermanos los cubanos retuvieran en su memoria todos los acontecimientos en la vida de la raza negra en todos los pueblos a que fue llevada; quisiéramos que a cada momento recordaran la historia, y en conciencia de sus propios actos, obren de acuerdo.   (Morúa Delgado 1957, 3: 49)
>
> (We wish that our Cuban brothers would retain in their memory all of the occurrences in the life of the black race in all the places to which they were taken; we wish that they would remember history in each moment, and conscious of their own actions, comport themselves accordingly.)

Morúa wants his readers to know the African presence was not limited to Cuba, but extended throughout the hemisphere. The diaspora was not isolated on the island, he reminds his readers, but was a part of a larger brotherhood, a *raza*, that extended throughout the Americas. For Morúa, knowing the history of enslaved people throughout the Americas, and sustaining continuous awareness of it, "a cada momento," was central to political change. He offers a kind of double address here: to the Afro-diasporic "we" conjured in his first person plural who must recognize their place within a hemispheric collective history; and also to their "brothers" in a figurative family long sustained by violent inequality, Spaniards and *criollo* Cubans and Latin Americans, who must look at themselves in the mirror and recognize their place (and actions) in the ongoing history of enslavement and unfree labor throughout the hemisphere (Morúa Delgado 1957, 3: 49). Morúa's call to memory and recognition thus served as the foundation for a wider political platform embracing the African diaspora throughout the Americas. Moreover, he argued that the place from which to center that platform and a new revolution was the Haitian Revolution, "cuya causa guarda entera analogía con la nuestra, pues que en general todos los cubanos damos vida en nuestros sentimientos a los sacratísimos principios de libertad e independencia" (Morúa Delgado 1957, 3: 49) (whose cause is a full analogy with ours, since in general all Cubans give life in our emotions to the most sacred principles of liberty and independence).[10]

Morúa refuses to remain at the level of analogy. He closely traces the history of the Haitian Revolution in order to educate those who do not know it, revealing it to be instructive for the Cuban case and the Americas more broadly (Morúa Delgado 1957, 3: 52–53). He argues that the reason for tracing Haitian history is to render readers able to understand that the prevailing narrative of the Haitian Revolution, presented as supposedly fueled by the racial hatred of enslaved people enacted upon whites, was not only erroneous but constituted a perverse racist construction by those who wished to delegitimize and diminish the revolution for their own political agendas (Morúa Delgado 1957, 3: 61). This false history was then applied to Cuba by Spanish authorities and loyalists. Morúa counters with a list of atrocities committed by the Spanish against indigenous people during colonial times and links them to atrocities perpetuated by Spaniards during the nineteenth century upon enslaved people to show that neither the events nor the oppressors had changed: Cuba did not need to fear Haitian history; it needed to fear its own history of violence perpetuated by a culture of enslavement and by plantation society.[11]

Morúa's true purpose is to bring his reader to acknowledge that slave uprisings throughout the Americas were, in fact, political acts against an unjust government. He recounts that African captives forcibly transported by the Spanish to Santo Domingo in 1506 revolted en masse as early as 1522: "Y en esto no ven los españoles más que un acto indigno e insubordinado, se extiende nuestra mirada y vemos la dignidad intuitiva del hombre, pugnando siempre por romper el yugo del despotismo y la soberbia dominadora" (Morúa Delgado 1957, 3: 68). (In this the Spanish only see an undignified act and insubordination. We extend our vision, and we see the intuitive dignity of man, striving always to break the yoke of despotism and a dominating arrogance.) Bringing the argument back to Cuban history and the role of eminent black men in the fight for independence, Morúa first refers to the Aponte Conspiracy of 1812.[12] For Morúa, it is called a slave conspiracy solely in order to take away from the roots of the uprising, which were independence. By noting that even before 1812 enslaved people fought back individually by either escaping into the mountains or refusing to submit to their oppression in fighting to the death against their enslavement, he stresses that "Todos estos hechos son una continua protesta contra el abominable gobierno español, autorizado tan sólo por el tan añejo como combatido derecho de conquista" (Morúa Delgado 1957, 3: 70). (All of these acts are a continuous protest against the abominable Spanish government, authorized by such an antiquated concept as the already defeated right of conquest.)

His goal, then, is to show that while the history of European countries had been framed as one in which men battled for their freedom from the political and economic oppressions they were experiencing, in the case of Haiti and Cuba, historians chose to present it not as a fight for the noble concept of freedom against political and economic oppression which drove men to the battlefield, but a war based on an identity. For it is only enslaved Africans (not aggrieved European colonists) who are said to hate whites when they undertake revolution. They are accused of fighting a race war rather than lauded for fighting for the universal and humanist principle of freedom: "¿por qué no dicen todos los que hasta hoy han tratado esta cuestión, que el negro ha protestado siempre contra la tiranía que se le ha impuesto, y no contra los individuos de la raza que no es la suya?" (Morúa Delgado 1957, 3: 71). (Why don't all who have discussed the issue until the present day say that the black man has protested always against the tyranny that has been imposed on him, and not against individuals from a race that is not his?)

In order to highlight the sleight of hand by the Spanish government in the Cuban case, he writes "Aponte fue acusado de enemigo de la raza blanca. Y ¿que mucho, cuando el mismo Saco lo fue de favorecedor de los negros, cosa que estaba él muy lejos de pensar?" (Morúa Delgado 1957, 3: 72). (Aponte was accused of being an enemy of the white race, and it doesn't mean very much, when even Saco was accused of favoring blacks, something that was very far from Saco's thinking.) Contemporary readers knew that José Antonio Saco (see Chapter 1) warned against immediate abolition and believed that Africans were inferior to Europeans. In presenting this example and making this analogy, Morúa shows how Saco was seen as a political dissident and exiled from Cuba for his opposition to the manner in which Spanish rule was conducted on the island. Meanwhile, Aponte, who also sought complete political change, was executed, because he was accused by Spanish colonists of having plotted against whites on account of his purported racial hatred for whites.[13]

Morúa then jumps to the Escalera Conspiracy of 1844 in order to further equate attempts to end enslavement with the quest for Cuban independence, thereby once again aligning slave uprisings with political actions against an oppressive government. He explains how in 1844 there had been a general uprising against colonial authorities throughout the island, and how the Captain General of Cuba, Leopoldo O'Donnell, strategically decided to use the fear of a race war to crush the separatist movement (Morúa Delgado 1957, 3: 80). Moreover, Morúa includes proponents of independence among those who were part of the problem, since they abandoned their Afro Cuban compatriots as soon as the accusation was made, so the latter received the full weight of the punishment (Morúa Delgado 1957, 3: 80): "A tan formidable enemigo, cual es todo un pueblo, vio O'Donnell que no podría resistir solo con la fuerza, y apeló al medio que ya se venía usando por todos sus antepasados en iguales circunstancias: la división de los cubanos: la guerra de raza" (Morúa Delgado 1957, 3: 80) (To such a formidable enemy, which was the entire people, O'Donnell who could not resist with force alone, appealed to the means that had already been used by his forefathers in similar circumstances: the division of Cubans: a race war). Morúa describes its immediate and pernicious outcome:

> Cambióse la escena. Ya no era la independencia la causa de las con-
> spiraciones en la Isla. Era el exterminio jurado de la raza blanca por
> la de color. Los verdaderos conspiradores comprendieron el golpe del
> gobierno, y el temor de ser arrollados por los *aristócratas de la sangre*

si algunos con dinero no los protegían, les hizo hacerse a un lado cobardemente y dejar caer todo el peso de aquella acusación, que aun pretende sostenerse sobre los negros de Cuba.

(Morúa Delgado 1957, 3: 80)

(The scene changed. Independence was no longer the cause of the conspiracies. It was the sworn extermination of the white race by the black race. The true conspirators understood the blow [against the movement] made by the government, and the fear of being crushed by the *aristocrats of blood* if someone with money did not defend them, made them cowardly step aside and allow the full weight of that accusation, that is still maintained, to fall upon black Cubans.)

The threat of a race war, Morúa claims, was a net laid by colonial authorities in which white Cubans allowed themselves and indeed chose to be caught as a result of their racism. This "surrender" was still operating to the present day: "Nada nuevo se operó en ésto por parte del gobierno. Lo mismo había sucedido ya en 1812…Nó. Sólo vemos un gobierno que acertó a lanzar una red en que se ha querido dejar coger un pueblo" (Morúa Delgado 1957, 3: 80). (The government did nothing new. The same had occurred in 1812…No. We only see a government that managed to cast a net in which a people have wanted to be caught.) They, thereby, became traitors to the cause for independence and betrayed their fellow Cubans, those who were enslaved, and freedmen of color.

Morúa goes as far as addressing the "return to Africa" initiative proposed by some Spaniards and propagated in the US. He bemoans that Cuba could even be compared to the United States, concluding that the most dangerous result of sending Cubans back to Africa would be a delayed independence: "Y cuenta que si hay negros en Cuba se hará la independencia; si no los hay, entonces, sin duda, tardará mucho menos en llegar a su ideal!" (Morúa Delgado 1957, 3: 90). (While there are blacks in Cuba independence will come to pass; if there are none, then, without doubt, the ideal will be majorly delayed!)

Morúa ends his analysis of race relations in Cuba with a condemnation of the political war then raging on the island during the interwar years, a rhetorical and social war that he saw as destroying the morality of the people and their love for freedom. He explains that both autonomism and annexationism were tools created to disenfranchise poor Cubans, regardless of race. Paralleling his depiction of the union between Magdalena and Gonzaga in *La familia Unzúazu*,

Morúa argues that autonomism would create a "magnate class" that would then gain control of the means of production and run toward annexation to the US: "Si Cuba deseara la anexión a los Estados Unidos, esto es, una esclavitud por otra esclavitud, entonces podría servirle la autonomía para asegurar el poder interior en unos cuantos magnates" (Morúa Delgado 1957, 3: 104). (If Cuba desired annexation to the United States, that is, replacing one enslavement for another, then autonomism would be useful since it would ensure the internal power of a few magnates.) In the end, those who support autonomism, he argued, were really dealing with their own racism, since at the root of autonomism there is a *social* preoccupation, i.e., a concern and fear for how Afro Cubans would fit into prescribed social categories that were founded on the necessarily inferior status of black Cubans. He ends "Ensayo político" by emphatically proclaiming "Gloria a la Independencia! ¡Loor a la República! ¡Salud patriotas!" (Morúa Delgado 1957, 3: 107). (Glory to Independence! Praise to the Republic! A toast, patriots!)

His position against autonomism changes drastically as he experiences exile politics, as argued in Chapter 4. This shift is most evident upon his return to Cuba in 1890. It is in *La Nueva Era* (1892)[14] that Morúa's integrationist politics and his suspicion of US-influenced Cubans come most to the fore. Not surprisingly, it is in its pages that he published his translation of Redpath's (1863) *Toussaint L'Ouverture: A Biography and Autobiography*, since he read L'Ouverture and the Haitian Revolution as the blueprint for a truly racially integrated hemisphere. The footprint of the translation is most salient in a series in the newspaper he called "Factores sociales" or "Social Factors," in which he discusses "el problema de la raza negra," setting off the phrase in quotation marks to stress its constructed nature by colonial authorities. "Factores sociales," published almost ten years after his "Ensayo político," served as another point in Morúa's continuum for thinking about the past, present, and future of race relations on the island; this time it is aligned with autonomism as a political platform.

In his introduction to the series, Morúa begins by defending those of African heritage:

> Ha figurado en las artes y en la literatura; ha participado, aunque en modesta proporción, en la industria y el comercio; ha contribuido gloriosamente al enaltecimiento de las armas nacionales y antinacionales,— lo que prueba más y más su posesión de la aceptada generalidad del

organismo humano,—y ha dado pruebas notables de no carecer de aptitudes para los ejercicios de la política y el funcionamiento de la administración. Ha dado, pues, todo lo que dan las demás razas que pueblan el mundo. Pagada su deuda inaugural en la civilización imperante ¿por qué no ha de ser exaltada al puesto que le corresponde?

(Morúa Delgado 1957, 3: 211)

(They are represented in the arts and in literature; they have participated, though in modest proportion, in industry and commerce; they have gloriously contributed to the exaltation of national and antinational armaments—which proves more and more their possession of the generally accepted human organism—and have given notable proof of not lacking aptitudes for politics and administration. They have given, then, all that the other races give that populate the world. Having paid their inaugural debt in the prevailing civilization, why should they not be exalted to their rightful place?)

Addressing the place of what he terms "mestizos," those with European fathers and enslaved mothers, he differentiates Africans and mestizos because he wishes to combat systems and not individuals, "persuadido como estoy de que aquéllos [i.e., systems] y no éstas [i.e., individual persons] son los que dominan en las colectividades civilizadas" (Morúa Delgado 1957, 3: 212) (persuaded as I am that those systems and not these individuals are what dominate in civilized collectivities). In defending the "mestizo" he contradicts those who constructed the false image of the "vengeful mulatto" that Beard and Redpath promulgate in their translation, as Daut (2015) has so aptly shown. Instead, Morúa argues that "esa clasificación es de origen esclavista" (Morúa Delgado 1957, 3: 213) (that classification originates with slavery and those who enslave). Providing a brief history of how enslaved women were forcibly transported to the New World by slave traffickers for reproductive purposes in order to increase the number of enslaved people, he highlights how, as more colonizers came to the New World, they raped enslaved women, because "del establecimiento de un régimen bastardo, solo bastardías habían de obtener unos y otros" (Morúa Delgado 1957, 3: 214) (from the establishment of a depraved regime, only depravity could be obtained one from the other), adding that the European man then chose to enslave his own children.[15] These children were then admitted as part of the black race in order falsely to deprive them of their Spanish citizenship and, ultimately, of being counted as Cuban: "Y así el mestizo que era cubano por su nacimiento, y español por innegable fuero originario, quedó prácticamente excluido de la población nacional, para aumentar el número de los extranjeros, de los esclavizados africanos" (Morúa Delgado 1957, 3: 215). (And in this fashion the mestizo who was Cuban by birth, and undeniably Spanish by his legal jurisdiction, ended up practically excluded from the national population, in order to increase the number of foreigners, of enslaved Africans.) In the end, he argues that whether they were classified as African or mestizo, the goal was to create a division between classes based on racial separation. The Spanish used terms and classifications to "create" Africans and mestizos as inferior to the white man in order to continue socially and politically enslaving them after abolition.[16] They also did so in order to "foreignize" them; this sleight of hand was created to doubly exclude Afro Cubans from the nation: while Cubans were arguing for a cultural nationalism through references to their birth on the island, meaning their "*criollo*" *cubanidad*, they were simultaneously excluding black Cubans who were born on the island from that same cultural nationalism. In Morúa's indictment, we see a critique of white Cubans acting like those Spaniards who refused to treat *criollos* or those born on the island as full Spanish citizens and instead treated them like colonized subjects.

Beginning his series of articles with these observations about the constructed nature of racial classifications signals the truly acerbic nature of his attack against the Directorio Central de las Sociedades de Color and its leaders, which is elaborated in the second half of this series of essays in *La Nueva Era*. The Directorio, organized and led by Juan Gualberto Gómez (1854–1933), sought to bring together Afro Cubans into a collective in order to gain political rights from the colonial administration of the time. By beginning the series with essays about how the artificial category of race was, in fact, imposed on those who were enslaved, Morúa equated the exclusivist nature of the Directorio with one that mirrored the separatist and divisive ideology of the recently eradicated institution of slavery and its proponents.

In denouncing Juan Gualberto Gómez's Directorio, Morúa condemns the organization from his own integrationist standpoint, noting that since 1879 he had held that any separation of races was deleterious for Cuba (Morúa Delgado 1957, 3: 228). Morúa writes that any separation by race led to thinking of those who were previously enslaved as a separate class, a phenomenon made possible by the long existence of the institution of slavery on the island to begin with and something that needed to be avoided at all costs, because those who opposed the black race would use "separation" to keep them in an inferior state: "Todo eso, vuelvo a repetirlo, no sirve más que para entronizar las preocupaciones que se combaten, para acentuar la línea divisorial y perpetuar a la raza negra y a las clases de color en la depresiva condición social y política que se les ha impuesto" (Morúa Delgado 1957, 3: 232–33). (All of that, I repeat it once again, only serves to enthrone the concerns that we are trying to combat, in order to accentuate a dividing line and perpetuate the low social and political position that has been imposed on the black race and the various classes of color.)

He also raged against the Directorio for asking its black members to refrain from voting in the upcoming local elections, arguing that the Autonomist party was the "Cuban" party while Cubans were under Spanish rule and that those with an independence ideology should vote in support of that party while they resided in Cuba, for other-wise individuals who would not serve their interests on the island would be elected (Morúa Delgado 1957, 13: 234). He dots the series of essays with phrases in English such as "*petty leaders*" or "*self candidates*" and "fantasiosos *politicians*"—these words are italicized in the article proper—to speak of the self-serving and rudderless directors of the Directorio. In doing so, he equates them with the New York Cubans who were planning revolution from abroad, since, as is well known, José Martí and Juan Gualberto Gómez were working together to organize black Cubans on the island in order to ensure their military participation once the new independence movement was launched under the leadership of the Partido Revolucionario Cubano, whose founder and president was José Martí himself. Morúa concludes by noting that separatism was not represented by a legitimate party on the island, but that autonomism was a viable option. Ultimately, he terms the Directorio as *inútil* (useless) and asks that schools should be founded in its stead (Morúa Delgado 1957, 3: 236), concluding sarcastically "¡Ojalá que cuando recomience sea para colmar de alabanzas a los que aún no he censurado cuanto por sus desaciertos merecen!" (Morúa Delgado 1957, 3: 237). (I hope that when I write again it will be to fill with praise those that I have as yet to deservedly censure for the errors they are committing!)

The intellectual and activist Rafael Serra responded to Morúa's attacks from New York in Gualberto Gómez's Havana-based paper *La Igualdad*. In these pages, Serra, who was born to emancipated parents, calls out Morúa for once believing that complete emancipation (political, civil, and social) for black Cubans would only be achieved by black Cubans (referencing indirectly Morúa's arguments in "Ensayo político") but now shifting to a support of autonomism, claiming that only autonomism could offer such rights for black Cubans. Morúa is said to have written that Serra was a "persona sin autoridad para intervenir en las cosas de nuestra patria" (a person without the authority to intervene in the concerns of the homeland).[17] Serra responds:

> Mi carta desagradó al Sr. Morúa. ¿Por qué? – Porque lo que más roe su corazón es que a pesar de considerarse una notabilidad política y literaria, el Sr. Morúa hasta ahora no ha podido hacer nada visible a favor de su raza, en bien de su patria y en provecho de la humanidad. Y como ve que Juan Gualberto Gómez goza de gran prestigio entre sus compatriotas de dentro y fuera de Cuba, y de respeto y de consideración entre sus enemigos decorosos, todo lo que se diga en honor de Gómez provoca su encono y despierta sus malos sentimientos.
>
> (*La Igualdad*, March 28, 1893)
>
> (My letter was disagreeable to Mr. Morúa. Why? Because what most gnaws his heart is that even though he considers himself a notable political and literary figure, Mr. Morúa until now has not been able visibly to do anything in favor of his race, for the good of his country, and for the benefit of humanity. And since he sees that Juan Gualberto Gómez enjoys great prestige with his compatriots in and outside of Cuba, and is respected and considered favorably by his decorous enemies, everything that is said in honor of Gómez provokes his rancor and awakens his evil sentiments.)

The accusations, while personal, revolved around the Directorio and autonomism as a political option for black Cubans. Serra defends his position and denounces Morúa as self-serving and as aligning himself politically with the highest bidder.

Most recently Jesse Hoffnung-Garskof summarizes these public debates most eloquently and places them in a trans-American framework in *Racial Migrations: New York City and the Revolutionary Politics of the Spanish Caribbean* (2019),[18] explaining that the founding of the Directorio in Cuba "touched off a bitter polemic over strategy, which reverberated among exiles in New York just as they began the work of building Martí's party" (Hoffnung-Garskof 173). Specifically, Morúa disagreed with the creation of a separate group defined by racial identity. As is evidenced by Morúa's arguments in "Factores sociales" (1892) and "Ensayo político (1883)," almost ten years earlier, and by his translation practice, Morúa did have a long-standing position as to the future of race relations in Cuba, as well as to the reasons why he believed an association like the Directorio would not achieve but instead would hinder both independence and the interests of Afro Cubans, within the insurrection and post-independence, and this view was formed by his time in the Jim Crow South. These arguments fall on an Afro Latina/o Continuum in which Toussaint Louverture and the history and legacy of the Haitian Revolution are central in its articulation.

After the war of 1895 and US intervention, militarily, politically, and socially, Morúa continued to advocate for a racially unified Cuba. He had been selected to take part in the Constitutional Assembly. He helped to draft the Cuban Constitution and voted for the Platt Amendment.[19] Those delegates who voted for the amendment were severely criticized in the Cuban press. Morúa defended his vote by noting that it was the only means of securing some form of independence for Cuba. He feared that Cuba would become a colony of the US. After his vote, he published an article titled "Toussaint L'Ouverture" in *Cuba y América* (1897–1917), a literary and political journal edited by his close friend Raimundo Cabrera. This article served as an apologia for Morúa's own decision to vote for the Platt Amendment in 1902. It also signals, once again, Morúa's vision for the role of black Cubans, this time in the first Cuban Republic. Not surprisingly, it is a vision inspired by Haiti and the figure of Toussaint L'Ouverture.

Morúa's Continuum (Take 3): Toussaint L'Ouverture

Morúa's article analyses the historiography on Toussaint L'Ouverture, ending with a defense of his universal importance. As he develops his argument, Morúa signals the pernicious influence of US racialized narratives that touted racial equality while legislating a separate but equal ideology. To counter this influence, Morúa places L'Ouverture and the black experience in the Americas on a continuum that simultaneously impacts the place and time of each endpoint—the US and Cuba. To do so, he begins by quoting Wendell Phillips and his 1861 speech "Toussaint L'Ouverture" (Phillips 1863). Placing the first endpoint in the US, Morúa then provides a corrective to the historiography on L'Ouverture, including Phillip's own speech. Morúa describes Phillips as:

> El más brillante, correcto y espontáneo de los oradores norteamericanos, pronunciando una inspirada conferencia político-social, dedicada a exponer ante la ilustrada sociedad de Boston la vida noble y la gloria incontestable de Toussaint L'Ouverture, a quien exaltó como un hombre ejemplar y superior por las peculiares circunstancias en que desarrolló sus facultades excepcionales.   (Morúa Delgado 1903, 316)

> (The most brilliant, correct and spontaneous of North American orators, who pronounced an inspired political-social lecture, dedicated to exposing before the learned society of Boston the noble life and the incontestable glory of Toussaint L'Ouverture, whom he exalted as an exemplary and superior man because of the peculiar circumstances in which he developed his exceptional faculties.)

He then provides a long quotation from Phillips, the last paragraph from his 1861 speech.[20] Yet Morúa quotes Phillips not to praise his work, but to correct his assertion that L'Ouverture was an "exception," an anomaly in the African race. Morúa subtly informs his reader that Phillips is to be questioned, since before Phillips's speech:

> Había sido universalmente reconocido en el Libertador de Haití, el carácter más perfecto que ha producido la civilización cristiana desde su excelso creador; siendo más altecedora su gloria porque, al contrario de las glorias todas que la fama ha consagrado, la de Toussaint L'Ouverture ha sido proclamada por sus propios enemigos, por los más apasionados detractors de su raza.   (Morúa Delgado 1903, 316)

> (It had been universally recognized in the Liberator of Haiti, the most perfect character that has been produced by Christian civilization, since its sublime creator; his glory being more exalted because, contrary to all the glories that fame has consecrated, that of Toussaint L'Ouverture was proclaimed by his very enemies, by the most passionate detractors of his race.)

Continuing his critique of Phillips and historians like him, as he had previously done in "Ensayo político," Morúa provides an assessment of the historiography on Haiti and the Haitian Revolution to date, questioning its facticity. He decries that instead of trying to understand the "factores singenéticos" (congenital factors) of Haitian history, historians overall have instead plagiarized from previous histories of Haiti, from authors that they "refuse to cite" (Morúa Delgado 1903, 316). Although Morúa does not name them, he signals historians who denigrated the now emancipated Haiti and questioned its citizens' ability for self-rule. In not citing their sources (most likely French, British, and Spanish historians), these writers thereby do not expose the prejudices with which they are producing their questionable narratives to begin with. I quote this passage at length below due to the importance of Morúa's reading of historiography on Haiti that purposely misleads:

> Haití ha sido presentado siempre, por la generalidad de los escritores que de su desarrollo han tratado, como un ejemplo de anarquía social, como una evidente demostración de la incapacidad política de la raza negra para la vida del derecho constitucional, seguramente porque la labor de los historiadores se halla todavía muy lejos de ser el resultado del estudio de los elementos que concurren á la formación de cada conglomerado social; siendo por el contrario, cuando no la copia más o menos mañosa de trabajos anteriores de no citados autores, la exposición mecánica de un producto social que en sus manifestaciones halaga ó desconsuela, según el caso, pero que no explica ni mucho menos el orígen y desenvolvimiento de los factores singenéticos de aquel producto.   (Morúa Delgado 1903, 316)

> (Haiti has always been presented, by most writers who have addressed its development as an example of social anarchy, as an evident demonstration of the political incapacity of the black race for constitutional rights, certainly because the labor of the historians is still very far from the result of a study of the elements that come together to form each social conglomerate; instead, on the contrary, when the work is not copied more or less craftily from previous works of uncited authors, the mechanical exposition of a social product that in its manifestations praises or discourages, based on each case, but that certainly never explains the origin or development of the congenital factors of that product.)

Morúa quotes the sociologist Ludwick Gumplicz in order to stress that the end result of such historiographical partiality is one in which:

> "Se puede decir, sin temor de engañarse, que la mayor parte de la historia escrita hasta el presente, no ha brotado más que de esta necesidad subjetiva de los hombres: de glorificar *lo que les es propio y lo*

que tienen más cerca, rebajando y denigrando lo que no les es propio y
lo que está alejado de ellos." (Italics in original)

(Morúa Delgado 1903, 317)

(It could be said, without any fear of deceiving oneself, that the major
part of the history written to the present day, has not flowed but from
the subjective necessity of man: to glorify *that which is proper to them*
and that which they have closest to them, lowering and denigrating that
which is not proper to them and that which is far from them.) (Italics in
original)[21]

Morúa here condemns how French, British, and Spanish historiography, representative of the three European nations directly involved
in the Haitian Revolution, had limited itself to writing about the
bloodiest scenes of the Haitian Revolution as committed, "según ellos"
(according to them), by the "salvajismo de los negros" (the savagery
of black men) (Morúa Delgado 1903, 317). This false assignation and
characterization reflected their own violence and their biased position, which Morúa signals with his use of quotation marks to set off
"salvajismo de los negros" in order to emphasize the artificial and
racist construction of these ascriptions by historians.

Morúa then moves to L'Ouverture's biography—highlighting the
coincidence of his birthdate and the founding of the Cuban Republic
(May 20, 1743 [L'Ouverture]) and May 20, 1902 (Cuba)) to further
emphasize his importance for Cuba's political past, present, and
future, a link established at an almost cosmological level. He lists a
series of figures who speak to the nobility and education of those
around L'Ouverture, including his father, who was the grandson of
an African king, and his teacher Juan Batista, who taught him French
and Latin. Referencing L'Ouverture's African heritage, he proceeds
to show how ethnographers have chosen to forget that Christian as
well as Greek and Roman civilization (and therefore all Western
civilization) arose from Ethiopian roots, something Eurocentric
historians wished to ignore. Morúa reviews the racist theories
that arose in relation to L'Ouverture, due to "el celo antropológico"
(Morúa Delgado 1903, 319) (anthropological jealousy), even in the
process of praising him, such as the proposition (by Phillips) that
L'Ouverture was "un producto incidental" (an incidental product)
of social communities in their process of development (Morúa
Delgado 1903, 319). He argues that to accept this thesis is to negate
the importance of each and every one of the other "caracteres
extraordinarios" (extraordinary figures) in history and up to the

present day (for example, Phillips cited George Washington as an exception). Discounting such theories as those that expound "ocasionalidad" (someone occurring only sporadically and without consistency) or "circunstancialidad etnogenética" (ethnogenetic circumstanciality), i.e., that it happened by chance (Morúa Delgado 1903, 320), he stresses that great men do not simply occur, since:

> cada hombre es hijo de su época y descendiente por línea recta de las épocas anteriores. No surgen por generación espontanea los grandes hombres, no los improvisan los acontecimientos incidentales de una época, sino que son el producto de una laboriosa gestación social en la marcha de los tiempos.   (Morúa Delgado 1903, 320)

> (Each man is a son of his epoch and a direct descendent of previous epochs. Great men do not rise up through spontaneous generation, incidental events of an epoch do not improvise them; instead they are a product of a laborious social gestation in the march of time.)

In other words, contra Phillips and other historians, men like L'Ouverture are not created by incidental events in the lives of countries. Instead, they are "observadores inteligentes" (intelligent observers) who are able to predict what will happen and then participate in history. Provocatively, Morúa gives the example of how the conde de Aranda warned Charles III that the US would turn on their previous allies, France and Spain, and would eventually take Florida in order to dominate the Gulf of Mexico.[22] Morúa concludes:

> Las Américas se conmovieron hasta independizarse de España, los Estados Unidos crecieron, se olvidaron de los beneficios recibidos de las dos potencias, se apoderaron de las Floridas y se tornaron, finalmente, en el coloso de América, que ha puesto en movimiento preventivo á todas las potencias del continente europeo.
> (Morúa Delgado 1903, 320)

> (The Americas were moved until they gained their independence from Spain, the United States grew, they forgot the benefits received from the two powers, they took over Florida, and they became, finally, the colossus of America, which has put into a defensive position all of the powers of the European continent.)

In referencing the conde de Aranda Morúa argues that L'Ouverture is not an exception, but a possibility inherent in all freedmen and those who were previously enslaved for rising up and leading a nation simply because it is the morally and ethically right thing to do. Afro Cubans could, as L'Ouverture did during his lifetime, simply *read* the political moment and act upon it. Simultaneously, Morúa places himself (and other black Cubans) in the position of harbingers, warning Cubans that the US was a formidable and insatiable neocolonial power, one to be feared, especially for its pernicious position on race relations: how they treated black Cubans was a barometer of how they would treat all Cubans in the future.

Crediting L'Ouverture with ending enslavement throughout the civilized world, which in turn led to the rights of all men to freedom, the end of the slave trade, the legal abolition of slavery, and the rehabilitation of those who had been enslaved throughout the Americas, he reminds his readers that in the US, Brazil, and Cuba the black individual is now a man and not a slave, and that in Cuba so much is particularly true, since "en ninguna parte como aquí participó de manera tan cumplida en la rectificación de los destinos de su patria" (Morúa Delgado 1903, 320) (in no place as here did [the black man] participate in a more dutiful manner in the rectification of the destiny of his homeland.) In this statement, he presents Afro Cubans as the exemplary case. In the past they had fought side by side with other Cubans in the multiple attempts at independence, serving as a model for what was possible. It was a model in which race was not a defining factor, since all men fought as Cubans. Now, in Republicanism, they would serve as a model once again, but this time for what was possible in civil society. They were exemplary of how to redeem the Americas, for they were proof that race as a social construction could be overcome in the name of the ideals of a free and democratic nation that was based on universal fraternity.

Morúa anchors what is in fact an Afro Latinx Continuum at one end when he credits Frederick Douglass, the abolitionist Peter Garner, and Booker T. Washington as individuals in the US who embody the moral and political synergy of the black race in the development of society. This is made possible, he argues, because of Toussaint L'Ouverture. He subsequently references the figure of Menelik II of Abissinia, the then emperor of Ethiopia who had defeated Italian forces in 1896 and had permanently established Ethiopia. As Ferrer (2014) demonstrates Ethiopia and Abyssinia were available to early black revolutionaries and insurrectionists because the history of Ethiopia was circulating in the Americas, and specifically, the United States (Boston, Virginia, and Savannah): "In the still new United States, black abolitionists and ministers spoke of the greatness of

Ethiopia. New black churches called themselves Ethiopian and Abyssinian" (Ferrer 2014 307). She goes on to state:

> If the presence of Ethiopia in Black Atlantic texts and institutions was already established in the last decades of the eighteenth century, those mentions acquired new meaning and force with the establishment in 1804 of an actual existing black state in the New World. Like Ethiopia, but immediate in time and space, Haiti had black emperors and kings and victorious black armies. Might Haiti then be a sign of a new age in the horizon? (Ferrer 2014, 308)

Morúa likewise makes a contemporaneous reference to Ethiopia with Melenik II. Might Haiti, once again, be a sign of a new age on the horizon for Cuba and the Americas? Just as Aponte envisioned the possibility of a freed Cuba through the history of Haiti, Morúa likewise envisioned a freed Cuba—from US rule—through black leadership that emerges from the popular classes and changes society.

He anchors the other point of his Afro-diasporic continuum, when he references various Afro Cubans who fought against Spanish colonialism, such as the martyred poet Plácido; the martyred Afro Cuban generals Antonio Maceo, Flor Crombet, and Guillermo Moncada; and Afro Puerto Ricans Rafael Cordero and Francisco "Pachín" Marín. He does so in order to emphasize universal fraternity that originates from black sacrifice, black leadership, and black experience, in which "la justicia es grande, alcanza para todos; el amor es inmenso, puede colmar el corazón de todos" (Morúa Delgado 1903, 320). (Justice is great; it is available to all; love is immense; it can fill the hearts of all.) This justice and love are a continuum established and made possible through black experience itself. In creating a continuum between African Americans, Afro Latina/os, and Afro Latin Americans, and then the African continent through Melenik II, he is making sure to equate black thinkers, writers, and leaders with their European counterparts, signaling their importance for humanity more broadly. He concludes: "Pues bien, esos hombres dan prestigio a su país y confianza al universo entero; porque la ilustración y las aspiraciones nobles constituyen una garantía inestimable en donde quiera que se manifiesten" (Morúa Delgado 1903, 320). (Well, those men give prestige to their countries and confidence to the whole universe; because culture and noble aspirations constitute an inestimable guarantee wherever they are manifested.)

In this article, Morúa thus aligns himself with L'Ouverture, using this figure to serve as a rationale for his own vote for the Platt Amendment. Morúa and other delegates were strongly criticized for tying the future of the republic to US economic interests. Morúa, in citing how historians had misread and miswritten L'Ouverture and his role in universal history, references his own situation as an Afro Cuban who is making decisions that would impact the future of all Cubans. Morúa's rhetorical moves allow us to understand the significance of the figure of L'Ouverture for Morúa's own vision regarding the place of the black experience in the past, present, and future of the Americas. In sum, by quoting Phillips's speech he highlights the prejudice of historians and their explicit racism when writing about Haiti and its history, even if their intentions are noble. He simultaneously alerts his readers to the pernicious manner in which race relations were legislated in the United States. For in referencing US abolitionist thinkers, he brings their concurrent vision of race relations into the Cuban sphere, noting in print how the two diverging ideologies regarding race relations were now forced to work side by side, something that Cubans should be cautious about. Next, in referencing important black figures in US history and then ending with a list of Cuban and Puerto Rican heroes (some of whom had spent time in the US) bound together by a prominent previously enslaved leader, L'Ouverture, Morúa rewrites contemporary historiography—for example, he is countering the increased "whitening" of Cuban soldiers in the press—in order to make relevant a broader black experience in the Americas. This experience is to serve as a foundation for imagining true political and social change in the hemisphere, since it would serve to potentially redeem and transform even US concepts of race relations. This redeeming work of the African experience in the Americas is expressed through Morúa's translation, journalism, and literary creations of the 1880s and 1890s. It culminates in this article from 1903. Ultimately, they create a Latina/o historiography of the Americas that sits on an Afro Latinx Continuum that situates the diasporic African experience of enslavement, resistance, and then freedom as the only means to redeem the body politic though justice and love.

*   *   *

Morúa went on to become president of the Cuban Senate and, as noted earlier, is now memorialized as a detested politician, since in 1910, after the organization of the Partido Independiente de Color, he proposed an amendment to the Cuban Constitution which made illegal the organization of any party based on race. This amendment was turned into law and has been considered one of the factors that led to the Race War of 1912.[23] Morúa partly defended his proposal on the basis of his fear of US-style racism taking hold of the country. On the Cuban Senate floor, he defended the need for the amendment, arguing that "lo que yo quiero evitar esto es que los cubanos se acostumbren a considerarse separados los unos de los otros" (Morúa Delgado 1957, 3: 243). (What I wish to avoid is that Cubans become accustomed to considering themselves separated one from another.) He claimed he wished to ensure that the Republic would survive in the face of US neocolonialism: "El caso es que ahora surgen dificultades, que asoman peligros para lo venidero y tengo la seguridad completa de que ha de sobrevenir,—si continuase—, la disolución de nuestra República" (Morúa Delgado 1957, 3: 244). (The case exists that difficulties are now emerging [from the US], that dangers are appearing for the future, and I am completely assured that the dissolution of our Republic will occur if they continue.) These new difficulties were caused by "aquellos pueblos que vinieron a nosotros" (Morúa Delgado 1957, 3: 244) (those peoples who have come to us). He sees this ideology as the instigator of a separation of races in Cuba:

> Harta desgracia hemos tenido con las preocupaciones que nos han separado en muchos casos, harta desgracia además de la nacional que hemos sufrido en nuestra vida política nacional las intervenciones, Enmiendas a nuestra Constitución y cauces determinados que se quieren imponer a nuestra sociedad, para aumentarla ahora, con una nueva que, no sé si aquellos que han tenido interés en crearnos dificultades, se sienten satisfechos por esa nueva que venían a estorbarnos el paso a la libertad a que todos propendemos.
>
> (Morúa Delgado 1957, 3: 243)

> (Disgrace enough have we experienced with concerns that have separated us in many cases, disgrace enough at the national level that our national political life has suffered with interventions, amendments to our Constitution and predetermined courses that want to be imposed on our society, to increase it now, with a new one that, which I am unsure if those who wish to create difficulties for us would be satisfied with the new one that would get in the way of the path to liberty for which we are aiming.)

For Morúa the "preoccupaciones" were social divisions established during colonial rule, legislating that Afro Cubans were inferior to white *criollos*, in order to retain economic and political control of the island by elite *criollos* and *peninsulares*. Upon this historical foundation of racism was now imposed a new danger, the US belief in the separation of races, as evidenced in the "predetermined course" being laid for the new Republic so that, as in the past, the same elites who sought to remain in power would continue to do so, but this time by aligning themselves with US interests. The end result mirrored the same tactic that Spain had used against Cuba in the nineteenth century, now deployed by the US as the agitators: "Blancos reunidos con exclusión de negros y negros reunidos con exclusión de blancos; y ahí está el gran conflicto que mi enmienda quiere evitar" (Morúa Delgado 1957, 3: 244). (Whites united by the exclusion of blacks and blacks united by the exclusion of whites; and that is the great conflict that my amendment wants to avoid.)

In arguing that the amendment would help to curb the foreign racist ideology permeating the country, Morúa further associated this pernicious separate but equal ideology with the US:

> Con esa enmienda [Ley Morúa] no se prohíbe a nadie que tenga su opinión, ni la expresión de ella, ni realice todos los actos que quiera, menos constituirse una clase nuestra, una raza nuestra aparte y en frente de la otra, que es el único punto donde yo veo un conflicto social; y como *nosotros nunca lo hemos tenido* debemos evitarlo ahora. (Italics mine)   (Morúa Delgado 1957, 3: 245)

> (With that amendment [the Morúa Law] it is not prohibited that anyone who has an opinion, nor the wish to express it, nor the actions that they wish to commit to obtain it, do so as long as they do not constitute our own class, a separate race that is in opposition to another race, which is the only point where I see a social conflict; and since *we have never had this*, we should avoid it now.)

In noting that Cuba had not had this type of ideological and political separation of the races before US intervention, he directly alludes to his own experience living in the post-Reconstruction US in the 1880s and witnessing the continuing racist legislation in the US employed to disenfranchise African Americans, especially in education. This experience had taught him about the pernicious intent behind the separation of races.

Morúa died from complications he experienced from Bright's disease two months after he gave these speeches on the Senate floor. He left his family penniless, since he did not engage in the rampant corruption that was such a mark of Cuban republicanism. He also did not witness the violent effects of his legislation, which was used to slaughter Afro Cubans in the eastern provinces in the summer of 1912. He did not witness the racial hatred that could still exist at the heart of Cuban society in his time and would allow such a slaughter to take place. Yet what I hope to have shown in this chapter on Morúa's journalism and translation is that his work and his political life should not be read through a narrow nationalist lens solely focused on his support of the Ley Morúa, since this disavows the historical importance of his many writings on race relations in Cuba and the black experience in the Americas more broadly. As Marlene Daut (2017, 199) argues in her study of the Baron de Vastey: "The Vastey I hope I have unveiled is the one whom we read rather than dismiss, and whose complicated humanism we contemplate rather than condemn." I hope I have done the same for Morúa. Deploying a trans-American and transcolonial framework for studying his life and works reveals a broader, more nuanced history, bequeathing an early Afro Latina/o political thinker with a prescient view of potentially liberatory futures for the hemisphere. Reading from the Latino Continuum allows us to decipher Morúa's belief that the black experience could be used as a model for redeeming previously colonized spaces, from Cuba to the wider purview of the Caribbean and Latin America. But Afro-diasporic history could also serve as a model for inspiring racial and political integration in the US.

In the end, by interpreting Morúa's life and work from this broader perspective, we see how he constructed, first, a vision for Cuba, parallel to but competing with Martí's, through the figure of a black military leader in the legacy of Toussaint L'Ouverture (someone like Flor Crombet). These figures would then serve as models for all black Cubans. And, second, in his choice of translation, which in turn impacted his literary endeavors, journalism, and political writings, we may recognize that Morúa found a means of conceptually integrating those who were enslaved and had previously been enslaved into the very foundation of the future Cuban nation, casting thereby the African diaspora as key to the future racial liberation of the Americas, including the US, and to universal humanity more broadly. The foundational fictions of Cuba and the US could not afford to exclude the African diaspora, he argued, for in its history lay the only possible future of true equality. Only by understanding and acknowledging Afro-diasporic history throughout the Americas—a history integral to and inextricable from the Latino Continuum—would the future realize the truth of its fullest possible destiny: that "la justicia es grande, alcanza para todos; el amor es inmenso, puede colmar el corazón de todos" (Morúa Delgado 1903, 320). (Justice is great; it is available to all; love is immense; it can fill the hearts of all.)

Conclusion

THE LATINX RETURN

In *Sofía* Martín Morúa Delgado would stress that clothes are markers: markers of taste, cultural inclinations, socioeconomic status. They are also markers of place and geographic identifications, as Morúa would observe about the inadequate clothing worn by Americanized Cubans upon their return to the island after extended stays in the US, noting that their use of "lanas y franelas sencillas...conservaban una graciosa reminiscencia del tipo extranjero impreso en ambos por su larga estancia fuera de su país natal" (Morúa Delgado 1891, 102) (simple wools and flannels...retained an amusing reminiscence of the foreign type stamped on both because of their long stay outside of their countries of birth). He was not the only Latina/o author who found himself moving between spaces, on a Latino Continuum, on which clothing, like texts and life events, served as markers of that experience. Take for example the martyred Cuban poet, Juan Clemente Zenea (1832–71), who, although on a diplomatic mission to the island, was executed by Spanish authorities as a traitor to the Spanish cause in Cuba. He would likewise comment on the experience of living in a new country, but this time through the lens of emotions and desire in the doomed love affair of a displaced couple who yearn for their homeland as they walk down *la Quinta Avenida* or dream of Cuba during day trips to Hoboken, New Jersey. In the novel *Lejos de la patria. Memorias de un joven poeta*, published in New York in 1859, Cuba and the US are united temporally and spatially through the love-making, musings, and yearnings found in its pages (Zenea 1859).

Or what of Adolfo and Federico Fernández Cavada, Cuban brothers raised in the US who fought for the Union, Federico (Cavada 1864) documenting his experiences in the war memoir *Libby Life: Experiences*

The Latino Continuum and the Nineteenth-Century Americas: Literature, Translation, and Historiography.
Carmen E. Lamas, Oxford University Press (2021). © Carmen E. Lamas. DOI: 10.1093/oso/9780198871484.003.0007

of a Prisoner of War in Richmond, Va., 1863–64, published in Philadelphia in 1864. He and Adolfo survived the US Civil War but died in the battlefields of Cuba during the Ten Years' War (1868–78). As with the case of Zenea, their travels to and from the island and their participation in multiple "Wars of Rebellion" (Alemán 2013), marked them in the nineteenth century and mark the Latinx experience up to the present day.[1] For when recovering and studying Latinx lives and experiences, we find markers—geographic, political, affective, aesthetic, and imaginative—that speak to the *comings and goings* of Latin Americans to the US and back again to their home countries— and simultaneously of the quickly and violently shifting borders, in their multiple manifestations beyond the spatial and temporal, that occurred and continue to occur throughout the Americas, not only on the US-Mexico border. They all speak of what I call the *Latinx return*, an endless circuit of arrivals and departures that characterized the nineteenth-century continuum explored in this book every bit as much as it speaks to the Latinx experience today.

Morúa, himself, living almost a decade in the US, mainly in Key West and later Tampa, traveling by train to New York and back in the post-Reconstruction United States, both witnessed and experienced firsthand the rise of the Jim Crow era. In *Sofía*, that is to say, he was describing more than clothing; he was grappling with his own experience and that of others like him, in which his life, marked by two stays in the US—one a decade, the other less than two years—profoundly changed him and made him something more than but also Cuban: it made him Latino. For his *latinidad* did not disappear upon his return to the island; indeed, it had changed him, and, through him and others like him, it changed Cuba *and* the US as well.

But what about someone like Ramón Meza y Súarez Inclán (1861–1911), a well-known Cuban novelist who resided briefly in the US while the final war of independence raged on the island, or Raimundo Cabrera (1852–1923), with a similar short residence in the United States? Like Meza y Súarez Inclán, Cabrera spent less than two years in the US, returning to Cuba in 1898, after the US takeover of the island. In Cabrera's case, his fictive war memoir *Episodios de la guerra. Mi vida en la manigua* (Cabrera 1897–98) demonstrates how he makes himself Latino, a process he wished to expedite in order to fit into the political maneuverings of the independence advocates of New York City. Taking part in the armed uprising then raging in Cuba was a sign of true patriotism, and Cabrera, who was an autonomist during the interwar years, had to "create" a Latina/o history that would document his dedication to the war effort. Under the pseudonym Ricardo Buenamar (an anagram of his name) he first published his memoir serially in a periodical he founded and edited in New York, *Cuba y América* (1897–98). *Episodios* was then published in book form in Philadelphia (Cabrera 1898a) and Mexico (Cabrera 1898b), thereby extending his Latina/o experience beyond the US and Cuba. Moreover, Cabrera, like the other Latinx authors studied here, was also a translator. In Cabrera (1889) he offered an annotated rendition of Andrew Carnegie's (1886) *Triumphant Democracy or Fifty Years' March of the Republic*, a text he rewrote as a Latina/o historiography that rejects a deep divide between Cuban and US history. Instead, Cabrera took on the persona of Carnegie, literally rewriting the text as a Cuban work.

Yet Cabrera was himself translated by a fellow Latina, longtime Philadelphia resident and niece of Eusebio Guiteras, Laura Guiteras. Laura translated Cabrera's well-known *Cuba y sus jueces*, which went through multiple editions between 1887 and 1896, including in Philadelphia in 1891. Laura dedicates her translation (now titled *Cuba and the Cubans* [Cabrera 1896]) to her beloved uncle, Eusebio Guiteras, thereby linking *Cuba y sus jueces* to *Rudo Ensayo*, a Latina textual intervention that inextricably binds the Americas. This translation signals yet another moment on the Latino Continuum as Laura Guiteras incorporates Cabrera and her uncle into the realities of the US, making them integral to US history, but does the same in the opposite direction, insisting that they are part of Cuba too. Laura Guiteras thus enacted another cycle of the Latinx return, bringing back and forth across the border, with her English-language edition, the lives and writing of her uncle and Cabrera.

It is through lives and texts like the ones studied here—biographies and works that cross and recross multiple spaces, languages, and genres, conflating time and space through memory and desire—that the Latino Continuum arrives finally at our own time of the Latinx Return. For when we enter the Americas archive—an archive that speaks to our inability definitively to place and limit an individual's experience and impact—the *latinidad* that emerges from these juxtapositions complicates the notion of being from a place or even a specific time. Instead, memory and affect, in addition to the political and social experiences of an individual and a collectivity, become defining factors. They bind groups, creating new histories across the Americas.

Cabrera's *latinidad*, particularly as embodied in his periodical *Cuba y América*, is unable to leave him; it has forever marked him. For he continues his periodical on the other side of the Florida Straits—just as Morúa had started *El Pueblo* in Matanzas and continued publishing it in Key West, and then founded *La Nueva Era* in Key West and continued publishing it in Havana. The vehicle Cabrera deployed in New York in 1897 to mark one experience now becomes a vehicle to mark yet another one, his *Latinx return*. For when he takes the periodical to Cuba, continuing to publish it there until 1917, Cabrera includes works written by Cubans during their previous stays in the US. Some returned to the island, as is in evidence in his publication of Ramón Meza y Súarez Inclán's (1899) *En un pueblo de la Florida* or Morúa's article "Toussaint L'Ouverture" (Morúa Delgado 1903). Others died before being able to choose their return, such as Eusebio Guiteras, who left the unpublished novel, *Gabriel Reyes*, which Cabrera published in *Cuba y América* in Havana from August 9, 1903 to September 23, 1904. These works and the vehicle for publishing them signal a new way of being that is always already and forever imprinted in Cabrera's experience and also on the Cuba to which Cabrera returns. His life, like those of the many Latina/os who either came back to their home countries or stayed in the US, remains still deeply integral to their home countries *and* vice versa, through publications such as these. In this simultaneous relocation, this bidirectional movement and inadvertent and/or purposeful recontextualization of the movement of people and texts, Cabrera makes these Latina/o authors Cubans once again, but also always already Latina/o. For in having to "make them" Cuban by reinscribing them into the Cuban national imaginary through their publication on Cuban soil for a new republican Cuban readership, he is reconstructing what was already there, an experience that moves on a continuum. And, unbeknownst to Cabrera, he captures the phenomenon I am discussing here. He is demonstrating how the Latinx experience is integral to the Cuban experience and vice versa, how the one cannot exist without the other. One does not leave one's *latinidad* at the door upon one's return to either one's home country or the US.

We might consider here the experience of Antonio José de Irissari (1786–1868), the "errant Latino," as Kirsten Silva Gruesz (2016) calls him, who was born in Guatemala City, travelled across the Americas (Chile, Colombia, Ecuador, and Curaçao) and finally settled in the US for nearly two decades, dying in New York City. These experiences never left him and impacted his life and writings. Or the experience of Juan Seguín (1806–90), who fought for Texas's independence at the Alamo, only to find himself cast out of Texas, through the racialization and violence experienced by *tejano* veterans who were now considered foreigners because they were labeled Mexican, as Seguín (1858) depicted in his *Personal Memoirs of John N. Seguín*, published in San Antonio, Texas in 1858. Or Vicente Pérez Rosales (1807–86), the Chilean miner, who was forever changed by his California experience during the Gold Rush, an experience underlying his *Diario de un viaje a California (1848–1849)* (Pérez Rosales 1949) and *Recuerdos del Pasado (1814–1860)* (Pérez Rosales 1886), as Juan Poblete (2016) has shown; or Civil War Latina/o soldiers such as the New Mexican James Santiago Tafolla, José Garza, and Francisco Martínez, who sided with the Confederacy but then deserted to Mexico, to be labeled foreigners, as Seguín had been thirty years earlier, but this time by the authorities in Mexico, even though Tafolla had been born in what was then Mexico in 1836. Alemán (2018, 216) refers to Tafolla and his fellow deserters as *mojados reversos*, their texts emblematic of "narratives of displacement" that do not simply serve as correctives to US history, but create an "alternative expressive culture that resists US empire through history, memory and transnationality by imagining Mexico and Mexican Americans in the United States despite their displacement from it".

With these examples in mind, and apart from the important recovery project that the Latino Continuum makes possible, I wish readers to understand the significance of its methodology for the present day, since the Americas archive it constitutes elicits new readings of US, Latinx, and Latin American texts and of the Latina/o experience itself. For the Latina/o experience—of multiple border crossings—does not "devour" them, as the Colombian author José Eustasio Rivera (1929, 343) said in *La vorágine* as his protagonists faced being devoured by the Amazonian jungle. The Chicano novelist Tomás Rivera (1971) offers a parallel experience of that confrontation in his aptly titled his novel…*y no se lo tragó la tierra* (…*And the Earth Did Not Devour Him*), a truly American text (in the hemispheric and trans-American sense of the term) in his now classic collection of short stories of the migrant farmer experience in the US. In the dialogue between these two texts (the Colombian Rivera and the Chicano Rivera), which is marked by the similarity of the last sentence of the earlier novel, "¡*Los devoró la selva!*" (The jungle devoured them!), to the title of the later work, we find that both speak of labor, of survival—physical, cultural, economic, political—and both speak of an experience that binds the Americas in its hemispheric and global dimensions, in the power relations that bring or force individuals and families across borders and back again, whether the crossing is successful or not, whether they are documented or without papers, whether they are imaginary or real. In these novels the characters seek to survive the death trap of the voracious rubber industry fueled by global market forces that push the worker into the abyss or the ever-hungry field in its treacherous grinding of migrant bodies, respectively. There is no division here between Colombia and Texas; they are mutually imbricated experiences of survival that link the hemisphere and the world. For just as Morúa argued for the continuity of the black experience across the Americas as the foundation for redeeming the Americas and constructing a truly raceless and just society, in these works we see similar structures, ones that speak of defiance, resistance, and survival. They are works and experiences that tenaciously move toward change, toward equality, toward justice, and love.

Moreover, this *latinidad* is present in other contemporary literary manifestations and experiences such as *American Visa* (1994) by the Bolivian Juan de Recacochea; *Paraíso Travel* (2001) by the Colombian Jorge Franco; and *La isla de amores infinitos* (2006) by the Cuban Daína Chaviano, to name only a few. One must also include authors who translate their own works, such as the Chilean María Luisa Bombal with *La última niebla* (1934), translated as *The House of Mist* (1947); *Eternal Curse on the Reader of These Pages* (1982) by the Argentinian Manuel Puig (this work was originally written in English, but Puig translated it to Spanish and first published it as *Maldición a quien lea estas páginas* (1980)); and Rosario Ferré with *Maldito amor* (1986), translated as *Sweet Diamond Dust* (1989). Or such recent translations as those by the Cuban American novelist Achy Obejas of the Dominican author Rita Indiana's *Papi* (2012, 2016) and *La mucama de omicumlé* (2015) as *Tentacle* (2018). Read in parallel with such English-language texts as *In Cuba I Was a German Shepherd* (2001) by Ana Menéndez; *Across a Hundred Mountains* (2007) by Reyna Grande; *When the Earth Turns in Its Sleep* (2007) by Sylvia Sellers-García;

The Deportation of Wopper Barraza (2014) by Maceo Montoya; *The Revolutionaries Try Again* (2016) by Mauro Javier Cárdenas; *The Fruit of the Drunken Tree* (2018) by Ingrid Contreras; *The Affairs of the Falcons* (2019) by Melissa Rivero; and *The Book of Lost Saints* (2019) by Daniel José Older, they speak of successful and failed comings and goings, forced leavings and altered returns.[2] At their core they speak to the same experience of *latinidad*, one that defines and defies the Americas, one that seeks to create new histories, one that sits on the Latino Continuum.[3]

For future study, I hope this book signals the importance of including Latinx authors and texts in theorizing world literature, not in order to show that these texts are "worthy" of being included in these debates. Instead, I invite scholars to move beyond the writings on the same by such scholars as Franco Moretti, David Damrosch, and Emily Apter, whose foundations for their theorization ultimately return to well-known European sources such as the writings of Walter Benjamin, Erich Auerbach, and Jacques Derrida. To put it simply, these contemporary scholars do not engage Latinx texts in their formulations of *distant reading*, *detached engagements*, and *translation zones*, respectively, thereby recreating the same lacuna one finds in American and Latin American literary studies and histories, but at the global level. Disavowing (by disregarding) the lives and texts of Latinx writers from these analyses creates and perpetuates the incomplete theorizations and histories that were produced in the nineteenth century to begin with. Alternatively, I hope readers of this book will turn to such philosophers and scholars as Gloria Anzaldúa, María Josefina Saldaña-Portillo, and Marlene Daut, thinkers who bring to light the unrecognized realities and perspectives that are forever present in the global histories that have been passed down to us.[4] For the latter—theories of the Latinx, indigenous, and African diasporic experience—are indispensable for formulating the former, theories of the global or world novel. The very act of excluding Latinx texts from contemporary theorizations of world literature is a sign of their constitutive, though unrecognized presence in that very enterprise. This is to say, then, that "world literature," the "global novel" too, must be conceived and theorized as and on a continuum.

As I hope I have shown, the Latino Continuum, as it proceeds through linguistic and cultural translations, across and beyond the spatial and the temporal, offers new ways of envisioning the Americas, especially in the much-needed corrective of making indigeneity and the African diaspora central and not incidental concerns of the movement of peoples and ideas across and within borders (physical, metaphorical, and disciplinary). This recovery and reconceptualization—from the Latino Continuum—fills past and present lacunae in American, Latin American, Cuban (in this case), and Latinx studies. By recuperating and reclaiming the complex and intertwining histories of the Americas and of Latina/os specifically in that history, we are able to recognize the deep and constitutive imprint that the Latinx experience, their lives and works, had and continue to have across the Americas and the world.

{NOTES}

Introduction

1. Gabriel de la Concepción Valdés (1809–44), whose literary pseudonym was "Plácido," was born free in Havana, Cuba. A well-known poet during his lifetime and a participant in the Del Monte *tertulias*, he was tortured and then executed during the Escalera Conspiracy (1844). Plácido maintained his innocence. In American literature he is best known because of the book *Blake, The Huts of America* (1859), by Martin Delaney, in which Plácido appears. In Latin American and Cuban literature he is considered an eminent Romantic poet and a martyr for the separatist cause, though his involvement in the planned uprising was never proven.

2. Juan Francisco Manzano (1797–1854) was born enslaved. In 1836 his freedom was purchased by the Del Monte group, of which Echeverría was a member. He was accused of taking part in the Escalera Conspiracy and was arrested in 1844, though freed a year later. The Irish abolitionist Richard Robert Madden published a heavily edited English-language version of Manzano's autobiography as *Poems by a Slave in the Island of Cuba* (1840). Willed to Del Monte's heirs, a Spanish version of the autobiography, considered the first and only slave narrative in the Americas, was finally published in Cuba in 1937. Another version—one highly edited by Del Monte's contemporary, Anselmo Suárez y Romero, and then transcribed by Nicolás Azcárate, was found in the Sterling Library at Yale University by Lee Williams in the 1980s. See William Luis (2007) for a detailed history of the production, translation, and transmission history of the work.

3. I addressed this disavowal in "Race and the Critical Trajectory of *Espejo de paciencia* (1608, 1838) in the Nineteenth Century" (2012), in which I argued that the nineteenth-century citations of the poem in literary anthologies, historical works, and novels indexed race and nation-based politics of the time. They also explain why the authenticity of the poem has been questioned (e.g., Poncet y de Cárdenas 1914; Pichardo Moya 1942; Saínz 1982) in the twentieth century, specifically because of the stanzas that relate Golomón's key role in the events portrayed in the poem, and by extension, the importance of enslaved and free Afro Cubans in Cuban history and literature.

4. This article was based on a presentation I gave at the inaugural conference of the Latina/o Studies Association in Chicago, IL (July 17–19, 2014).

5. Alemán has also authored dozens of essays that question the narrative of US exceptionalism in constructing US history and its literature. For example, in "Wars of Rebellion: US Hispanic Writers and Their American Civil Wars" (2013), he argues that "the US Civil War can be viewed as a larger historical event that put into play micro-Wars of identity for US Hispanics precisely because they were already caught between the US, Mexico, Cuba and the Confederacy" (57). In other words, the literature of Latina/os during this time period shows how the Civil War impacted and was impacted by other rebellions in the Americas.

6. In the introduction to *Bridges, Borders, and Breaks: History, Narrative, and Nation in Twentieth-Century Chicana/o Literature* (2016), editors William Orchard and Yolanda Padilla stress the importance of redirecting the narrative analysis of Chicana/o texts to the field of Chicano/o literary studies. I agree with their claim that Chicana/o literary study, or Cuban American literary study in the case of the examples offered in *The Latino Continuum*, should serve to "direct us to new archives in need of investigation, new concepts that require further elaboration, and new methods that not only renovate the study of Chicana/o literature but may also invigorate the intellectual fields that are adjacent to it" (21). I argue that the Latino Continuum, as a methodology, aids in uncovering the inextricable links between different Latina/o groups in the US while simultaneously serving to recover new archives within distinct national-origin literary productions.

7. I must stress here that travelling with these mainly male figures were wives, children, servants, and enslaved workers. Though they are absent from some of the texts I study in this book, the methodological approach that brings to light the existence of a Latino Continuum makes the recovery of these figures and the histories in which they participated possible in the future.

8. For further reading on the use of Latinx see the 2017 special issue of *Cultural Dynamics*, "Theorizing LatinX", edited by Claudia Milian. Also, see Catalina M. De Onís's "What's in an 'x'? An Exchange about the Politics of 'Latinx'" (2017) and the issue of the *Latino Studies* journal dedicated to exploring the concept of "Latinx" (October 2018), with a foreword by editor-in-chief, Lourdes Torres and especially the articles "Latinx Thoughts: Latinidad with an X" by Salvador Vidal-Ortiz and Juliana Martínez and "Crossed Out by LatinX: Gender Neutrality and Genderblind Sexism" by Nicole Trujillo-Pagán.

9. Recent works that address the inextricable ties between Cuban and Cuban American literature and culture include *Impossible Returns: Narratives of the Cuban Diaspora* (2015) by Iraida H. López; Albert Laguna's *Diversión: Play and Popular Culture in Cuban America* (2017); and the anthology *Let's Hear Their Voices: Cuban American Writers of the Second Generation* (2019), edited by Iraida H. López and Eliana Rivero. Earlier iterations that highlight the complexities of these ties include *Life on the Hyphen: The Cuban American Way* (1995) by Gustavo Pérez Firmat and Isabel Álvarez Borland's *Cuban American Literature of Exile: From Person to Persona* (1998). Luis A. Pérez, Jr. catalogs the cultural and historical ties between Cubans in the US and the island as well as between the US and Cuba in *On Becoming Cuba: Identity, Nationality and Culture* (2008). Lisandro Pérez's *Sugar, Cigars, and Revolution: The Making of Nineteenth Century New York* (2018) focuses on the movement of Cubans to New York City and back to the island in the nineteenth century.

Chapter 1

1. Silva Gruesz (2012, 36) engages the "primacy of *first-ness*" in constructing literary histories in her article "Tracking the First Latino Novel: *Un matrimonio como hay muchos* (1849) and Transnational Serial Fiction."

2. Parts of this chapter were previously published as "Father Félix Varela and the Emergence of an Organized Latina/o Minority in Early Nineteenth-Century New York" (157–75) in *The Cambridge History of Latina/o American Literature* (2018), edited by John Morán Gonzalez and Laura Lomas.

3. José Ignacio Rodríguez. *Vida del Presbítero Don Félix Varela*. New York: Imprenta de "O Novo Mundo," 1878. Rodríguez cites a eulogy published in the *New York Freeman's Journal and Catholic Register* 13.38 March 19, 1856.

4. Scholasticism argued that there were God-decreed universal truths that governed the cosmos, a cosmos in which everything was in perfect balance. Catholicism was at the core of structuring and understanding of the universe. While scholasticism in Western Europe was debunked during the Renaissance, the Protestant Reformation, and the Enlightenment, late scholasticism continued to structure philosophical and political arguments in Spain and its colonies into the late eighteenth and early nineteenth centuries. The new science, meanwhile, privileged reason over faith in understanding the cosmos and promoted the scientific method in the "natural sciences," by which they referred to experiments and empirical observation in scientific investigations and philosophical argumentation that served to explain reality.

To understand Varela's position in relation to scholasticism and the new science emerging from Europe, see Travieso (1942); Amigo (1947); Vitier (1970); and Leal (1971). See also Coronado (2013), who addresses the emergence of the new science in the context of early nineteenth-century Latina/o writing.

5. See Hernández's introduction ("Félix Varela: el primer cubano") to the compilation *El Habanero: papel político, científico, y literario* in Varela (1997).

6. José Saco (1797–1879) was one of the anti-annexationist editors of the influential *Revista Bimestre Cubana* (1831–34). Exiled to Spain from 1834 because of his political beliefs—he was a reformist who rejected absolutist monarchical rule—Saco is the well-known author of *Historia de la esclavitud desde los tiempos más remotos hasta nuestros días* (1875–77). Varela and Saco held different views on slavery. Saco advocated for the end of the slave trade and pushed for an increase in white immigration and white labor to the island in order to counter the large number of enslaved persons who were brought to Cuba in the early nineteenth century. Varela wanted to end the slave trade but also called for a gradual abolition coupled with indemnification to slaveholders, citing a fear of slave revolts due to the large number of enslaved people already on the island as the reason for abolition. Both Varela's and Saco's positions regarding the end of the slave trade and slavery are deplorable at best, but Varela, in particular, was at least an early advocate for abolition. A more detailed analysis of Varela's views of slavery and abolition is yet to be completed. However, Luis (1990), Williams (1994), Reid-Vázquez (2011), and Aching (2015) provide introductory explanations and comparisons of these two authors' respective positions.

7. Ravitch (1974), Shea (2004), and Gjerde (2012) offer useful summaries of the New York public-school debates of 1840–42.

8. The McCaddens' biography (1969) provides a positive picture of Archbishop Hughes and his role in the New York public school debates; however, they stress the tactical differences between Hughes and Varela, noting Hughes's polarizing position and Varela's more conciliatory approach (106–10). Meanwhile, Travieso in *Biografía* (1949, 409–33) presents Hughes as an individual who marginalized Varela's more conciliatory strategy altogether.

9. The preface to the Spanish edition of *Jicoténcal* published by Arte Público Press includes an extended introduction by Luis Leal and Rodolfo Cortina (1995) regarding the authorship of the novel. However, Leal first published his findings in the academic journal *Revista Iberoamericana* 25.4 (1960): 9–31.

10. All translations are mine.

11. The latest edition of *The Norton Anthology of American Literature* (Levine 2017), for example, does not include Latina/o writing in Volume B, in its nineteenth-century (1820–65) compilation.

12. For example, Varela speaks to the dangers of expansionism by any invasion (US, Mexican, or Colombian) of the island in *El Habanero* in his article "Paralelo entre la revolución que puede formarse en la isla de Cuba por sus mismos habitantes y la que se formará por la invasión de tropas extranjeras." He concludes: "En una palabra: todas las ventajas económicas y políticas están en favor de la revolución echa exclusivamente por los de casa, y hacen que deba preferirse a la que pueda practicarse por el auxilio extranjero" (Varela 1997, 201) (In a word: all of the economic and political benefits favor a revolution made exclusively at home, and make it so it is to be preferred to the one that might occur with foreign help.) For a detailed analysis of Martí and his writings as those of "migrant Latina/os", see Laura Lomas (2009) foundational study *Translating Empire: José Martí, Migrant Latino Subjects and American Modernities.*

13. Two scholars that have given attention to *Jicoténcal* are Silva Gruesz (2001) and Brickhouse (2004). While they do not speak in detail to the wider significance of the figure of Varela in Latina/o literature and history, their books are essential reading for those interested in Latinx studies from a hemispheric perspective. Lazo (2020) has provided the most comprehensive reading of Varela's US works and their significance in *Letters from Filadelfia*. However, he does not believe that Varela was the author of *Jicoténcal* because Varela had written in *El Habanero* against the secrecy practiced by Cuban Masonic groups when challenging colonial rule (184).

14. Tyler Anbinder's book titled *Five Points: The 19ᵗʰ-Century New York City Neighborhood That Invented Tap Dance, Stole Elections, and Became the World's Most Notorious Slum* (2001) concentrates on this neighborhood and its importance for Irish-American and US history. Yet Varela is absent from his book.

15. These biographical details and many others are compiled from Varela's three book-length biographies (Rodríguez 1878, Travieso 1949, and McCadden and McCadden 1969), as well as the introduction of *Letters to Elpidio* by Felipe Estévez (Varela 1989). The last-mentioned is the first English translation of *Cartas* in its entirety.

16. *Impiedad* (volume 1) of *Cartas a Elpidio* was also published in Madrid in 1836. In the twentieth century, *Impiedad* and *Superstición* were published in Cuba in 1944. In 2001, *Cartas a Elpidio* (both *Impiedad* and *Superstición*) was included in volume 3 of Varela's complete works, published by the University of Havana and edited by Eduardo Torres-Cuevas et al.

17. His presentation to the Spanish Cortes (1822–23), but primarily his articles in *El Habanero*, speak to his call for Spanish American and Cuban independence.

18. Oxx (2013) dedicates an entire chapter to the Ursuline Convent burning and cites primary sources that signal the rise of nativism in the US in its religious context in the early nineteenth century. Franchot (1994) provides a detailed account of the newspaper coverage of the arson case as well as the court proceedings surrounding the case. Her endnotes (398–401) are particularly useful for those wishing to read primary sources related to this event. Billington (1938) also offers a useful summary from a religious perspective.

19. Along with Oxx (2013) and Franchot (1994), see Hatch (1989) and Fessenden (2007) for a full discussion of disestablishment and the secularization of religion in the nineteenth century.

20. This last edit, a comment on human nature, speaks directly to Varela's concerns subsequently expressed in *Cartas a Elpidio*, which he will draft almost a decade later. In *Manual* he warns Spanish Americans, as well as those in the US who were long-time residents and even US citizens, that accepting American democracy as the ideal model for political governance was precarious in nature, since the best model lay not in what the US had constructed but in what the new Spanish American Republics could construct based on their own colonial histories, their emerging political presents, and their many hopes for representative governance in the future.

21. Varela's first known writing on slavery appeared in 1823. He prepared a speech on the topic to be presented to the Cortes, along with a detailed project for abolition. The presentation called for slow abolition for enslaved persons with financial compensation for slaveholders: "Proyecto y memoria para la extinción de la esclavitud en la isla de Cuba," (Varela 2001, 2: 113–19), in a limited manner, humanized enslaved individuals, reminding those listening to his speech that their legally sanctioned status is what has led to their "degraded state"; reminding the Cortes and slaveholders that many of those who were enslaved were in fact fathered by their owners, and that while many enslaved persons were brought directly from Africa, there were now many who were "habaneros" or those born on the island and therefore "criollos de este país", or people born in this country, i.e., Spain. Varela advocated for slow abolition with indemnification of slave owners. In doing so, Varela simultaneously extended by analogy the concept of slavery to the colonization of Cuba by Spain.

And yet, after living in the US for over a decade, Varela's views of slavery in Cuba shifts. In an 1834 letter to González del Valle, one of his students, he warns that due to the influence of the planter class in Cuba abolition was only possible in an undetermined future. The importance of this letter, which was not circulated until 1935, has yet to be studied at length. Only Piqueras (2007) gives it a detailed reading.

22. For more information on Irish Americans and their perspectives on slavery during the nineteenth century, see Ignatiev (1995); Roediger (1991); and Murphy (2010).

23. Lisandro Pérez refers to many of these figures in *Sugar, Cigars, and Revolution: The Making of Cuban New York* (2018).

24. Silva Gruesz (2001) argues for the network of trans-American texts and lives that are part of the Latina/o experience. Brickhouse (2004) addresses the trans-American relations of which Latina/o and US writers were a part.

Chapter 2

1. Other works by these scholars that inform my analysis include Bassnett (1980, 2014); Gentzler (2017); Lefevere (1992, 2016); and Venutti (1998, 2000).

2. US citizens owned businesses, coffee plantations and sugar mills in the region (Ponte Domínguez 1959). The reason for this phenomenon is that Matanzas was at the heart of sugar production and slavery in Cuba. It was also a transportation hub: sugar and other goods were brought to Matanzas by rail and were shipped out of the country through the port of Matanzas. This also led to US tourism to the region: US nationals could travel easily to Matanzas, arriving in Havana and then taking a ferry to the area. Two critical editions speak directly of the US presence in Matanzas in the mid-nineteenth century: *Impressions of Cuba in the Nineteenth Century: The Diary of Joseph J. Dimock* [1859], edited by

Luis A. Pérez (1998) and *A Bristol, Rhode Island and Matanzas, Cuba, Slavery Connection: The Diary of George Howe* [1832–35], edited by Rafael Ocasio (2019). Stephen Chambers writes about the early alliance between Cuban and US slavery in *No God but Gain: The Untold Story of Cuban Slavery, the Monroe Doctrine and the Making of the United States* (2015). An earlier resource is Laird Bergard's *Cuban Rural Society in the Nineteenth Century: The Social and Economic History of Monoculture in Matanzas* (1990).

3. *Costumbrismo* was a literary genre popular in Cuba in the 1840s and 1850s. It emphasized the creation of picturesque characters and landscapes that reflected and embodied national types. A well-known book of the time, *Los cubanos pintados por si mismos* (1852), was modeled on the Spanish book *Los españoles pintados por si mismos* (1843–44). *Costumbrismo* is said to have developed from the "sketch" literary portraits of late eighteenth-century England, then moving to France, and finally arriving in Spain in the 1820s, before moving to the Spanish Americas (Garcha 2012; Pérez Salas 2005; Moriuchi 2018; Ucelay Da Cal 1951). Some literary historians have placed the origins of Spanish *costumbrismo* in seventeenth-century Spain (Soria Ortega 1949). As in Cuba, an important contemporaneous and representative work in Mexico was *Los mexicanos pintados por si mismos* (1854–55). Scholarly works that study Cuban *costumbrismo* include Salvador Bueno (1985) and Rafael Ocasio (2012). In Latinx studies, John Alba Cutler is the only scholar to address this genre in "Toward a Reading of Nineteenth-Century Latina/o Short Fiction" (2016). Since these pieces were published in newspapers of the era, many of which are found in the archive only as fragments, he refers to them as existing in *fugitive archives*. Ultimately, he links US modernism to Latin American *modernismo*, arguing that a study of nineteenth-century Latina/o short fiction reveals that the latter preceded and made possible the former: "This more comprehensive history would need to acknowledge that in the United States *modernismo* precedes modernism, and that Latino/a writers were interested in many of the same thematic and formal innovations that now-canonical U.S. writers would take up a generation later" (Cutler 2016, 141).

4. Lazo (2005, 124–29) provides a hemispheric picture of Tolón's person and writings. He clarifies that only part 1 of *Lola Guara* was every published and that part 2 was advertised as forthcoming in *La Verdad* (216, no.82). The second part of *Lola Guara* may have been written in the US, since the editors (Joaquín Lorenzo Luaces and José Fornaris) of *La Piragua*, a journal in Matanzas (1856–57), provide a biography of Tolón, noting that Tolón is working on the second volume (78–9). Tolón was living in the US at the time.

5. Specifically, Tolón was implicated in the *Mina de la Rosa Cubana* uprising, a filibustering attempt to annex Cuba to the United States. The Mina de las Rosa Cubana was an annexationist conspiracy planned for 1848 in which 5,000 veterans from the US-Mexico War of 1846–48, headed by William J. Worth, would take over the island. Narciso López and José Ignaza were the Cuban leaders on the island, while the Consejo Cubano in New York led the organizing and financial efforts. US President James Polk was in negotiations to buy Cuba from Spain. When he heard of the conspiracy, he informed the US consul in Havana, who then informed the Spanish government on the island. They in turn suppressed the conspiracy and executed or exiled its organizers and supporters.

6. According to Linda S. Hudson, Jane McManus actually coins the term, although it has been attributed to O'Sullivan. See *Mistress of Manifest Destiny: A Biography of Jane Cazneau McManus, 1807–1878* (2001). McManus used the pseudonym "Cora Montgomery" when she edited the English-language edition of the annexationist newspaper *La Verdad*. Tolón edited the Spanish edition from 1848 to 1852.

7. These dates are based on the introductory chapter of Tolón's collected works titled *Miguel Teurbe Tolón. Poesía reunida*, compiled and edited by Diego Ropero-Regidor (Tolón 2004).

8. Jesse Alemán (2012) addresses these types of elisions in US history that are then recovered by Latinx writings. Specifically, he presents *Xicoténcatl* as a counternarrative:

> But we can also read this coalition [across indigenous states in *Xicoténcatl*] as an allegory of the text's anonymous authorship and the transnational possibilities it raises as a hispanophone text penned and published in the United States but linked to the independence movements in Cuba and Mexico. If Varela penned the text, for instance, then the narrative links Cuba's fledgling independence movements in the 1820s and 1830s to Mexico's post-independence turmoil and sees them as equally susceptible to the duplicity of the United States as a model republic and emergent empire.
>
> (Alemán 2012, 91)

9. Textbook publishing was a thriving industry in the 1830s and 1840s, and historical maps, Willard's specialty, paralleled this boom. Inexpensive technologies allowed printers to incorporate maps in books to an unprecedented degree, the inclusion of which appealed to mass audiences and specialists alike. The "spread of education" also led to their increasing popularity (Schulten 2012, 11). This, in turn, allowed for Willard's innovative use of historical maps to create a narrative of a divinely ordained past and future for the US.

10. Willard's textbooks continued to sell well in the South during the Civil War and up to the time of her death in 1870. According to Joyce (2015), Southerners called for the production of their own versions of American history both in the antebellum period and during the Civil War. To some degree, a status quo in the textbook trade was preserved by the economic circumstances of the market, for the textbook trade was firmly established in the Northeast, as was teacher training. In addition, the Civil War and its aftermath did not severely impact the textbook market, since books in use in the South were produced in the North, where the means of production were not affected directly by the war. Some authors did write American histories from a Southern perspective: Martin Kerney's *Catechism of the History of the United States* (1850), for example; or Bartholomew R. Carroll's *Catechism of United States History* (1858); or William Gilmore Simms's *History of South Carolina…Designed for the Instruction of the Young* (1840). Sales of textbooks by the likes of Willard and A. H. Grimshaw, the latter the son of the well-known historian of the period William Grimshaw, were not affected, however. While William Grimshaw wrote acerbically against slavery, his son used a more conciliatory tone toward the South and about the issue of slavery than his father, and he "ended the narrative with the events of the Mexican War in order to [in A.H. Grimshaw's own words] 'avoid the excitement of political imputations, or the discussion of recent events… which appear unadvisable in a work designed peculiarly for the instruction of youth'" (Joyce 2015, 240). Joyce suggests that:

> the lessons that students were to learn from these and other events was that the subsequent American Union had persevered through the spirit of conciliation and compromise. The school histories . . . now stressed compromise as a key theme in the history of the United States (as opposed to the story of America).
>
> (Joyce 2015, 244)

Like A. H. Grimshaw's, Willard's histories also were constructed as narratives of compromise. And as Joyce (2015, 244) argues—and I agree with him—the enduring popularity of her textbooks in the South had as much to do with the fact that they did not critically address the question of slavery as with the fact that textbook production was historically tied geographically to the Northeast.

11. Paula Rebert in *La Gran Línea* (2001) provides a detailed accounting of the erasure of Native Americans and Mexican nationals from both sides of the US-Mexico border based on the differences between the surveys completed by the US and Mexico when mapping the border throughout the nineteenth century. Rachel St. John (2011) in *Line in the Sand* likewise notes this difference, and links it to the earlier and contested border mapping originating with the Adams-Onís treaty of 1819.

12. While it was first published in her *History of the United States or Republic of America* in the 1850 edition, it was not included in the *Abridged History* until 1860. It is also in that edition of the *Abridged History* that she included a description of her plans for bringing enslaved Africans in the US South to the Northeast, which signals implicitly the role of slave labor in the construction of the US nation.

13. As in what was constructed with the use of a preface to frame the history of Native Americans in the US in her earlier history, whereby they were excluded from that history, Willard initially depicts California and the US Southwest as a space separate from US history in *Last Leaves*. It is only when immigrants occupy that space that the Southwest becomes part of the US imaginary. The preface speaks of the necessity of historical truth by citing Washington Irving, from an anecdotal conversation she had had with him. Supposedly, Irving said, "Pure truth is as difficult to be obtained as pure water; though clear in appearance, it is ever found by the chemist to contain extraneous substances" (Willard 1849, 3). By citing this anecdote Willard seeks to garner validity for her work, as it emphasizes her close relationship with Irving, who, along with George Bancroft and W. H. Prescott, was considered one of the most prominent of historians of the US and the Americas in her day. She concludes the short preface by noting that "My object is not, however, to glorify individuals; but so to present my country's history, both to her friends and her foes, that it shall make its proper impression" (Willard 1849, 4). Earlier in the preface she notes that her text possibly contains errors—here she may be addressing the likes of Marcius Willson, whom she publicly declaimed for plagiarism after he published a scathing attack on her histories, listing the errors he found within them. She continues; "But whenever an error is found, of whatever nature, and whether pointed out by a friend to serve, or a foe to injure, that error will be corrected as soon as discovered" (Willard 1849, 4). This also adds the sense that she is writing as history is unfolding, and so it speaks to the Journalistic nature of this part of her work.

14. *Last Leaves* concludes with ten pages of advertisements for books. According to Joyce (2015, 45–55) these books were marketed to the West Coast, and we can imagine the didactic nature of the works in relation to establishing the idea of an American Republic imaginary now reaching across the continent.

15. In the preface to her *Abridged History* (as of 1844) she explains that the volume is meant as a textbook in which time and space come together visually in order to aid memory and recall. Yet it has another purpose: "We have, indeed, been desirous to cultivate the memory, the intellect, and the taste. But much more anxious have we been to sow the seeds of virtue" (Willard 1844, iv). With this goal as a guide Willard explains that her textbook offers narrative details regarding virtuous acts, but will only speak of the effects of bad acts. She wished to combat those "who rashly speak, as if in despair of the fortunes of our republic; because, say they, political virtue has declined" (Willard 1844, iv). Her answer to their concern is to offer a text that would "infuse patriotism into the breasts of the coming

generation." And, ultimately, she hoped her book would lead "our future citizens, to become its enlightened and judicious supporters" (Willard 1844, vi).

16. In *Fugitives, Smugglers, and Thieves: Piracy and Personhood in American Literature*, Sharada Balachandran Orihuela (2018) links citizenship and the land rights of *californios*, rightly proposing that the latter marked access to the full rights of the former, and not the other way around, as it has been understood to date. She writes: "Because of the foundational ties between citizenship and property...dispossessing Mexicans of their land is the foundation for dispossession of citizenship, rather than the other way around" (Orihuela 2018, 134). This important book astutely brings together, through the lens of property and ownership, such events as *californio* dispossession and the Civil War, that is, the experience of Mexican Americans with previously enslaved African Americans.

17. While Tolón claims to render the 1850 edition, the format he generally follows is that of the *Abridged History* that Emma Willard published in 1852, since the *Compendio* incorporates California within a chapter proper of the narrative—as it is found in the 1852 edition—instead of including it as an epilogue to the text, as is found in the 1850 edition.

18. The link between the creation of the Texas Rangers and the legacy of Spanish *cazadores* (light infantry) in the region has yet to be made by scholars. One must recall that *cazadores* may also refer to *voluntarios* or volunteer militiamen who were not part of the military but simply recruited to deal with a given "political" problem. On the military nature of *cazadores*, see the entry "cazadores" in Mellado (1851, 758–66). Conde de Clonard (1851, 70) refers to the 1843 deployment of *cazadores* in Matanzas, Cuba, to intervene in the Escalera Conspiracy.

19. It is important to note here that an earlier book of Willard's, titled *Universal Geography*, which she co-wrote with the cartographer William Woodbridge, was strongly criticized by New York Catholics for its blatant anti-Catholicism.

20. Regardless of the influence of his translation work on his political views, there is still a good chance that Tolón would have turned against Cuban annexation, as many of his Cuban cohorts did. But translating Willard's nearly contemporaneous historical account with all of its biases must have given him further pause when considering annexation for Cuba.

21. The US-Mexico War was the first major war in which US soldiers fought on foreign territory, apart, of course, from the many battles waged against Native Americans on Native American lands.

Chapter 3

1. This is the title given to the work by Thomas Buckingham Smith (1810–71) in 1863. The original title and the one recognized by Mexican historiographers is *Descripción geográfica, natural y curiosa de la Provincia de Sonora por un amigo del Servicio de Dios y del Rey Nuestro Señor año 1764*.

2. One is held at the Huntington Library in San Marino, California (Nentvig 1762); two are held at the *Archivo General de la Nación* in Mexico City (Nentvig 1764a); and the fourth is held in Madrid at the *Real Academia de la Historia* (Nentvig 1764b). The Spanish copy is thought to be the earliest copy of the work, according to Nentvig (1980), and it is the one from which Smith published the first US edition.

3. Mary Lindsay Van Tine in "Translated Conquest: Archives, History and Territory in Hemispheric Literatures, 1823–1854" (2016) provides the most extensive account of the

relationships between different antiquarians and historians in the US and Mexico during this time period.

4. Smith was also a corresponding member of the New York Historical Society, the American Ethnological Society, and the New England Historical-Genealogical Society.

5. A memoir of Smith written by John Gilmary Shea, "the father of American Catholic History," and appearing in an 1871 publication of Smith's English translation of the *Narrativa de Alvar Núñez Cabeza de Vaca* [1542, 1851] notes that his sister Hannah, who was also born in Florida, was referred to as Anita, during her lifetime. This anecdote signals how the Spanish language and the experience of living in Florida and Mexico may have impacted Smith's interest in indigenous languages and the legacy of Spanish culture in what became part of the US, first with Florida and then the US Southwest with the Treaty of Guadalupe Hidalgo. Van Tine (2016) provides a detailed account of how Smith's translation of Cabeza de Vaca is related to the contested boundary between the US and Mexico after the US-Mexico War. Kagan (2019) situates Smith as an early proponent of the importance of Floridian history for US history. Smith was one of the founders of the Historical Society of Florida (1856).

6. The publication of the first English translation of Cabeza de Vaca's manuscript in particular cannot be brushed aside as a simple happenstance mirroring Smith's distinct intellectual curiosity. Instead, it must be understood as a pointed political and cultural intervention, for three reasons.

First, the territories that Cabeza de Vaca's narrative (the Spanish title of which was *Narrativa de Alvar Núñez Cabeza de Vaca*, hereafter referred to as the *Narrative*) covers were newly acquired ones that were of interest to general readers and political decision-makers alike: Cabeza de Vaca traveled for eight years from Florida to Mexico, gathering the local fauna and flora of the area while documenting the lives and customs of the different populations that inhabited it at the time.

Second, given the scope and nature of the *Narrative*, the act of translation served to bring these Spanish territories and their legacy into the US imaginary as part and parcel of the United States. Indeed, the introduction to the first publication of the translation by George W. Riggs, Jr. says as much:

> This account of one of the earliest explorations of territory within the limits of the United States, and of its inhabitants, has been deemed worthy of selection from the works of America of the sixteenth century, for presentation in this form, to a few personal friends, whose tastes and whose studies induce them to examine the history of our country from the beginning.   (Smith 1851, n.p.)

(George W. Riggs, Jr. was a member of the banking firm Corcoran and Riggs. This firm's investment in the US-Mexico War was lucrative (Riggs Family Papers, Library of Congress). Thus, we can better understand his interest in translating the work. While it may be in part due to his conversion to Catholicism and his interest in the Spanish and Catholic history of these territories, the translation simultaneously serves as a potential guide for colonizing and settling the area and its peoples.)

Simply, the text itself, through its appearance in English and the act of translation by such a figure as Smith, serves to interpellate the Florida Territory and the US Southwest into the US imaginary as conquered spaces. Smith too notes as much, when, at the end of the translation, he clarifies that while Cabeza de Vaca's text is dated, the information he shared about the peoples in the area remained accurate:

In the Second part of De Bry's Voyages and Discoveries, there are pictures descriptive of the Indians and their customs, such as were observed by the French chiefly about the entrance of the Saint John's River, and not long after the middle of the sixteenth century, which may be found interesting to examine in connection with this account. The volume of Bernard Romans, "A Concise History of East and West Florida," Printed in 1775 ... shows the customs and character of the tribes along the Gulf coast, seventy-five years ago, to have differed but little from those that Cabeza had before described.

(Smith 1851, 126)

Third, the *Narrative*, whose publication dates to 1542 (though the events in the narrative are from 1528–1536), is considered by scholars as one of the foundational texts for establishing a Latina/o literary genealogical tradition (Leal 1973; Novoa 1993), because Cabeza de Vaca's account is "marked forever by...his American alterability," i.e., his being Spanish, but "distinguished...from other Spaniards" by his experience and life among the many indigenous peoples he met in his travels from Florida, through Texas, and then to Mexico City (Novoa 1993, 16). Indeed, according to Novoa, Cabeza de Vaca's experience is comparable to those of contemporary Chicanos, who must negotiate their Mexican and US identities in a similar fashion to Cabeza de Vaca with his Spanish and indigenous identities:

There is, however, vacillation...as to the proper place under which the immigrants fall...There is an apparent surface acceptance as long as the immigrants maintain a discreet distance and a respect for native institutions. And, of course, there is an insistence on categorizing us as a floating population—always the foreigners—while in Mexico they view us as *descastados*, too assimilated to the "American way of Life."

(Novoa 1993, 22)

He concludes: "the most disturbing thing about Alvar Núñez Cabaza de Vaca and his descendants is that they reveal in their alterity the inherent instability of an identity system [whether US American or Mexican], and they make out of it a virtue and a source of great pride" (Novoa 1993, 22).

7. In addition, that *Rudo Ensayo* was produced by Joel Munsell, a well-known printer in Albany, New York and a key member of the American Antiquarian Society, signals the importance of the text for delineating a "[US] history to compare to that of Europe's nations" (Gura 2012, 21–2), one of the chief missions of the Society. As Phillip Gura argues in *The American Antiquarian Society, 1812–2012: A Bicentennial History* (2012), in order to establish this history, the society understood their work as necessarily including the study of "early European settlements on the continent, meaning Spanish, French, Dutch, Portuguese, Danish and Swedish as well as English" and the "continent's civil antiquities," i.e., "the establishment and growth of European society in the New World" (Gura 2012, 22). Both were seen as integral to the historical trajectory of the young nation.

8. All translations of *Rudo Ensayo* are by Eusebio Guiteras.

9. The editor of the volume of the *Records of the American Catholic Historical Society* in which *Rudo Ensayo* appears, Lawrence F. Flick, placed the text geographically in the US imaginary of the 1890s, describing it as "an early historical and descriptive account of that portion of Mexico, which lies North of the Yaqui River, and West of the Sierra Madre Mounts, and that part of the present territory of Arizona which lies West and South of the Gila River" (Flick 1894b, 109). He also places Nentvig in contemporaneous US history and in Catholic history more generally:

The territory included in the description was casually visited by Catholic missionaries as early as 1548, and was brought under the dominion of the Cross as early as 1690...the description was written by a Jesuit Father, who had labored in the district, and who had traveled over it probably in the capacity of Provincial. It is dated 1763, and while it deals chiefly with the country and Indians as they were at that time, it also gives much interesting information of an earlier date.   (Flick 1894b, 109)

While this introduction was written after Guiteras's death, it speaks directly to the purpose of the piece: to demonstrate the historical importance of Catholic missionaries to the history of the US, and, as I will soon argue, their continued importance to American history.

10. After the US Civil War ended various Apache groups, along with Navajos, Tontos, and Yamarais, found themselves on the verge of extinction not only due to the corruption and negligence of the Bureau of Indian Affairs and the effects of such congressional legislation as the Dawes Act of 1887 and the Indian Appropriation Act of 1896, but also as a result of the attacks by settlers and the US military as expansion into Apache reservations brought with it violent clashes between these groups. By the time Guiteras began his translation, the Apache were considered "pacified", but their integration into US society was still to be accomplished.

11. In Cuba, annexationists and reformers had become disillusioned with the church. After the exile of Father Félix Varela and the death of Bishop Juan José Díaz de Espada y Landa, the church leadership in Rome in collaboration with the Spanish monarchy and Cuba's governors sent pro-Spanish priests to the island in order to curb revolution. This led Cubans to leave Catholicism altogether, a step against which Félix Varela warned in *Cartas a Elpidio* (Varela 1944). Guiteras's separation from the church in Cuba, followed by his reconciliation in a US context, away from the complications of Cuban politics, speaks to this historical reality.

12. Important in this historical moment are the surrender of Geronimo and the forced migration of the Apache to reservations. While the Apache Wars continued until 1924, when Native Americans were given the right to vote, Americans read daily accounts of their so-called savagery and the need to "pacify" and, most of all, educate them.

13. Interestingly, Nolan devotes an entire paragraph detailing the conversion of the son of Leland Stanford to Catholicism. He writes:

Father Casanova informed us that young Leland Stanford was received into the Catholic Church in Florence, three months before his death. Whether the good Father's assertion was founded on mere hearsay or on more reliable testimony, we have not been able to ascertain. The Late Senator Stanford and his wife always manifested a warm interest in the church during their frequent visits to the Hotel Del Monte and Father Casanova referred gratefully to the then recent gift by Mrs. Stanford of a valuable carpet for the sanctuary.   (Nolan 1894, 94)

Of importance is his aligning Stanford, as a senator, with the Catholic presence in the West and in particular with his contributions to the education of Americans, since immediately following the above paragraph, Nolan writes:

Remarking on the religious, not to say Catholic character of the pictures in the chapel of the University, which now did not seem so strange, we were informed that they had all been selected by the boy himself and were hung there in compliance with what his parents knew would have been his wish.   (Nolan 1894, 94)

14. A microcosm of the experience of Cubans in the US is presented by Lisandro Pérez (2018) in his *Sugar, Cigars and Revolution: The Making of Cuban New York*.

15. An extensive and much-needed biography of Guiteras does not exist, and much of Guiteras's life in the US is yet to be recovered. Of particular interest would be a deeper knowledge of his political views in these decades, which might be accessed through his personal correspondence. As Aguilera Manzano notes in his introduction to Guiteras's 1842–45 travel diary, "Hopefully in the future all of the correspondence that Eusebio Guiteras maintained with all of the intellectuals of his time and that remains unedited will be published" (Aguilera Manzano 2010, 42).

Presently, however, much can nevertheless be known of Guiteras's life, all that is known being culled from three texts that speak in limited detail: Laura Guiteras's previously mentioned "Brief Sketch of the Life of Eusebio Guiteras" which was published in the US in the *Records* in 1894; Ramón Meza y Súarez Inclán's *Eusebio Guiteras: Estudio biográfico*, published in Cuba in 1908; and, most recently, the introduction by the scholar José María Aguilera Manzano to Guiteras's travel diaries from 1842–45. The transcription of the diaries is titled *El pensamiento liberal cubano a través del diario de viaje de Euesbio Guiteras Font* (2010). That Guiteras and his brothers chose not to return to Cuba after the Ten Years' War may signal his politics, suggesting that he was most likely a separatist. His biographers do not place him clearly in any political camp. Instead, scholars tend to concentrate on Guiteras's role as an educator and on the impact of his Spanish-language readers on Cubans and on the construction of a Cuban national identity in the nineteenth century. It is only Aguilera Manzano in his introduction to *Pensamiento liberal* who explains that "Eusebio Guiteras was a moderate liberal autonomist who believed in maintaining the island of Cuba within the Spanish state, but with its own autonomous government that would permit the oligarchy of the island to preside over local issues. But this line of thinking was repressed by the centralized government" (Aguilera Manzano 2010, 12). Aguilera Manzano's introduction, nevertheless, centers exclusively on the liberal politics of Guiteras during the 1840s, the dates of his travels in the US, Europe, and the Middle East. He does not address Guiteras's political beliefs in the 1870s and 1880s, after the outbreak of the Ten Years' Wars and its subsequent failure. Laura Guiteras in her "Brief Sketch" (1894, 107) stressed that "any one who had the happiness of knowing my uncle, must be aware how opposed to his views was anything like revolt against the exisiting authorities, whatever they might be" [*sic*].

16. In the first chapters he notes that he first arrived in New York in September. From his mentioning, as he there does, of the still present aftereffects there of the Civil War on the United States (Guiteras n.d., 20), the reader can infer that he begins his narrative with a memory from 1869. Yet his experiences as recounted therein bring him at least to 1886, because he refers, among other events, to the construction of the Brooklyn Bridge, completed in 1883 (Guiteras n.d., 16–17), to observations about the twenty-four "urban trains" operating in New York in 1885, and to his personal reflections on the Statue of Liberty, completed in 1886 (Guiteras n.d., 142).

17. *Un invierno en Nueva York*, which was published in Barcelona by Gorgas y Compañia is undated. Amores (2015, 20) notes that it is registered in La Biblioteca Nacional as published in 1888.

18. For details about the differences between the two autonomist positions, see Rafael Rojas (2013).

19. Immediately following this observation about the impact of the history of slavery and skin color on race relations in the US, Guiteras narrates his experience in the smoking salon of the steamer Providence, in which he was travelling in order to visit Bristol. He notes that there were two seats in the room, and they were occupied by "un mulato joven y de buen talle. Vestía con elegancia, y llevaba el sombrero un tanto inclinado hacia la oreja izquierda: entre los labios, cubiertos de un poblado bigote, saboreaba un cigarro" (Guiteras n.d., 26) (a young mulatto, of good figure. Dressed elegantly, he wore a hat slightly inclined toward his left ear: between his lips, covered by a bushy mustache, he enjoyed a cigar.) In comparison, the second seat was taken by a small "blanco" (white man) who was "mal vestido y hasta un si es no es sucio" (Guiteras n.d., 26) (poorly dressed and even dirty) and smoking a pipe. Guiteras condemns the use of the pipe, since he prefers Cuban cigars that do not make others nauseous. It is of note that Guiteras and "un caballero de buen porte, que tal vez era senador de Massachusetts ó gobernador de Maine" (Guiteras n.d., 26) (a gentlemen of good appearance, he may have been a senator from Massachusetts or a governor from Maine) had to wait until the seats were unoccupied to be able to sit down and enjoy their cigars. Guiteras is here providing a lesson to his Cuban reader that race and class should not matter and that the cultured mulatto is to be preferred to the small, poorly dressed, and dirty white man.

20. More study is necessary to understand the role of Ewer in this narrative. It is of interest that he was born in Nantucket, Massachusetts, but migrated to California in 1849 as an agent of the Pacific Company. He was unwilling to join his father, who was participating in the Gold Rush, so he stayed in San Francisco, becoming a journalist. He is credited with publishing the first monthly literary journal in California, *The Pioneer*. In 1858 he is confirmed as an Episcopalian minister and leads Grace Church until 1860, when he returns east and settles in New York City. In relation to Guiteras's interest in education, Ewer was one of the board members in San Francisco who ensured the displacement of Catholics from the school board and that public funds would not be divided between Catholic and Protestant schools but instead fall under the purview of the school board, which in turn defunded Catholic education.

21. Some critics argue that the tradition can be traced into the twentieth century through the vanguard, regional novels popular in Latin America in the 1920s and 1930s.

22. Guiteras was most likely a sensualist, according to Aguilera Manzano (2012, 28–9). Sensualism was a popular Western European philosophical tradition in the early nineteenth century. It was introduced into Cuba by José Agustín Caballero (1762–1835) and his student Félix Varela (1788–1853). Guiteras was influenced by Varela, and he must have read Abbé de Condillac and particularly Antoine Destutt de Tracy, philosophers Varela studied and taught.

Chapter 4

1. Parts of this chapter were previously published as "The Black Lector and Martín Morúa Delgado's *Sofía* (1896) and *La familia Unzúazu* (1901)" in *Latino Studies* 13.1 (2015): 113–30.

2. I will not offer a detailed accounting of the many critical works published on "Nuestra América" in multiple countries and languages. The 1891 essay, which appeared in New York in the *Revista Ilustrada* and in *El Partido Liberal* in Mexico, argues for the necessity of standing up to US imperialism by returning to the cultural roots of Latin America—its indigenous communities. In this essay, Martí encourages Latin American intellectuals to

distance themselves from foreign and European models and instead return to their indigenous roots in order to come together to face US expansionism and neocolonialism. Fernández Retamar (1979), Belnap and Fernández (1998), and Rojas (2000) are some of the many examples of studies that critically engage "Nuestra América" and its significance for hemispheric studies.

3. Biographies of Martí are many. Early biographies include Jorge Mañach (1932), who referred to him as El Apostol (the apostle), Gonzalo Quesada y Miranda (1940), Felix Lisazo (1940), and Márquez Sterling (1942).

4. For a detailed study of the role of Serra and Figueroa in *Patria*, see Hoffnung-Garskof's (2019) *Racial Migrations: New York City and the Revolutionary Politics of the Spanish Caribbean*. Nicolas Kanellos (2016) writes about the place of Afro Caribbean writers in Latina/o history and specifically Sotero Figueroa in "Sotero Figueroa: Writing Afro Caribbeans into History in the Late Nineteenth Century". In *Unbecoming Blackness: The Diaspora Cultures of Afro-Cuban America*, Antonio López (2012) uncovers the important role of Afro Latina/o literature and performance in constructing a transnational *cubanidad*. His groundbreaking monograph links Afro-diasporic Cuban American and Afro Latina/o cultures, arguing for their indispensability for thinking through race not only in Cuba/US relations but in the hemisphere more broadly. Nancy Mirabal (2017) has also addressed the ties between Afro Cuban, Afro Latina/os, and African Americans in *Suspect Freedoms: The Racial and Sexual Politics of Cubanidad in New York, 1823–1957*. More recently, Monika Gosín (2019) focuses on the tensions and coalitions between African Americans, Cubans, and Afro Cubans through racial politics in Miami in *The Politics of Racial Division: Interethnic Struggles for Legitimacy in Multicultural Miami*.

5. A now well-established critical tradition exists that recognizes Martí as one of the founders of *modernismo*. Iván Schulman has studied the implications of this identification. His most cited works on the topic are *Génesis del modernismo* (1966) and *Martí, Darío y el modernismo* (1969).

6. Allen (2018) lists four books translated by Martí for Appleton & Co: *Greek Antiquities* by J. P. Mahaffy; *Roman Antiquities* by A. S. Wilkins; *Notions of Logic* by W. Stanley Jevon; and *Called Back* by Hugh Conway (1883). Allen also mentions a recent discovery by Jorge Camacho—a 300-page transcript of a brief submitted to then US President Grover Cleveland regarding an arbitration issue in Latin America. It is titled *Argument for the Argentine Republic in regard to the Territory of Misiones* (1894).

7. Martí was so invested in translation that in a letter dated April 9, 1895, just over a month before his death, he offered an entire program to María Mantilla, who historians believe may have been his daughter from an extramarital affair.

8. See Rotker (1992), (2000); Allen (2002); Fernández Retamar and Rodríguez (2003); Fountain (2003); and Fountain (2014).

9. Some of the best-known book-length texts on Martí's translation practice include Cuesta (1996), Arencibia Rodríguez (2000), and Lomas (2009). These authors dedicate some of their study to *Ramona* but a longer in-depth analysis is still lacking.

10. George Ticknor (1791–1871) was a professor at Harvard who published a three-volume *History of Spanish Literature* in 1849, which was based on lectures he gave at Harvard in the 1820s. For a study of Martí's critique of historiography produced in the US, see Rojas (2018).

11. The plot line of *Ramona* involves Ramona, the orphaned daughter of a Scotsman and a Native American woman, who is taken in by the *californio* Señora Romero, who does not love her. Ramona falls in love with Alessandro, a Native American man who comes to work

on Señora Moreno's ranch. The two elope, and the novel details the hardships they endure at the hands of ruthless US settlers and as a result of US policy toward Native Americans and the land rights of *californios*. Ultimately, Alessandro loses his mind and is killed by a settler. Ramona returns to the Morenos' ranch and marries their son Felipe. The two move to Mexico with Ramona's and Alessandro's surviving daughter, aptly named Ramona.

12. A critical edition of José Martí's translation of *Ramona* was published by Jonathan Alcántar and Anne Fountain in 2018 as *Ramona: Helen Hunt Jackson, traducida del inglés por José Martí*. Ana María Kerekes (2009) completed an MA thesis that was a comparative analysis of Martí's translation with Jackson's original, titled "Poder y belleza de la palabra: análisis de la traducción martiana de la novela *Ramona* de Helen Hunt Jackson".

13. Scholarly works that address border literature continues to grow. Seminal texts include *Borderlands/La Frontera: The New Mestiza* (1987) by Gloria Anzaldúa; *Border Matters: Remapping American Cultural Studies* (1997) by José David Saldívar; *When We Arrive: A New History of Mexican America* (2003) by José Aranda; *The Borderlands of Culture: Américo Paredes and the Transnational Imaginary* (2006) by Ramón Saldívar, and *Border Renaissance: The Texas Centennial and the Emergence of Mexican American Literature* (2009) by John Morán González.

14. Paul Estrade (1987) questioned Martí's conceptualization of the indigenous in his formulation of "Nuestra América" in *José Martí 1853–1895: Les Fondements de la démocratie en Amérique Latine*. This work was translated into Spanish in 2000 as *José Martí: Los fundamentos de la democracia en Latinoamérica*. More recently, Jorge Camacho (2013) has questioned the place of the indigenous in Martí's writings and thinking in *Etnografía, política y poder a finales del siglo XIX: José Martí y la cuestión indígena*.

15. For a corrective to how Mexicanists continue to neglect a study of the northern border, see Lori Celaya (2013).

16. Robert McKee Irwin (2003, 559–60) further explains that "without conquest and colonization, the borderlands and therefore Mexico and *Nuestra America* remain vulnerable to Yankee imperialism."

17. For a discussion of the transnational and hemispheric connection between Du Bois's and Martí's conceptualization of race, see David Luis-Brown's (2008) *Waves of Decolonization: Discourses of Race and Hemispheric Citizenship in Cuba, Mexico, and the United States* and Juliet Hooker's (2017) *Theorizing Race in the Americas: Douglas, Sarmiento, Du Bois and Vasconcelos*.

18. In this chapter, I follow Morúa in his use of L'Ouverture for Louverture. Morúa's interpretation of Louverture's life and autobiography occurred through Beard's and Redpath's mediated texts.

19. I follow here Ed Morales's (2018) discussion of the *collective black* in *Latinx: The New Force in American Politics and Culture*. Morales bases his theorization on Eduardo Bonilla-Silva's "tripartite racial structure" (Morales 2018, 246). Morales explains: "The use of the term and category 'collective black' has the potential to unify those who, whether African American or not, experience exclusion from white privilege and are exposed to the worst ravages of racism and lack of access to social justice" (Morales 2018, 246). See Eduardo Bonilla-Silva's "From Bi-Racial to Tri-Racial: Toward a New System of Racial Stratification in the US" (2004) and *Racism without Racists: Color-Blind Racism and the Persistence of Racial Inequality in America* (2003).

20. Two previous attempts for independence had failed: the Ten Years' War (1868–78) and the Guerra Chiquita (1879–80).

21. For a study of Cuban Autonomism, see De la Torre Molina (1997); Elorza and Sandoica (1998); and Bizcarrondo and Elorza (2001).

22. See Portuondo Linares (1950); Fermoselle (1974); Pérez (1986); Fernández Robaina (1990); Helg (1995); Fuente (2001); and Castro Fernández (2002).

23. Estimates of the number of black Cubans who were killed vary. Since most were buried in common graves, it is difficult to determine the death toll.

24. Morúa's letter also demonstrates his simultaneous apprehension toward Máximo Gómez and Antonio Maceo. After meeting Gómez in New Orleans in November 1884, just a month after Martí's own meeting with the generals, from the pages of his newspaper *El Pueblo*, Morúa recalls the occasion and refers to Gómez as a man with "acerado apegamiento a sus opiniones, cuyo hábito de mando militar le interceptaba la entrada en el palacio de la diplomacia" (a steely attachment to his opinions, whose habit of military leadership intercepted his entrance into the palace of diplomacy). He describes Gómez as violent and someone who threatened to leave the leadership of the movement, if he was not recognized as the "jefe supremo" (supreme leader) (April 30, 1887). He was also wary of Maceo. When Maceo purchased a black suit for himself, while the insurrectionists were ill, hungry, and without proper shoes, Morúa described this action, along with Maceo demanding another $2,500 from the revolutionary clubs in the US, as a final blow to these types of interventions led by generals, noting "El pueblo había perdido la confianza. Cada nuevo esfuerzo excitaba nuevas y más duras censuras contra los jefes. La mutación se había operado" (The people had lost their confidence. Every new initiative incited new and harsher criticism of the leaders. The change had occurred.) (May 28, 1887).

25. *Cecilia Valdés* (Villaverde 1992) recounts the tale of two lovers, the white, wealthy *criollo* Leonardo Gamboa and the mulatta Cecilia Valdés. Their affair produces a daughter. While neither of the lovers discovers that the other is a sibling, the black characters, the narrator, and the reader know of the incestuous nature of the love affair. As their doomed relationship develops, Villaverde decries the horrors of slavery and its effect on Cuban society. The novel concludes with the murder of Leonardo by a free mulatto José Dolores Pimienta, who is in love with Cecilia and seeks to avenge Leonardo's abandonment of her.

26. See Castellanos (1935); Stubbs (1985); Poyo (1989); Stebbins (2007); Tinajero (2007); and Poyo (2014) for descriptions of the political and revolutionary roles of readers in cigar factories.

27. On the narrative strategies of late nineteenth-century black writers, also see Carby's (1988) introduction to *The Magazine Novels of Pauline Hopkins*.

28. Choosing the name Amalia is also instructive because of José Mármol's *Amalia* (1851), a novel that allegorized the cultural and political challenges facing Argentina in the nineteenth century. Amalia may also intimate a reference to "Emilia" Casanovas, Villaverde's wife and political collaborator. In addition, the names Albina and América and their sibling status signal possible alterative but inextricably tied trajectories, because of the racialized dimensions of the name Albina and its link to América. As whiteness goes north (Albina), either it forgets its past and incorporates itself to the capitalist North Americans or it returns south (América), implying that there might be a true continental inheritor, but Morúa makes sure to show América's return occurs only to regain her goods from the Spanish authorities and not necessarily to forge a new nation. It is implied that, like Albina, she is there to get what was hers without seeking to change Cuban society and race relations in particular.

29. Before joining his brother-in-law's firm, Gonzaga worked in a clothing store in New York City. Occupations related to fashion, such as tailors, were held by freedmen in Havana.

In *Cecilia Valdés* the character Francisco de Paula Uribe is a tailor. He is described as being a mulatto with a dark complexion. Consequently, in *Sofía* this profession may be said to position Gonzaga as an inferior individual in the US social and racial hierarchy, thereby signaling Morúa's critique that Villaverde had chosen not to learn about race matters, even though he had lived in the US for close to thirty years.

30. I thank José B. Fernández for alerting me to the Quaker connection in a conversation at the Recovering the US Hispanic Literary Heritage Project Conference in Houston, Texas on October 19, 2012.

31. For a detailed account of Irish immigration and anti-immigration sentiments in the US, see Higham (1971); Rodgers (2007); and Murphy (2010).

32. In *Las Novelas del Señor Villaverde* Morúa criticized the lack of intelligence and naivety with which Villaverde depicted the enslaved woman María de la Regla, who tells the daughter of her owner of her plight, insinuating that Cecilia was the daughter of el Señor Gamboa, Leonardo's father in the process: "María de Regla es inteligente, y siéndolo...no iba a referir...una historia tan peligrosa para ella que buscaba el cese de su prolongado castigo" (Morúa Delgado 1892, 47) (María de Regla is intelligent, and being so...she was not going to reference...a story so dangerous for her who was looking for an end to her prolonged punishment.) That Morúa titles his second novel *La familia Unzúazu* also signals the collective disavowal by Americanized-criollos of the potential political impact of Afro Cubans in the future life of the Republic. In addition, it signals their collective attempt at keeping Afro Cubans in subservient positions that kept them politically and economically disenfranchised.

33. Jorge Camacho (2015, 2018) demonstrates that Martí along with other revolutionaries at the time argued that black Cubans would never rise against white Cubans because they were grateful that white Cubans had died for them in the battlefields during the Ten Years' Wars. As I will show in Chapter 5, Morúa is skeptical of this rhetoric, instead claiming that because black Cubans were fighting to free Cuba from Spain, they would not rise up against their Cuban brothers either during the military campaign or once the country was freed from colonial rule, but it had nothing to do with a one-sided gratitude. Meehan and Miller (2006) frame the contradiction at the heart of Martí's writing regarding blackness.

34. See Iglesia (1895); López Leiva (1930); Pérez (1986); Schwartz (1989); Paz Sánchez et al. (1993); Ripoll (1998); Balboa Navarro (2003); and Baker (2015).

35. It is important to highlight here the narrative link with *libertino* and Liberato. As Liberato had raped Ana María, Gonzaga is positioned as economically raping América and Magdalena. Although he is said to love Magdalena, his lack of moral character, since he is having an affair with her and is exploiting his own wife América in order hide his moral depravity, haunts the novel. In this way, Gonzaga and Liberato are not so subtly linked in the novel.

36. Debates on what constitutes American studies include Porter (1994); McClennen (2005); Levander and Levine (2006); Castronovo and Gillman (2009); Pease (2009); Edwards and Gaonkar (2010); Fluck et al. (2011); and Gilles (2011). Scholars who have challenged and expanded the US literary canon as it relates to nineteenth-century Latina/o literature include Saldívar (1997); Silva Gruesz (2002); Brickhouse (2004); Lazo (2005); Nwankwo (2005); Alemán and Streeby (2007); Lazo (2020); Lazó and Alemán (2016); Lomas (2009); Morán González (2010); Morán González (2016); Morán González and Lomas (2018); Saldívar (2011); and Coronado (2013). For a more extensive list, see my

bibliographic article "Nineteenth-Century Literature" (Lamas 2019) in *Latino Studies* in *Oxford Bibliographies Online*.

37. William Wells Brown's (1853) *Clotel; or, the President's Daughter: A Narrative of Slave Life in the United States* is considered the first novel by an African American author. The work details the plight of enslaved women under US slavery. Specifically, it narrates the perilous life of a mistress of Thomas Jefferson, her two daughters, and his granddaughter, thereby condemning the duplicity of the Founding Fathers in their claiming equal rights for all, while enslaving others. It pages are immersed in the history of Haiti and the Haitian Revolution, since Brown transcribes multiple phrases from Beard's *Life of Toussaint L'Ouverture* in the novel.

Chapter 5

1. Morúa uses "L'Ouverture" throughout his writings to refer to Louverture. Consequently, I will use "L'Ouverture" in order to retain Morúa's vision of Louverture, which is mediated by his translation of Redpath's (1863) rendition of Beard (1853).

2. These works were written to support abolition in the US. In detailing the life of L'Ouverture, Beard (1853) and Redpath (1863) advocated for the humanity of enslaved people and condemned the inhumanity of enslavement and those individuals and governments that supported the institution of slavery. For a detailed analysis of John R. Beard's and James Redpath's biographies of L'Ouverture, see Daut (2015).

3. Lazo (2020) and Johnson (2012) study texts that predate Morúa's historical moment. Cuba was under Spanish colonial rule when Morúa completed and/or published his novels and translation, which makes the use of their methodological approaches appropriate as a means of approaching his work.

4. I will use Redpath/Beard to refer to Redpath's 1863 edition of Beard's 1853 texts, since the former makes multiple editorial interventions in his rendition. Consequently, both Redpath and Beard may be said to be the authors of the work.

5. Morúa's translation is reprinted in full in *Martín Morúa Delgado. Obras completas*. Alberto Baeza-Flores, ed. Volume 5. Numbers 1–2 Havana, Cuba. Edición de la Comisión Nacional del Centenario de Martín Morúa Delgado, 1957.

6. Guillaume Thomas Raynal (1713–96) published and then expands his *L'Histoire philosophique et politique des établissements et du commerce des Européens dans les deux Indes* (Philosophical and Political History of the Two Indies), which he coauthored with Denis Diderot and various other writers. In it he discussed the future of the European powers in relation to their colonies in the Far East and the New World, covering such topics as the plight of indigenous peoples and the institution of slavery in South America, the Caribbean, and the British colonies in what would become the United States. The excluded passage runs from page 30 to page 36 in Beard (1853). Beard himself footnotes that he had omitted certain "revengeful" parts of Raynal's work (Beard 1853, 36). The section that he does include speaks to the injustices perpetuated by those individuals who enslave Africans. He lists the series of responses slave owners give in order to support the institution and then acerbically condemns slave traffickers and slave owners.

7. In 1880 gradual abolition was instituted in Cuba though a patronage system that would last until 1886. This patronage system was called the *patronato* because it was said that those who were enslaved needed to be trained for freedom. It simply delayed the

emancipation of those thousands of Cubans still enslaved on the island. In 1886, when slavery was finally legally abolished, the last 70,000 enslaved Cubans were legally freed.

8. We must recall that Morúa was born and raised in Matanzas, Cuba. This was the province in which the largest number of people from the US resided. It was also the stronghold of the Cuban plantation industry. In other words, Morúa experienced US attitudes toward those who were enslaved and freedmen and freedwomen first-hand, in Cuba, in addition to his time in the US South.

9. *El Separatista* was founded in 1883 with monies from the Club Independiente in New York, which was headed by Salvador Cisneros Betancourt. The newspaper, founded by José Leocadio Bonachea (1845–85), was meant to raise awareness and funds for another military insurrection, headed by Bonachea. Along with Flor Crombet and Francisco Varona Tournet (who also found themselves in New York), these veterans of the Ten Years' War had continued to fight for Cuban independence after the signing of the Pacto del Zanjón. The mostly Afro Cuban contingent continued fighting for fourteen months after the signing of the truce because it did not offer abolition to those who were enslaved.

From *El Pueblo* (Key West, 1886–87), in the series "Ideas sobre la política del último movimiento," which detailed the events surrounding the failed Sánchez-Varona and Gómez-Maceo expeditions, today's readers can further note how Morúa criticized Martí for not supporting the expeditions and a military invasion. For example, Morúa wrote that "el señor Martí, por razones que decía tener, combatió con insistencia la idea, siendo de opinión que era prematura la medida que se quería adoptar" (Quoted in Pérez Landa and Rosell Pérez 1957, 64. March 5, 1887) (Mr. Martí, for reasons that he said he held, insistently combated the idea, being of the opinion that the measure we wished to adopt was premature.) He adds that when Gómez travels to New York in 1884, "encontró lo que su ardorosa imaginación no acertaba a explicarse; las contrariedades de los pequeños nacidas de la rivalidad y el exagerado celo militar de los engrandecidos." (Quoted in Pérez Landa and Rosell Pérez 1957, 65. March 22, 1887) (He found what his ardent imagination could not to explain; the opposition of the small born from rivalry and an exaggerated military jealousy of those who think too highly of themselves.) Questioning the morality of the New York Cubans, including Martí, he wrote "conocíamos aquella emigración lo bastante para suponer con alguna razón hasta donde era capaz de avanzar en su moral y material apoyo" (*El Pueblo*, April 2, 1887) (We knew that community of immigrants well enough to assume, with good reason, the point to which it was capable of advancing in its moral and material support.) Finally, he describes the New York Cubans as wasting away from "el marasmo que nuevamente se iba apoderando de los cubanos en el extranjero" (*El Pueblo*, April 16, 1887) (the paralysis that was once again taking over the Cubans who lived abroad). I thank Gerald Poyo for making this archive available to researchers and for providing access to the same.

10. Morúa was not the only journalist to present the history of Haiti as a positive example for Cuba. Ada Ferrer (1999) cites an article from February 25, 1893 published in Juan Gualberto Gómez's *La Igualdad* to show as such. She explains the revolutionary nature of such an analogy since it worked against two conventional visions of the Haiti:

> Parallels to Haiti, needless to say, were standard ammunition in Spanish counterinsurgency. Among nationalists, on the other hand, Haiti usually figured only insofar as it allowed authors to assert dissimilarities and to establish a suitable distance between the two societies and republics. "Only crass ignorance," said Martí, would lead some to draw comparisons between the two islands. In the article written for the black paper, however, Haiti was invoked to lay claim to political and social rights.   (Ferrer 1999, 134)

11. I refer to Antonio Benítez Rojo's (1989) concept of a Plantation society in his well-known book *La isla que se repite: El Caribe y la perspectiva posmoderna*.

12. José Antonio Aponte (1790?–1812) was a Cuban-born freedman who organized a mass rebellion that linked freed and enslaved individuals throughout Cuba in a plot to take down colonial rule on the island and the institution of slavery. The plot was uncovered, and he, along with other organizers, was executed. The colonial authorities framed it as a slave rebellion against their white owners instead of enslaved people rising up against the corrupt government that was oppressing and enslaving them. For a detailed history of the Aponte Conspiracy and its ties to Haiti, see Ferrer's (2014) *Freedom's Mirror: Cuba and Haiti in the Age of Revolution*. Specifically, Morúa references the significance of the rebellion in a similar fashion as Ferrer frames it, the former noting specifically how slave insurrections must be read as political acts, a point Ferrer makes about Aponte's reconceptualization of history as made evident through Aponte's now lost *libros de pintura*. Ferrer explains, "Aponte drew on New World, European, and African intellectual and political currents to create a revolutionary movement that would make real the era's promise of meaningful transformation. For these revolutionaries, making that promise real meant, without a doubt ending slavery and, very likely, ending colonial rule" (Ferrer 2014, 275). Ferrer signals to Juan Arnao, a Cuban exile "writing from Brooklyn" in 1877, as an example of the "powerful historiographical tradition" that understood the Aponte rebellion not only as antislavery but as an act against the Crown (Ferrer 2014, 294). Morúa, a contemporary of Arnao, extends this analogy to *all* slave uprisings on the island before and after Aponte.

13. It is important to note here how historians have written extensively about Saco but purposely erased Morúa. As shown in Chapter 1, Saco had written about the inferiority of black Cubans and did not support immediate abolition.

14. Morúa published a US version of *La Nueva Era* in Key West in 1889 that focused on the strikes by tobacco workers in Key West and New York. Few copies of this US edition are currently available. I have found only one issue from 1889. I would like to thank Isis Campos (University of Houston) for her help in locating this journal in the Recovering the US Hispanic Heritage archives.

15. I am reminded of the double entendre driving *bastardo/bastardías* and its link to Gonzaga's and Magdalena's child who was born out of wedlock in *La familia Unzúazu*.

16. "Ensayo político" (1883) and "Factores sociales" (1892) deserve more extended study and contextualization in Morúa's *oeuvre* because of the complex observations Morúa makes about race relations and the impact of the legacy of enslavement on civic life, observations that need to be further contextualized in US, Cuban, Caribbean, Latin American, and Latina/o histories of the 1880s and 1890s.

17. In "En defense propria" an article published in *La Igualdad*, March 28, 1893, Serra quotes Morúa's attack. I thank Jesse Hoffnung-Garskoff for generously sharing his primary sources regarding this debate.

18. *Racial Migrations* (Hoffnung-Garskof 2019) is an important book that brings together the late nineteenth-century political organizing of black Cubans, black Puerto Ricans, and African Americans in the US. Another work that delineates their cooperation during this time period is Nancy Mirabal's (2017) *Suspect Freedoms. The Racial and Sexual Politics of Cubanidad in New York, 1823–1957*.

19. The Platt Amendment was added to the Cuban Constitution, drafted in 1901 and effective as of 1902. The amendment stipulated that the US could interfere militarily in Cuban affairs if it believed that their economic interests on the island were at peril due to

political instability. This led contemporary thinkers to speak of the first Republican era (1902–33) as the "mediated Republic."

20. I include the English original below since Morúa provides a literal translation. The only change is in the use of "prejudices" by Phillips. Morúa opts for "preocupaciones" or preoccupations to signal his belief that prejudices like racism were social constructs:

> You see me as a fanatic tonight, for you read history, not with your eyes, but with your prejudices. But fifty years hence, when Truth gets a hearing, the Muse of History will put Phocion for the Greek, and Brutus for the Roman, Hampden for England, Fayette for France, choose Washington as the bright, consummate flower of our earlier civilization, and John Brown the ripe fruit of our noonday, then, dipping her pen in the sunlight, will write in the clear blue, above them all the name of the soldier, the statesman, the martyr, Toussaint L'Ouverture.   (Phillips 1863, 494)

21. Morúa cites from Ludwig Gumplowicz's *La lucha de razas* (n.d.). Gumplowicz is considered one of the founders of European sociology. He argued that no pure race existed, since all races were mixed. He decried a biological basis for understanding race, instead emphasizing that race was a cultural and social construction in which a necessary conflict for dominance must occur. Some critics have argued that, as with Herbert Spencer, Gumplowicz adhered to a form of "scientific racism" in which racial struggle was inevitable and the survival of the fittest was preeminent, so that racial extermination of one group by another was not only possible but necessary (McGovern, 1941; Weikhart, 2003) However, others have argued that Gumplowicz's tenets regarding the conflict between groups have been misread (Adamek and Radwan-Praglowski 2006). It appears that Morúa emphasized Gumplowicz's conception that race and racial enmity were socially and culturally constructed, choosing to ignore or simply unable to envision the violent ends for which theories of social conflict, such as Gumplowicz's, could be utilized. For a brief summary of Gumplowicz's works and ideas, see Konieczny 2015.

22. Morúa is referring here to the Adam-Onís Treaty of 1819 that ceded Florida to the US. Florida would be admitted as a slave state in 1845.

23. The amendment read: "No se considerará, en ningún caso, como partido político o grupo independiente, ninguna agrupación constituida exclusivamente por individuos de una sola raza o color, ni por individuos de una clase con motivo de nacimiento, la riqueza o el título profesional" (In no case will it be considered, as a political party or independent group, any grouping constituted exclusively by individuals of one race or color, nor by individuals of one class based on their birth, their wealth or their professional title.)

Conclusion

1. Jesse Alemán (2016) provides an illuminating and detailed discussion of the brothers Adolfo and Federico Fernández Cavada in "From Union Officer to Cuban Rebels: The Story of the Brothers Cavada and Their American Civil Wars".

2. Memoirs and texts that depict these multiple types of crossings are an indispensable and integral part of the Latino Continuum. See, for example, *The Devil's Highway: A True Story* (2004) by Luis Alberto Urrea; *Finding Mañana: A Memoir of a Cuban Exodus* (2006) by Mirta Ojito; and *Unaccompanied* (2017) by Javier Zamora.

3. Theorizations about contemporary Latina/o literature and narrative abound. See, for example, the collection of essays *Critical Latin American and Latino Studies* (2003), edited

by Juan Poblete; Ralph Dalleo and Elena Machado Sáez's groundbreaking study *The Latina/o Canon and the Emergence of Post-Sixties Literature* (2007); *The Latino Body: Crisis Identities in American Literary and Cultural Memory* (2007) by Lázaro Lima; Marta Santangelo's *On Latinidad: US Latino Culture and the Construction of Ethnicity* (2007) and *Documenting the Undocumented: Latino Narratives and Social Justice in the Era of Operation Gatekeeper* (2016); *Latining America: Black-Brown Passages and the Coloring of Latina/o Studies* (2013) by Claudia Milian; the award-winning *Chicana/o and Latina/o Fiction: The New Memory of Latinidad* (2016) by Ylce Irizarry; *Latinx Literature Unbound: Undoing Ethnic Expectation* (2018) by Ralph E. Rodríguez; *Negotiating Latinidad: Intralatina/o Lives in Chicago* (2019) by Francis R. Aparicio; and *Latinx Literature Now: Between Evanescence and Event* (2020) by Ricardo L. Ortiz. Recent collected essays and companions include *The Cambridge Companion to Latina/o American Literature* (2016), edited by John Morán González; *The Cambridge History of Latina/o American Literature* (2018), edited by John Morán González and Laura Lomas; *Contemporary U.S. Latinx Literature in Spanish* (2018), edited by Amrita Das, Katheryn Quinn-Sánchez, and Michele Shaul; *Mapping South American Latina/o Literature of the United States: Interviews with Contemporary Writers* (2018) by Juanita Heredia; and *The Routledge Companion to Latino/a Literature* (2012) edited by Suzanne Bost and Frances R. Aparicio.

4. Two other works that accomplish this type of recovery are Yarimar Bonilla's *Non-Sovereign Futures: French Caribbean Politics in the Wake of Disenchantment* (2015) for Guadalupe and Dixa Ramírez's *Colonial Phantoms: Belonging and Refusal in the Dominican Americas, from the 19th Century to the Present* (2018) for the Dominican Republic.

{WORKS CITED}

Aching, Gerard. *Freedom from Liberation: Slavery, Sentiment and Literature in Cuba.* Bloomington, IN: Indiana University Press, 2015.

Adamek, Wojciech and Janusz Radwan-Praglowski. "Ludwik Gumplowicz: A Forgotten Classic of European Sociology." *Journal of Classical Sociology* 6.3 (2006): 381–98.

Aguilera Manzano, José María, ed. *El pensamiento liberal cubano através del diario de viaje de Eusebio Guiteras.* Seville, Spain: Junta de Andalucía, 2010.

Alcántar, Jonathan and Anne Fountain, eds. *Ramona: Helen Hunt Jackson, traducida del inglés por José Martí.* Buenos Aires: Stock Cero, 2018.

Aldama, Frederick. *The Routledge Concise History of Latino/a Literature.* New York and London: Routledge, 2013.

Alemán, Jesse. "The Invention of Mexican America." In *The Oxford Handbook of Nineteenth-Century American Literature*, edited by Russ Castronovo, 81–96. Oxford: Oxford University Press, 2012.

Alemán, Jesse. "From Union Officers to Cuban Rebels: The Story of the Brothers Cavada and Their American Civil Wars." In *The Latino Nineteenth Century*, edited by Rodrigo Lazo and Jesse Alemán, 89–109. New York: New York University Press, 2016.

Alemán, Jesse. "Narratives of Displacement in Places that Once Were Mexican." In *The Cambridge History of Latina/o American Literature*, edited by John Morán González and Laura Lomas, 216–31. Cambridge: Cambridge University Press, 2018.

Alemán, Jesse. "Wars of Rebellion: US Hispanic Writers and Their American Civil Wars." *American Literary History* 25.1 (Spring 2013): 54–68.

Alemán, Jesse and Shelley Streeby, eds. *Empires and the Literatures of Sensation. An Anthology of Nineteenth-Century Popular Fiction.* New Brunswick, NJ: Rutgers University Press, 2007.

Allen, Esther. "'He Has Not Made Himself Known to Me': José Martí, U.S. History, and the Question of Translation." In *Syncing the Americas: José Martí and the Shaping of National Identity*, edited by Ryan Anthony Spangler and Georg Michael Schwarzmann, 29–50. Lanham, MD: Bucknell University Press, 2018.

Allen, Esther, trans. *José Martí. Selected Writings.* New York: Penguin Books, 2002.

Álvarez Borland, Isabel. *Cuban American Literature of Exile: From Person to Persona.* Charlottesville, VA: University of Virginia Press, 1998.

Amores, Montserrat. "Eusebio Guiteras Font y las paradojas de la sociedad norteamericana." In *Mosaico Transatlántico. Escritoras, artistas e imaginarios (España-EE.UU. 1830–1940)*, edited by Beatriz Ferrús and Alba del Pozo, 15–38. Valencia, Spain: Universidad de Valencia, 2015.

Amigo, Gustavo. *La posición filosófica del Padre Félix Varela* (1947). Miami: Editorial Cubana, 1991.

Anbinder, Tyler. *Five Points: The 19th-Century New York City Neighborhood that Invented Tap Dance, Stole Elections and Became the World's Most Notorious Slum* (2001). New York: Free Press, 2010 [reissue].

Anzaldúa, Gloria. *Borderlands/La Frontera: The New Mestiza* (1987). San Francisco, CA: Aunt Lute Books, 2007.

Aparicio, Frances R. *Negotiating Latinidad: Intralatina/o Lives in Chicago.* Urbana, IL: University of Illinois Press, 2019.

Apter, Emily. *The Translation Zone: A New Comparative Literature.* Princeton, NJ: Princeton University Press, 2006.

Aranda, José. *When We Arrive: A New History of Mexican America.* Tucson, AZ: University of Arizona Press, 2003.

Arencibia Rodríguez, Lourdes. *El traductor Martí.* Pinar del Río, Cuba: Hermanos Loynaz, 2000.

Arencibia Rodríguez, Lourdes. "Un traductor llamado José Martí: una valoración necesaria." *Temas* 15 (1998): 96–108.

Baeza-Flores, Alberto. "Introduction." In *Obras completas de Martín Morúa Delgado.* Vol 4.1, edited by Alberto Baeza-Flores, 5-13. Havana: Edición de la Comisión Nacional del Centenario de Martín Morúa Delgado, 1957.

Baker, Pascale. *Revolutionaries, Rebels and Robbers. The Golden Age of Banditry in Mexico, Latin America and the Chicano Southwest, 1850–1950.* Cardiff, Wales: University of Wales Press, 2015.

Balboa Navarro, Imilcy. *La protesta rural en Cuba. Resistencia cotidiana, bandolerismo y revolución (1878–1932).* Madrid: CSIC, 2003.

Bassnett, Susan. *Translation Studies.* London: Routledge, 1980.

Bassnett, Susan. *Translation: The New Critical Idiom.* London: Routledge, 2014.

Bassnett, Susan and André Lefevere, eds. *Translation, History and Culture.* London: Cassell, 1990.

Baym, Nina. "*Women in the Republic: Emma Willard's Rhetoric of History.*" *American Quarterly* 43.1 (1991): 1–23.

Beard, John R. *The Life of Toussaint L'Ouverture: The Negro Patriot of Hayti: Comprising an Account of the Struggle for Liberty in the Island, and a Sketch of Its History to the Present Period.* London: Ingram, Cooke, and Co., 1853.

Beecher, Lyman. *A Plea for the West.* New York: Leavitt, Lord & Co., 1835.

Belnap, Jeffrey and Raúl Fernández, eds. *José Martí's "Our America": From National to Hemispheric Cultural Studies.* Durham, NC: Duke University Press, 1998.

Benítez Rojo, Antonio. *La isla que se repite. El Caribe y la perspectiva posmoderna.* Hanover, NH: Ediciones del Norte, 1989.

Benjamin, Walter. "The Task of the Translator." In *Illuminations: Essays and Reflections,* 69–82. New York: Schoken, 2007.

Bennett, David H. *The Party of Fear: From Nativist Movements to the New Right in American History* (1988). New York: Vintage, 1988.

Bentham, Jeremy. *Tactique des assembleées législatives, suivie d'un traité des sophismes politiques,* translated by Étienne Dumont. 2 vols. Geneva and Paris: J. J. Paschoud, 1816.

Bergard, Laird W. *Cuban Rural Society in the Nineteenth Century: The Social and Economic History of Monoculture in Matanzas.* Princeton, NJ: Princeton University Press, 1990.

Betancourt Cisneros, Gaspar. *Thoughts upon the Incorporation of Cuba into the American Confederation, in Contra Position to Those Published by José Antonio Saco.* New York: La Verdad, 1849.

Billington, Ray. *The Protestant Crusade 1800–1860: A Study of the Origins of American Nativism.* New York: Palgrave Macmillan, 1938.

Bizcarrondo, Marta and Antonio Elorza. *Cuba/España. El dilema autonomista, 1878–1898*. Madrid: Editorial Colibrí, 2001.

Bombal, María Luisa. *The House of Mist (La última niebla)*, translated by María Luisa Bombal. New York: Farrar, Straus, 1947.

Bombal, María Luisa. *La última niebla. El Arbol*. (1935). Santiago de Chile: Andres Bello, 1990.

Bonilla, Yarimar. *Non-Sovereign Futures: French Caribbean Politics in the Wake of Disenchantment*. Chicago: University of Chicago Press, 2015.

Bonilla-Silva, Eduardo. "From Bi-Racial to Tri-Racial. Toward a New System of Racial Stratification in the USA." *Ethnic and Racial Studies* 27.6 (November 2004): 931–50.

Bonilla-Silva, Eduardo. *Racism without Racists: Color-Blind Racism and the Persistence of Racial Inequality in the United States*. Lanham, MD: Rowman & Littlefield, 2003.

Bost, Suzanne and Frances R. Aparicio. *The Routledge Companion to Latino/a Literature*. New York: Routledge Press, 2012.

Brickhouse, Anna. *Transamerican Literary Relations and the Nineteenth-Century Public Sphere*. Cambridge: Cambridge University Press, 2004.

Brown, William Wells. *Clotel; or, the President's Daughter: A Narrative of Slave Life in the United States* (1853), edited by Robert Levine. Boston, MA: Bedford/St. Martin's Press, 2000.

Bueno, Salvador. *Costumbristas cubanos del siglo XIX*. Caracas, Venezuela: Biblioteca Ayachucho, 1985.

Cabrera, Raimundo. *Cuba and the Cubans*, translated by Laura Guiteras. Philadelphia, PA: Levytype Company, 1896.

Cabrera, Raimundo. *Cuba y sus jueces: rectificaciones oportunas*. 1st ed. Havana: Imp. "El Retiro," 1887.

Cabrera, Raimundo. *Cuba y sus jueces: rectificaciones oportunas*. 7th ed. Philadelphia, PA: Levytype Company, 1891.

Cabrera, Raimundo. (Ricardo Buenamar). "Episodios de la guerra. Mi vida en la manigua." *Cuba y América* Año 1 Número 1–Año 2 Número 31 (April 1, 1897—March 26, 1898).

Cabrera, Raimundo. *Episodios de la guerra. Mi vida en la manigua (Relato del coronel Ricardo Buenamar)*. Philadelphia, PA: Compañía Levytype, 1898a.

Cabrera, Raimundo. *Episodios de la guerra. Mi vida en la manigua*. Mexico: Tip. El Continente Americano, 1898b.

Cabrera, Raimundo. *Los Estados Unidos. Reducción de la obra "Triumphant Democracy" de Mr. Andrew Carnegie, con notas, aplicaciones y comentarios*. Havana: Imp. de Soler Álvarez, 1889.

Camacho, Jorge. *Amos, siervos y revolucionarios: la literatura de las guerras de Cuba (1868–1898). Una perspectiva transatlántica*. Madrid: Iberoamericana, 2018.

Camacho, Jorge. *Etnografía, política y poder a finales del siglo XIX: José Martí y la cuestión indígena*. Chapel Hill, NC: University of North Carolina Press, 2013.

Camacho, Jorge. *Miedo negro, poder blanco en la Cuba colonial*. Madrid: Iberoamericana, 2015.

Carby, Hazel B. *The Magazine Novels of Pauline Hopkins*. New York: Oxford University Press, 1988.

Cárdenas, Mauro Javier, *The Revolutionaries Try Again*. Minneapolis, MN: Coffee House Press, 2016.

Carnegie, Andrew. *Triumphant Democracy or Fifty Years' March of the Republic*. New York: Scribners, 1886.

Carroll, Bartholomew R. *Catechism of United States History*. Charleston, SC: McCarter & Co., 1858.

Castellanos, Jesús. *Motivos de Cayo Hueso.* Havana: Ucar, García y Cia., 1935.

Castro Fernández, Silvio. *La masacre de los Independientes de Color en 1912.* Havana: Editorial de Ciencias Sociales, 2002.

Castronovo, Russ and Susan Gillman, eds. *States of Emergency: The Object of American Studies.* Chapel Hill, NC: University of North Carolina Press, 2009.

Cavada, Federico Fernández. *Libby Life: Experiences of a Prisoner of War in Richmond, Va., 1863–64.* Philadelphia, PA: King & Baird, 1864.

Celaya, Lori. *México visto desde su literatura del norte: identidades propias de la transculturación y la migración.* Pittsburgh, PA: University of Pittsburgh Press, 2013.

Chambers, Stephen. *No God but Gain: The Untold Story of Cuban Slavery, the Monroe Doctrine and the Making of the United States.* New York: Verso, 2015.

Chávez Álvarez, Clara. *Hacedora de la bandera cubana. Emilia Margarita Teurbe Tolón y Otero.* Havana: Ediciones Boloña, 2010.

Chaviano, Daína. *La isla de amores infinitos.* Barcelona: Grijalbo, 2006.

Clonard, Conde de. *Historia orgánica de la armas de infantería y caballeria españolas desde la formación del ejército permanente hasta el día.* Vol. 8. Madrid: Imp. del *Boletín de Jurisprudencia,* 1851.

Contreras, Ingrid, *The Fruit of the Drunken Tree.* New York: Doubleday Press, 2018.

Conway, Hugh. (Frederick John Fargus) *Called Back.* Bristol, UK: J.W. Arrowsmith, 1883.

Coronado, Raúl. *A World Not to Come: A History of Latino Writing and Print Culture.* Cambridge, MA: Harvard University Press, 2013.

Craton, Michael. "Forms of Resistance to Slavery. The Slave Societies of the Caribbean." In *General History of the Caribbean,* edited by Franklin Knight, 222–70. London: UNESCO Publishing, 1997.

Cuesta, Leonel Antonio de la. *Martí, traductor.* Salamanca, Spain: Universidad Pontificia de Salamanca, 1996.

Cutler, John Alba. "Toward a Reading of Nineteenth-Century Latina/o Short Fiction." In *The Latino Nineteenth Century,* edited by Rodrigo Lazo and Jesse Alemán, 124–45. New York: New York University Press, 2016.

Dalleo, Ralph and Elena Machado Sáez. *The Latina/o Canon and the Emergence of Post-Sixties Literature.* New York: Palgrave Macmillan Press, 2007.

Damrosch, David. *What Is World Literature?* Princeton, NJ: Princeton University Press, 2003.

Das, Amrita, Katheryn Quinn-Sánchez, and Michele Shaul. *Contemporary U.S. Latinx Literature in Spanish.* Cham, Switzerland: Springer Nature Press, 2018.

Daut, Marlene. *Baron de Vastey and the Origins of Black Atlantic Humanism.* New York: Palgrave McMillan, 2017.

Daut, Marlene. *Tropics of Haiti. Race and the Literary History of the Haitian Revolution in the Atlantic World, 1789–1865.* Liverpool, UK: University of Liverpool Press, 2015.

Delany, Martin R. *Blake, or The Huts of America* (1859, 1861–62), edited by Jerome McGann. Cambridge, MA: Harvard University Press, 2017.

Dimock, Wai Chee. *Through Other Continents: American Literature Across Deep Time.* Princeton, NJ: Princeton University Press, 2006.

Dumont, Étienne, trans. and ed. *Tactique des assembleées législatives, suivie d'un traité des sophismes politiques* by Jeremy Bentham. 2 vols. Geneva and Paris: J. J. Paschoud, 1816.

Edwards, Brian T. and Dilip P. Gaonkar, eds. *Globalizing American Studies.* Chicago, IL: University of Chicago Press, 2010.

Elorza, Antonio and Elena Hernández Sandoica. *La guerra de Cuba (1895–1898)*. Madrid: Alianza, 1998.

Estrade, Paul. *José Martí 1853–1895: Les Fondements de la démocratie en Amérique Latine*. Paris: Éditions caribéennes, 1987.

Estrade, Paul. *José Martí. Los fundamentos de la democracia en Latinoamérica*. Madrid: Casa de Velázquez, 2000.

Fermoselle, Rafael. *Política y color en Cuba: la guerrita de 1912*. Madrid: Editorial Colibrí, 1974.

Fernández Retamar, Roberto. *Calibán y otros ensayos*. Havana: Editorial de Arte y Literatura, 1979.

Fernández Retamar, Roberto and Pedro Pablo Rodríguez. *En los Estados Unidos: el periodismo de 1881–1892 de José Martí*. Madrid: ALLCA XX, 2003.

Fernández Robaina. Tomás. *El negro en Cuba. 1902–1958: apuntes para la historia de la lucha contra la discriminación racial*. Havana: Editorial de Ciencias Sociales, 1990.

Ferré, Rosario. *Maldito amor y otros cuentos* (1988). New York: Vintage Español, 1998.

Ferré, Rosario. *Sweet Diamond Dust and Other Stories* (*Maldito amor y otros cuentos*), translated by Rosario Ferré. New York: Plume Press, 1996.

Ferrer, Ada. *Freedom's Mirror: Cuba and Haiti in the Age of Revolution*. New York, NY: Cambridge University Press, 2014.

Ferrer, Ada. *Insurgent Cuba: Race, Nation and Revolution, 1868–1898*. Chapel Hill, NC: University of North Carolina Press, 1999.

Fessenden, Tracy. *Culture and Redemption: Religion, the Secular, and American Literature*. Princeton, NJ: Princeton University Press, 2007.

Fletcher, David M. *The Diplomacy of Trade and Investment: American Economic Expansion in the Hemisphere (1865–1900)*. Columbia, MO: University of Missouri Press, 1998.

Flick, Lawrence F. "The Papago Indians and Their Church." *Records of the American Catholic Historical Society* 5.3 (1894a): 385–416.

Flick, Lawrence F. "*Rudo Ensayo*. Preface." *Records of the American Catholic Historical Society*. 5.2 (1894b): 109–110.

Fluck, Winfired, Donald E. Pease, and John Carlos Rowe, eds. *Re-Framing the Transnational Turn in American Studies*. Hanover, RI: Dartmouth College Press, 2011.

Foreman, Gabrielle. "Reading Aright: White Slavery, Black Referents, and the Strategy of Histotextuality in *Iola Leroy*." *Yale Journal of Criticism* 10.2 (1997): 327–54.

Forero Quintero, Gustavo, ed. *Xicotencatl. Anónimo*. Madrid: Iberoamericana, 2012.

Fountain, Anne. *José Martí and US Writers*. Gainesville, FL: University Press of Florida, 2003.

Fountain, Anne. *José Martí, the United States, and Race*. Gainesville, FL: University Press of Florida, 2014.

Franchot, Jenny. *Roads to Rome. The Antebellum Protestant Encounter with Catholicism*. Berkeley, CA: University of California Press, 1994.

Franco, Jorge. *Paraíso Travel*. Bogotá, Colombia: Editorial Planeta Colombia, 2001.

Fuente, Alejandro de la. *A Nation for All: Race, Inequality and Politics in Twentieth-Century Cuba*. Chapel Hill, NC: University of North Carolina Press, 2001.

Garcha, Amanpal. *From Sketch to Novel. The Development of Victorian Fiction*. Cambridge: Cambridge University Press, 2012.

Gentzler, Edwin. *Translation and Identity in the Americas: New Directions in Translation Theory*. London: Routledge, 2008.

Gentzler, Edwin. *Translation and Rewriting in the Age of Post-Translation Studies.* London: Routledge, 2017.

Gibbs, Jenna. "Columbia the Goddess of Liberty and Slave-Trade Abolition (1807–1820)." *Sjuttonhundratal: Nordic Yearbook for Eighteenth-Century Studies* (2011): 156–68.

Gilles, Paul. *The Global Remapping of American Literature.* Princeton, NJ: Princeton University Press, 2011.

Gillman, Susan. *Blood Talk: American Race, Melodrama and the Culture of the Occult.* Chicago, IL: University of Chicago Press, 2003.

Gillman, Susan "Whose Protest Novel? *Ramona*, the *Uncle Tom's Cabin* of the Indian." In *The Oxford Handbook of Nineteenth-Century American Literature*, edited by Russ Castronovo, 376–91. New York: Oxford University Press, 2012.

Gjerde, Jon. *Catholicism and the Shaping of Nineteenth-Century America.* New York: Cambridge University Press, 2012.

González, Julián. *Martín Morúa Delgado. Impresiones sobre su última novela y su gestión en la Constituyente de Cuba.* Havana: Impr. de Rambla y Bouza, 1902.

González Acosta, Alejandro. *El enigma de Jicoténcal. Dos estudios sobre el héroe de Tlxacala.* Mexico, D.F.: Instituto Tlaxcalteca de Cultura, 1997.

Gosin, Monika. *The Politics of Racial Division: Interethnic Struggles for Legitimacy in Multicultural Miami.* Ithaca, NY: Cornell University Press, 2019.

Grande, Reyna, *Across a Hundred Mountains.* New York: Washington Square Press, 2007.

Guerra, Lillian. *The Myth of Martí: Conflicting Nationalisms in Early Twentieth-Century Cuba.* Chapel Hill, NC: University of North Carolina Press, 2005.

Guillén, Nicolás. *Martín Morúa Delgado ¿Quién fue?* . . . Havana: Ediciones Unión, 1984.

Guiteras, Eusebio. "Gabriel Reyes." *Cuba y América* 12–16 (August 9, 1903–September 23, 1904).

Guiteras, Eusebio. *Guía de la Cueva de Bellamar. Guide to the Caves of Bellamar.* Matanzas, Cuba: Imp. de la Aurora del Yumurí, 1863.

Guiteras, Eusebio. *Irene Albar, novela cubana.* Barcelona: Imp. de L. Tasso Serra, 1885.

Guiteras, Eusebio. *Libro de lectura.* Philadelphia, PA: J. K. and P. G. Collins, 1856.

Guiteras, Eusebio. *Libro segundo de lectura.* Philadelphia, PA: J. K. and P. G. Collins, 1857.

Guiteras, Eusebio. *Libro tercero de lectura.* Philadelphia, PA: J. K. and P. G. Collins, 1858.

Guiteras, Eusebio. *Libro cuarto de lectura.* Matanzas, Cuba: Sánchez & Co., 1868.

Guiteras, Eusebio. "*Libros de viaje.*" In *El pensamiento liberal cubano através del diario de viaje de Eusebio Guiteras*, edited by José María Aguilera Manzano. Sevilla, Spain: Junta de Andalucía, 2010.

Guiteras, Eusebio. trans. "*Rudo Ensayo.*" *Records of the American Catholic Historical Society.* 5.2 (1894): 109–240.

Guiteras, Eusebio. *Un invierno en Nueva York. Apuntes de viaje y esbozos de pluma.* Barcelona: Gorgas y Co., n.d. (1869–1890).

Guiteras, Laura. "Brief Sketch of the Life of Eusebio Guiteras." *Records of the American Catholic Historical Society* 5.2 (June 1894): 99–108.

Guiteras, Pedro José. *Vidas de poetas cubanos.* Havana: UNEAC, 2001.

Gumplowicz, Ludwig. *La lucha de razas.* Madrid: La España Moderna, n.d.

Gura, Phillip. *The American Antiquarian Society, 1812–2012: A Bicentennial History.* Worcester, MA: American Antiquarian Society, 2012.

Gutiérrez, Ramón A. "Comment: A Response to 'Gay Latino Cultural Citizenship." In *Gay Latino Studies: A Critical Reader*, edited by Michael Hames-García and Ernesto Javier Martínez, 198–203. Durham, NC: Duke University Press, 2011.

Handley, George B. "Reading Behind the Face. Martín Morúa Delgado, Charles W. Chesnutt, and Frances E.W. Harper." In *Postslavery Literatures in the Americas: Family Portraits in Black and White*, 75–111. Charlottesville, VA: University of Virginia Press, 2000.

Hartman, Saidiya V. *Scenes of Subjection: Terror, Slavery and Self-Making in Nineteenth-Century America*. Oxford: Oxford University Press, 1997.

Hatch, Nathan O. *The Democratization of American Christianity*. New Haven, CT: Yale University Press, 1989.

Helg, Aline. *Our Rightful Share: The Afro-Cuban Struggle for Equality*. Chapel Hill, NC: University of North Carolina Press, 1995.

Heredia, Juanita, *Mapping South American Latina/o Literature of the United States: Interviews with Contemporary Writers*. Cham, Switzerland: Springer Nature Press, 2018.

Higham, John. *Strangers in the Land. Patterns of American Nativism, 1860–1925*, 2nd ed. New York: Atheneum, 1971.

Hoffnung-Garskof, Jesse. *Racial Migrations: New York City and the Revolutionary Politics of the Spanish Caribbean*. Princeton, NJ: Princeton University Press, 2019.

Hooker, Juliet. *Theorizing Race in the Americas: Douglas, Sarmiento, Du Bois and Vasconcelos*. New York: Oxford University Press, 2017.

Horrego Estuch, Leopoldo. *Martín Morúa Delgado. Vida y mensaje*. Havana: Editorial Sánchez, 1957.

Hudson, Linda S. *Mistress of Manifest Destiny: A Biography of Jane Cazneau McManus, 1807–1878*. Austin, TX: Texas Historical Association, 2001.

Hunt Jackson, Helen. *Ramona, a Story*. Boston, MA: Roberts Brothers, 1884.

Hulbert, William Henry. "The Poetry of Spanish America." *North American Review* 142 (January 1849): 129–60.

Iglesia, Álvaro de la. *Manuel García (El rey de los campos de Cuba). Su vida y sus hechos*. Havana: La Comercial, 1895.

Ignatiev, Noel. *How the Irish Became White*. New York: Routledge, 1995.

Imbert, E. Anderson. *Historia de la literatura hispanoamericana* (1954). Vol. 1 *La Colonia. Cien años de república*, 9th reprint. Mexico, D.F.: Fondo de Cultura Económica, 1995. 221–2.

Indiana, Rita, *La mucama de omicumlé*. Caceres, Spain: Editorial Periferica, 2015.

Indiana, Rita *Papi*. Caceres, Spain: Editorial Periferica, 2012.

Indiana, Rita. *Papi*, translated by Achy Obejas. Chicago: University of Chicago Press, 2016.

Indiana, Rita. *Tentacle (La mucama de omicumlé)*, translated by Achy Obejas. Sheffield, UK: And Other Stories Press, 2018.

Irizarry, Ylce, *Chicana/o and Latina/o Fiction: The New Memory of Latinidad*. Champaign, IL: University of Illinois Press, 2016.

Jackson, Richard. *Black Writers in Latin America*. Albuquerque, NM: University of New Mexico Press, 1979.

Jaksic, Iván. *The Hispanic World and American Intellectual Life, 1820–1880*. New York: Palgrave Macmillan, 2007.

James, C. L. R. *The Black Jacobins: Toussaint L'Ouverture and the San Domingo Revolution* (1963). New York: Vintage Books, 1989.

Jefferson, Thomas. *Manual of Parliamentary Practice for the Use of the Senate of the United States (1801)*. Washington, DC: Davis & Force, 1820.

Jenson, Deborah. *Beyond the Slave Narrative: Politics, Sex, and Manuscripts in the Haitian Revolution*. Liverpool: Liverpool University Press, 2012.

Johnson, Sarah E. *The Fear of French Negroes: Transcolonial Collaboration in the Revolutionary Americas*. Berkeley, CA: University of California Press, 2012.

Joyce, Barry. *The First U.S. History Textbooks. Constructing and Disseminating the American Tale in the Nineteenth Century*. Lanham, MD: Lexington Books, 2015.

Kagan, Richard L. *The Spanish Craze: America's Fascination with the Hispanic World, 1779–1939*. Omaha, NE: University of Nebraska Press, 2019.

Kanellos, Nicolás. "Sotero Figueroa: Writing Afro-Caribbeans into History in the Lote Nineteenth Century." In *The Latino Nineteenth Century*, edited by Rodrigo Lazo and Jesse Alemán, 323–40. New York: New York University Press, 2016.

Kerekes, Ana María. "Poder y belleza de la palabra: análisis de la traducción martiana de la novela *Ramona* de Helen Hunt Jackson." MA thesis, Concordia University, Montreal, 2009.

Kerney, Martin J. *Catechism of the History of the United States*. Baltimore, MD: J. Murphy & Co., 1850.

Kleppner, Paul. *The Third Electoral System, 1853–1925. Parties, Voters, and Political Cultures*. Chapel Hill, NC: University of North Carolina Press, 1979.

Konieczny. Matthew J. "Ludwig Gumplowicz (1838–1909)". In *The Wiley Blackwell Encyclopedia of Race, Ethnicity, and Nationalism*, edited by John Stone, et al . 951–3. Boston, MA: Wiley Blackwell, 2015.

Kutzinski. Vera M. *Sugar's Secret: Race and the Erotics of Cuban Nationalism*. Charlottesville, VA: University of Virginia Press, 1993.

La piragua: periódico de literature dedicado a la juventud cubana, edited by José Fornaris and Joaquín L. Luaces. Havana: Impr. del Tiempo, 1856–57.

Labrador Rodríguez, Sonia. "Estrategias discursivas en la narrativa antiesclavista cubana." Dissertation, State University of New York at Stony Brook, New York, 1993.

Laguna, Albert. *Diversión: Play and Popular Culture in Cuban America*. New York: New York University Press, 2017.

Lamas, Carmen. "Americanized-criollos: Latina/o Figures in Late Nineteenth-Century Cuban Literature." *Revista Hispánica Moderna* 61.1 (2008): 69–87.

Lamas, Carmen. "The Black *Lector* and Martín Morúa Delgado's *Sofia* (1891) and *La familia Unzúazu* (1901)." *Latino Studies* 13.1 (Spring 2015): 113–30.

Lamas, Carmen. "Father Félix Varela and the Emergence of an Organized Latina/o Minority in Early Nineteenth-Century New York City." In *The Cambridge History of Latina/o American Literature*, edited by John Morán González and Laura Lomas, 157–75. New York: Cambridge University Press, 2018.

Lamas, Carmen. "Nineteenth-Century Literature." In *Oxford Bibliographies in Latino Studies*, edited by Ilán Stavans. New York: Oxford University Press, 2019. https://www. oxfordbibliographies.com/view/document/obo-9780199913701/obo-9780199913701-0135.xml

Lamas, Carmen. "Race and the Critical Trajectory of *Espejo de paciencia* (1608, 1838) in the Nineteenth Century." *Latin American Research Review* 47.1 (Spring 2012): 115–35.

Lamas, Carmen. "Raimundo Cabrera, the Latin American Archive and the Latina/o Continuum." In *The Latino Nineteenth Century*, edited by Rodrigo Lazo and Jesse Alemán, 210–29. New York: New York University Press, 2016.

Lauter, Paul, ed. *The Heath Anthology of American Literature: Volume B: Early Nineteenth Century*, 7th ed. Boston, MA: Cengage Learning, 2014.

Lazo, Rodrigo. "La famosa Filadelfia": The Hemispheric American City and Constitutional Debates." In *Hemispheric American Studies*, edited by Caroline F. Levander and Robert S Levine, 57–74. Rutgers University Press, 2008.

Lazo, Rodrigo. *Letters from Filadelfia. Early Latino Literature and the Trans-American Elite*. Charlottesville, VA: University of Virginia Press, 2020.

Lazo, Rodrigo. *Writing to Cuba: Filibustering and Cuban Exiles in the United States*. Chapel Hill, NC: University of North Carolina Press, 2005.

Lazo, Rodrigo and Jesse Alemán, eds. *The Latino Nineteenth Century*. New York: New York University Press, 2016.

Leal, Luis. "Félix Varela and Liberal Thought." In *The Ibero-American Enlightenment*, edited by Alfred Owen Aldridge, 234–42. Champaign, IL: University of Illinois Press, 1971.

Leal, Luis. "A Historical Perspective: Theorizing Aztlan" (1973). In *A Luis Leal Reader*, edited by Ilán Stavans, 14–27. Evanston, IL: Northwestern University Press, 2007.

Leal, Luis. "*Jicoténcal*, primera novela histórica en castellano." *Revista Iberoamericana* 25.49 (1960): 9–31.

Leal, Luis and Rodolfo Cortina, eds. *Jicoténcal* by Félix Varela. Houston, TX: Arte Público Press, 1995.

Lefevere, André. *Translating Literature: Practice and Theory in a Comparative Literature Context*. New York: Modern Language Association of America, 1992.

Lefevere, André. *Translation, Rewriting and the Manipulation of Literary Fame*. London: Routlege, 2016.

Levander, Caroline and Robert Levine. "Introduction: Hemispheric American Literary History." *American Literary History* 18.3 (2006): 397–405.

Levine, Robert S., ed. *The Norton Anthology of American Literature: Volume B*, 9th ed. New York: W. W. Norton & Co., 2017.

Lima, Lázaro, *The Latino Body: Crisis Identities in American Literary and Cultural Memory*. New York: New York University Press, 2007.

Linkh, Richard M. *American Catholicism and the Nationality Question, 1880–1900*. Staten Island, NY: Center for Migration Studies, 1975.

Lint Sagarena, Roberto Ramón. *Aztlán and Arcadia. Religion, Ethnicity and the Creation of Place*. New York: New York University Press, 2014.

Lisazo, Félix. *Martí, místico del deber*. Buenos Aires: Losada, 1940.

Lomas, Laura. *Translating Empire: José Martí, Migrant Latino Subjects, and American Modernities*. Durham, NC: Duke University Press, 2009.

López, Antonio. *Unbecoming Blackness: The Diaspora Cultures of Afro-Cuban America*. New York: New York University Press, 2012.

López, Iraida H. *Impossible Returns: Narratives of the Cuban Diaspora*. Gainesville, FL: University Press of Florida, 2015.

López, Iraida H. and Eliana S. Rivero, eds. *Let's Hear Their Voices: Cuban American Writers of the Second Generation*. Albany, NY: SUNY Press, 2019.

López, Marissa K. *Chicano Nations: The Hemispheric Origins of Mexican American Literature*. New York: New York University Press, 2011.

López Leiva, Francisco. *El bandolerismo en Cuba*. Havana: Imp. "El Siglo XX", 1930.

Los cubanos pintados por sí mismos. Colección de tipos cubanos. Havana: Imp. y Papelería Barcina, 1852.

Los españoles pintados por sí mismos. Madrid: I. Boix, 1843–44.

Los mexicanos pintados por sí mismos: tipos y costumbres nacionales, edited by M. Murguía and D. H. Iriarte. Mexico City: Imp. de Murguía y Comp, 1854–55.

Luis, William, ed. *Autobiografía del esclavo poeta y otros escritos*. Madrid: Iberoamericana, 2007.

Luis, William. *Literary Bondage: Slavery in Cuban Narrative*. Austin, TX: University of Texas Press, 1990.

Luis-Brown, David. *Waves of Decolonization: Discourses of Race and Hemispheric Citizenship in Cuba, Mexico, and the United States*. Durham, NC: Duke University Press, 2008.

Mañach, Jorge. *Martí, el apostol*. Madrid: Espasa-Calpe, 1932.

Manfra, Jo Ann. "Hometown Politics and the American Protective Association, 1887–1890." *The Annals of Iowa* 55.2 (Spring 1996): 138–66.

Manzano, Juan Franciso. *Autobiografía del esclavo poeta y otros escritos*, edited by William Luis. Madrid: Iberoamericana, 2007.

Manzano, Juan Francisco. *Poems by a Slave in the Island of Cuba, Recently Liberated*, edited and translated by Richard Robert Madden. London: Thomas Ward & Co., 1840.

Máquez Sterling, Manuel. *Martí: maestro y apóstol*. Havana: Secane, Fernández & Cia, 1942.

Martí, José. *Obras completas*. 27 volumes. Havana: Editorial Nacional de Cuba, 1963.

McCadden, Joseph and Helen M. McCadden. *Félix Varela. Torch Bearer for Cuba*. (1969), 2nd ed. San Juan, Puerto Rico: Ramallo Bros., 1984.

McClennen, Sophia A. "Inter-American Studies or Imperial American Studies?" *Comparative American Studies* 3.4: (2005): 393–413.

McGovern, William H. *From Luther to Hitler: The History of Nazi-Fascist Philosophy*. Cambridge, MA: Harvard University Press, 1941.

McKee Irwin, Robert. "*Ramona* and Postnationalist American Studies. On "Our America" and the Mexican Boderlands." *American Quarterly* 55.4 (Dec. 2003): 539–67.

Meehan, Kevin and Paul B. Miller. "Martí, Schomburg y la cuestión racial en las Américas." *Afro-Hispanic Review* 25.2 (2006): 73–88.

Mellado, Francisco. *Enciclopedia moderna. Diccionario universal de literatura, ciencias, artes, agricultura, industria y comercio*. Vol. 7. Madrid: P. Mellado, 1851.

Menéndez, Ana. *In Cuba I Was A German Shepherd*. New York: Grove Press, 2001.

Merchán, Rafael. "La población de color en Cuba (A propósito de una novela)." *Variedades* 1 (1894): 472–510.

Mesa Rodríguez, Manuel. *Martín Morúa Delgado. Discurso*. Havana: Academia de la Historia de Cuba, 1956.

Mestre y Domínguez, José Manuel. *De la filosofía en la Habana*. Havana: Imp. "La Antilla," 1862.

Meza y Súarez Inclán, Ramón. "En un pueblo de la Florida." *Cuba y América* (March-June 1899).

Meza y Súarez Inclán, Ramón. *Eusebio Guiteras: Estudio biográfico*. Havana: Impr. Avisador Comercial, 1908.

Milian, Claudia. *Latining America: Black-Brown Passages and the Coloring of Latina/o Studies*. Athens, GA: University of Georgia Press, 2013.

Milian, Claudia. *LatinX*. Minneapolis, MN: University of Minnesota Press, 2019.

Milian, Claudia, ed. "Theorizing LatinX." Special Issue. *Cultural Dynamics* 29.3 (August 2017).

Mirabal, Nancy. *Suspect Freedoms: The Racial and Sexual Politics of Cubanidad in New York City, 1823–1957*. New York: New York University Press, 2017.

Montejano. David. *Anglos and Mexicans in the Making of Texas*. Austin, TX: University of Texas Press, 1987.

Montoya, Maceo, *The Deportation of Wopper Barraza*. Albuquerque, NM: University of New Mexico Press, 2014.

Morales, Carlos Javier, ed. Lucía Jerez *de José Martí*. Madrid: Cátedra, 1994.

Morales, Ed. *Latinx: The New Force in American Politics and Culture*. New York: Verso, 2018.

Morán González, John. *Border Renaissance: The Texas Centennial and the Emergence of Mexican American Literature*. Austin, TX: University of Texas Press, 2009.

Morán González, John, ed. *The Cambridge Companion to Latina/o American Literature*. New York: Cambridge University Press, 2016.

Morán González, John. *The Troubled Union: Expansionist Imperatives in Post-Reconstruction American Novels*. Columbus, OH: Ohio State University Press, 2010.

Morán González, John and Laura Lomas, eds. *The Cambridge History of Latina/o American Literature*. New York: Cambridge University Press, 2018.

Morell de Santa Cruz, Agustín. *Historia de la isla y catedral de Cuba* (1760s). Preface by Francisco de Paula Coronado. Havana: Academia de la Historia de Cuba, Imp. "Cuba Intelectual," 1929.

Moretti, Franco. *Distant Reading*. New York: Verso Books, 2013.

Moriuchi, Mei-Yen. *Mexican Costumbrismo: Race, Society and Identity in Nineteenth-Century Mexican Art*. University, Park, PA: Penn State University Press, 2018.

Morris, Charles R. *The Grand American Catholic Compromise*. New York: Times Books, 1998.

Morúa Delgado, Martín. *La familia Unzúazu. Novela cubana*. Havana: Impr. La Prosperidad, 1901.

Morúa Delgado, Martín. *Martín Morúa Delgado. Obras completas*, edited by Alberto Baeza-Flores. 5 volumes. Havana. Edición de la Comisión Nacional del Centenario de Martín Morúa Delgado, 1957.

Morúa Delgado, Martín. *Las novelas del Sr. Villaverde*. Havana: Impr. de A. Alvarez y Compañía, 1892.

Morúa Delgado, Martín. *Sofía*. Havana: Impr. de A. Alvarez y Compañía, 1891.

Morúa Delgado, Martín. "Toussaint L'Ouverture." *Cuba y América* 11 (1903): 316–21.

Muller, Dalia Antonio. *Cuban Emigres and Independence in the Nineteenth-Century Gulf World*. Durham, NC: University of North Carolina Press, 2017.

Murphy, Angela F. *American Slavery, Irish Freedom: Abolition, Immigrant Citizenship and the Transatlantic Movement for Irish Repeal*. Baton Rouge, LA: Louisiana State University Press, 2010.

Nentvig, Juan. *Descripción geográfica natural y curiosa de la provincia de Sonora, circa 1762*. San Marin, CA: Huntington Library, HM4267, 1762.

Nentvig, Juan. *Descripción geográfica, natural y curiosa de la Provincia de Sonora por un amigo del Servicio de Dios y del Rey Nuestro Señor año 1764*. Vols. 16 and 393. Mexico City, Mexico: Archivo General de la Nación, 1764a.

Nentvig, Juan. *Descripción geográfica, natural y curiosa de la provincial de Sonora por un amigo del Servicio de Dios y del Rey Nuestro Señor año 1764*. In *Memorias de la Nueva España*. Vol 16. Madrid, Spain: Real Academia de la History, 1764b.

Nentvig, Juan. *Descripción geográfica, natural y curiosa de la Provincia de Sonora por un amigo del Servicio de Dios y del Rey Nuestro Señor año 1764*. In *Documentos para la historia de México*, edited by Joaquín García Icazbalceta. Vol. 4, 489–616. Mexico: Imp. de Vicente García Torres, 1856.

Nentvig, Juan. *Rudo Ensayo, tentativa de una prevencional descripcion geographica de la provincia de Sonora, sus terminos y confines; ó mejor, Coleccion de materiales para hacerla quien lo supiere mejor. Compilada así de noticias adquiridas por el collector en sus viajes por casi toda ella, como subministrdas por los padres missioneros y practicos de la tierra. Dirigida al remedio de ella, por un amigo del bien comun*, transcribed by Thomas Buckingham Smith. St. Augustine, FL, 1863.

Nentvig, Juan. "*Rudo Ensayo*, Translated into English from the Spanish, by Eusebio Guiteras." *Records of the American Catholic Historical Society of Philadelphia* 5.2. (1894): 109–240.

Nentvig, Juan. *Rudo Ensayo: A Description of Sonora and Arizona in 1764 by Juan Nentvig*, edited and translated by Alberto Francisco Pradeau and Robert R. Rasmussen. Tucson, AZ: University of Arizona Press, 1980.

Nolan, Edward J. "Certain Churches in the West." *Records of the American Catholic Historical Society* 5.1 (1894): 88–98.

Novoa, Juan Bruce. "Shipwrecked in the Seas of Signification. Cabeza de Vaca's Relación and Chicano Literature." In *Reconstructing a Chicano/a Literary Heritage. Hispanic Colonial Literature of the Southwest*, edited by María Herrera-Sobek, 3–23. Tucson, AZ: University of Arizona, Press, 1993.

Núñez Rodríguez, Mauricio. "El espacio americano en la novela de José Martí." *ISLAS* 45.136 (April–June 2003): 48–58.

Núñez Rodríguez, Mauricio. "Prólogo." In *Lucía Jerez o Amistad funesta* by José Martí, 1–24. Havana: Editorial Letras Cubanas, 1997.

Nwankwo. Ifeoma Kiddoe. *Black Cosmopolitanism. Racial Consciousness and Transnational Identity in the Nineteenth-Century Americas*. Philadelphia, PA: University of Pennsylvania Press, 2005.

Ocasio, Rafael, ed. *A Bristol, Rhode Island and Matanzas, Cuba Slavery Connection: The Diary of George Howe*. Lanham, MD: Lexington Books, 2019.

Ocasio, Rafael. *Afro-Cuban Costumbrismo: From Plantations to the Slums*. Gainesville, FL: University of Florida Press, 2012.

Offner, John L. *An Unwanted War: The Diplomacy of the United States and Spain over Cuba (1895–1898)*. Chapel Hill, NC: University of North Carolina Press, 2001.

Ojito, Mirta. *Finding Mañana: A Memoir of a Cuban Exodus*. New York: Penguin Books, 2006.

Older, Daniel José, *The Book of Lost Saints*. New York: St. Martin's Press, 2019.

Onís, Catalina M. de "What's in an 'x'? An Exchange about the Politics of 'Latinx.'" *Chiricú Journal. Latina/o Literatures, Arts, and Cultures* 1.2 (2017): 78–91.

Orchard, William and Yolanda Padilla, eds. *Bridges, Borders, and Breaks: History, Narrative, and Nation in Twenty-First-Century Chicana/o Literary Criticism*. Pittsburg, PA: University of Pittsburg Press, 2016.

Orihuela, Sharada Balachandran. *Fugitives, Smugglers, and Thieves: Piracy and Personhood in American Literature*. Chapel Hill, NC: University of North Carolina Press, 2018.

Ortiz, Ricardo L. *Latinx Literature Now: Between Evanescence and Event*. Cham, Switzerland: Springer Nature Press, 2020.

Oxx, Katie. *The Nativist Movement in America. Religious Conflict in the Nineteenth Century*. New York: Routledge, 2013.

Paine, Thomas. *Common Sense*. Philadelphia: R. Bell, 1776.

Pampín, María Fernanda. "'Ese don raro de asir la música y el espíritu en las lenguas.' Los mecanismos implícitos en el proceso de traducción en la obra de José Martí." *Anclajes* 15.2 (December 2012): 59–71.

Paz Sánchez, Manuel, José Fernández Fernández, and Nelson López Novegil. *El bandolerismo en Cuba: 1800–1933. Presencia canaria y protesta rural*. Tenerife, Canary Islands: Centro Popular Canaria, 1994.

Pease, Donald E. *The New American Exceptionalism*. Minneapolis, MN: University of Minnesota Press, 2009.

Pellón, Gustavo. "El intelectual hispanoamericano como 'fruto sin mercado' en *Lucía Jerez* de José Martí." In *Cajón de textos. Ensayos sobre literatura hispanoamericana*, edited by Carmenza Kline, 201–208. Bogotá, Colombia: Fundación General de la Universidad de Salamanca, 2007.

Pérez, Lisandro. *Sugar, Cigars, and Revolution. The Making of Cuban New York*. New York: New York University Press, 2018.

Pérez, Jr. Luis A, ed. *Impressions of Cuba in the Nineteenth Century: The Diary of Joseph J. Dimock* (1859). Lanham, MD: Rowman and Littlefield, 1998.

Pérez, Jr. Luis A. *Lords of the Mountain: Social Banditry and Peasant Protest in Cuba, 1878–1918*. Pittsburgh, PA: University of Pittsburgh Press, 1986.

Pérez, Jr. Luis A. *On Becoming Cuban: Identity, Nationality and Culture*. Chapel Hill, NC: University of North Carolina Press, 2008.

Pérez Firmat, Gustavo. *Life on the Hyphen: The Cuban American Way*. Austin, TX: University of Texas Press, 1994.

Pérez Landa, Rufino and María Rosell Pérez. *Vida pública de Martín Morúa Delgado*. Havana: Academia de la Historia, 1957.

Pérez Rosales, Vicente. *Diario de un viaje a California (1848–1849)*. Santiago de Chile: Bibliofilos Chilenos, 1949.

Pérez Rosales, Vicente. *Recuerdos del pasado (1814–1860)*. Santiago de Chile: Imp. Gutenberg, 1886.

Pérez Salas, María Esther. *Costumbrismo y litografía en Mexico. Un nuevo modo de ser*. Mexico City: Universidad Nacional Autónoma de Mexico, 2005.

Peters, Samuel. *A general history of Connecticut, from its first settlement under General Fenwick, Esq., to its latest period of amity with Great Britain, including a description of the country, and many curious and interesting anecdotes. To which is added, an appendix wherein new and the true sources of the present rebellion in America are pointed out, together with the particular part taken by the people of Connecticut in its promotion, by a gentleman of the Province*. London: J. Bew, 1781.

Phillips, Wendell. "Toussaint L'Ouverture" (1861). In *Speeches, Lectures, and Letters*, 468–94. Boston, MA: James Redpath Publisher, 1863.

Pichardo Moya, Felipe. "Estudio crítico" (1942). In *"Espejo de paciencia": Edición facsímil y crítica*, edited by Cinto Vitier, 27–39. Havana: Comité Nacional de la UNESCO, 1961.

Pierrot, Grégory. *The Black Avenger in Atlantic Culture*. Athens, GA: University of Georgia Press, 2019.

Piqueras, José Antonio. *Félix Varela y la prosperidad de la patria criolla*. Madrid: Fundación MAPFRE, 2007.

Poblete, Juan. "Citizenship and Illegality in the Global California Gold Rush." In *The Latino Nineteenth Century*, edited by Rodrigo Lazo and Jesse Alemán. New York, 278–300: New York University Press, 2016.

Poblete, Juan, ed. *Critical Latin American and Latino Studies*. Minneapolis, MN: University of Minnesota Press, 2003.

Ponce de León, Néstor. "Los primeros poetas de Cuba." *Revista Cubana* 15 (1892): 385–99.

Poncet y de Cárdenas, Carolina. *El romance en Cuba*. Havana: Imp. Siglo XX, 1914.

Ponte Domínguez, Francisco José. *Matanzas. Biografía de una provinica*. Havana: Siglo XX, 1959.

Porter, Carolyn. "What We Know We Don't Know: Remapping American Literary Studies. *American Literary History* 6.3 (1994): 467–526.

Portuondo Linares, Serafín. *Los independientes de color: historia del Partido Independiente de Color*. Havana: Librería Selecta, 1950.

Poyo, Gerald. *Exile and Revolution. José D. Poyo, Key West and Cuban Independence*. Gainesville, FL: University Press of Florida, 2014.

Poyo, Gerald. *"With all and for the Good of All": The Emergence of Popular Nationalism in the Cuban Communities of the United States, 1848–1898*. Durham, NC: Duke University Press, 1989.

Pradeau, Alberto Francisco and Robert R. Rasmussen, eds. and trans., *Rudo Ensayo: A Description of Sonora and Arizona in 1764 by Juan Nentvig*. Tucson, AZ: University of Arizona Press, 1980.

Puig, Manuel. *Eternal Curse on the Reader of These Pages*. New York: Random House, 1982.

Puig, Manuel. *Maldición a quien lea estas páginas*. Barcelona: Seix Barral, 1980.

Quesada y Miranda, Gonzalo. *Martí, hombre*. Havana: Seoane, Fernández y Cía, 1940.

Rama, Angel. *La ciudad letrada*. Hanover, NH: La Edición del Norte, 1984.

Ramírez, Dixa. *Colonial Phantoms: Belonging and Refusal in the Dominican Americas, from the 19th Century to the Present*. New York: New York University Press, 2018.

Ravitch, Diane. *The Great School Wars. New York City (1805–1973): A History of the Public Schools as Battlefield of Social Change*. New York: Basic Books, 1974.

Raynal, Guillaume Thomas. *L'Histoire philosophique et politique des établissements et du commerce des européens dans les deux Indes,* 3rd ed. 10 vols. Geneva: Jean-Leonard Pellet, 1780–84.

Rebert, Paula. *La Gran Línea. Mapping the United States-Mexico Boundary, 1849–1857*. Austin, TX: University of Texas Press, 2001.

Recacoechea, Juan de. *American Visa*. Cochabamba-La Paz, Bolivia: Liberia-Editorial Los Amigos del Libro, 1994.

Redpath, James. *Toussaint L'Ouverture: A Biography and Autobiography*. Boston, MA: James Redpath Publisher, 1863.

Reid-Vázquez, Michele. *The Year of the Lash: Free People of Color in Cuba and the Nineteenth-Century Atlantic World*. Athens, GA: University of Georgia Press, 2011.

Rexach, Rosario. *El pensamiento de Félix Varela y la formación de la conciencia cubana*. Havana: Editorial Lyceum, 1950.

Riggs Family Papers. Washington, DC: Library of Congress. George Washington Riggs, 1813–81. MSS37895.

Ripoll, Carlos. *El bandolerismo en Cuba: desde el descubrimiento hasta el presente*. New York: Editorial Dos Ríos, 1998.

Rivera, John-Michael. *The Emergence of Mexican America: Recovering the Stories of Mexican Peoplehood in U.S. Culture*. New York: New York University Press, 2006.

Rivera, José Eustacio. *La vorágine* (1924). New York: Editorial Andes, 1929.

Rivera, Tomás. . . . *y no se lo tragó la tierra* (1971). Houston, TX: Arte Público Press, 1995.

Rivero, Melissa, *The Affairs of the Falcóns*. New York: Harper Collins Press, 2019.

Robinson, Cedric. *Black Marxism: The Making of the Black Radical Tradition* (1983). Chapel Hill, NC: University of North Carolina Press, 2000.

Rodgers, Nini. *Ireland, Slavery and Anti-Slavery, 1612–1865*. New York: Palgrave Macmillan, 2007.

Rodríguez, Jaime Javier. *The Literatures of the US-Mexican War: Narrative, Time, and Identity*. Austin, TX: University of Texas Press, 2010.

Rodríguez, José Ignacio. *Vida del Presbítero Don Félix Varela*. 1878. New York: Imprenta de "O Novo Mundo," 1878.

Rodríguez, Ralph E. *Latinx Literature Unbound: Undoing Ethnic Expectation*. New York: Fordham University Press, 2018.

Rodríguez Morell, Jorge Luis. "Razones para una metodología de análisis de la traducción martiana en *Ramona*." *Anuario del Centro de Estudios Martianos* 18 (1995–96): 133–40.

Roediger, David. *The Wages of Whiteness: Race and the Making of the American Working Class*. New York: Verso, 1991.

Roig de Leuchsenring, Emilio. *Ideario cubano Félix Varela, precursor de la revolución libertadora cubana*. Havana: Oficina del Historiador de la Ciudad, 1953.

Rojas, Rafael. "Bancroft, Motley, Martí, and American Renaissance Historiography." In *Synching the Americas: José Martí and the Shaping of National Identity*, edited by Ryan Anthony Spangler and Georg Michael Schwarzmann, 129–38. Landham, MD: Bucknell University Press, 2018.

Rojas, Rafael. "La esclavitud liberal. Liberalismo y abolicionismo en el Caribe hispano." *Secuencia. Revista de historia y ciencias sociales* 86 (May-Aug. 2013): 29–52.

Rojas, Rafael. *José Martí. La invención de Cuba*. Madrid: Colibrí, 2000.

Ropero Regidor, Diego. "Vida y obra del poeta Cubano Miguel Teurbe Tolón." In *Miguel Teurbe Tolón. Poesía reunida*, 7–128. Moguer, Spain: Junta de Andalucía. Fundación Juan Ramón Jiménez, 2004.

Rosa Corsa, Gabino and Mirta T. González. *Casadores de esclavos: Diarios*. Havana: Fundacion Fernando Ortiz, 2004.

Roth, Wendy D. *Race Migrations: Latinos and the Cultural Transformation of Race*. Palo Alto, CA: Stanford University Press, 2012.

Rotker, Susan. *Fundación de una escritura: las crónicas de José Martí*. Havana: Casa de las Américas, 1992.

Rotker, Susan. *The American Chronicles of José Martí: Journalism and Modernity in Spanish America*, translated by Jennifer French and Katherine Semler. Hanover, NH: University Press of New England, 2000.

Ruiz de Burton, María Amparo. *The Squatter and the Don (1885)*, edited by Rosaura Sáncez and Beatrice Pita. 2nd edn. Houston, TX: Arte Público Press, 1997.

Saco, José Antonio. *Historia de la esclavitud de la raza africana en el nuevo mundo y en especial en los paises hispano-americanos*. Vol. 1. Barcelona: Imp. de Jaime Jepús, 1877.

Saco, José Antonio. *Historia de la esclavitud desde los tiempos más remotos hasta nuestros días*. 3 vols. Paris, Tipografía Lahure, 1875; Paris: Imp. de Kugelmann, 1875; Barcelona: Imp. de Jaime Jepús, 1877.

Saco, José Antonio. *Ideas sobre la incorporación de Cuba en los Estados-Unidos*. Paris: Imprenta de Panckoucke, 1848.

Saínz, Enrique. *Silvestre de Balbo y la literatura cubana*. Havana: Editorial Letras Cubanas, 1982.

Saldaña-Portillo, María Josefina. *Indian Given: Racial Geographies across Mexico and the United States*. Durham, NC: Duke University Press, 2016.

Saldívar, José David. *Border Matters: Remapping American Cultural Studies*. Berkeley, CA: University of California Press, 1997.

Saldívar, José David. *TransAmericanity: Subaltern Modernities, Global Coloniality, and the Cultures of Greater Mexico*. Durham, NC: Duke University Press. 2011.

Saldívar, Ramón. *The Borderlands of Culture: Américo Paredes and the Transnational Imaginary*. Durham, NC: Duke University Press, 2006.

Sánchez, Marta E. *A Translational Turn: Latinx Literature into the Mainstream*. Pittsburgh, PA: University of Pittsburgh Press, 2018.

Santangelo, Marta, *Documenting the Undocumented: Latino Narratives and Social Justice in the Era of Operation Gatekeeper*. Gainesville, FL: University Press of Florida, 2016.

Santangelo, Marta. *On Latinidad: US Latino Culture and the Construction of Ethnicity.* Gainesville, FL: University Press of Florida, 2007.

Schulman, Iván. *Génesis del modernismo: Martí, Nájera, Silva, Casal.* Mexico: Colegio de México, 1966.

Schulman, Iván, ed. *Lucía Jerez* by José Martí. Buenos Aires: Stock Cero, 2005.

Schulman, Iván. *Martí, Dario y el modernismo.* Madrid: Editorial Gredos, 1969.

Schulten, Susan. "Emma Willard and the Graphic Foundations of American History." *Journal of Historical Geography* 33 (2007): 542–64.

Schulten, Susan. *Mapping the Nation: History and Cartography in Nineteenth-Century America.* Chicago, IL: University of Chicago Press, 2012.

Schwartz, Rosalie. *Lawless Liberators: Political Banditry and Cuban Independence.* Durham, NC: Duke University Press, 1989.

Seguín, Juan Nepomuceno. *Personal Memoirs of John N. Seguín from the Year 1834 to the Retreat of General Woll from the City of San Antonio in 1842.* San Antonio, TX: Ledger Book & Job Office, 1858.

Sellers-Garcia, Sylvia. *When the Earth Turns in Its Sleep.* London: Riverhead Books, 2007.

Serpa, Gustavo. *Apuntes sobre la filosofía de Félix Varela.* Havana: Editorial Ciencias Sociales, 1983.

Shea, John Gilmary. "Memoir of Thomas Buckingham Smith." In *Alvar Núñez Cabeza de Vaca. Relation of Alvar Nuñez Cabeza de Vaca translated from the Spanish by Buckingham Smith,* edited by Thomas W. Field , 255–63. Albany, NY: J. Munsell for H. C. Murphy, 1871.

Shea, William. *The Lion and the Lamb: Evangelicals and Catholics in America.* New York: Oxford University Press, 2004.

Silber, Nina. *The Romance of Reunion: Northerners and the South (1865–1900).* Chapel Hill, NC: University of North Carolina Press, 1997.

Silva Gruesz, Kirsten. *Ambassadors of Culture. The Transamerican Origins of Latino Writing.* Princeton, NJ: Princeton University Press, 2002.

Silva Gruesz, Kirsten. "*El Gran Poeta* Longfellow and a Psalm of Exile." *American Literary History* 10.3 (Autumn 1998): 395–427.

Silva Gruesz, Kirsten. "The Errant Latino: Irisarri, Central Americanness, and Migration's Intention." In *The Latino Nineteenth Century,* edited by Rodrigo Lazo and Jesse Alemán, 20–48. New York: New York University Press, 2016.

Silva Gruesz, Kirsten. "Tracking the First Latino Novel: *Un matrimonio como hay muchos* (1849) and Transnational Serial Fiction." In *Transnationalism and American Serial Fiction,* edited by Patricia Okker, 36–63. New York: Routledge, 2012.

Simms, William Gilmore. *History of South Carolina... Designed for the Instruction of the Young,* Charleston, SC: S. Babcock & Co., 1840.

Smith, Thomas Buckingham, trans. *Narrative of Alvar Nuñez Cabeza de Vaca.* Washington, DC: George W. Riggs, 1851.

Smith, Thomas Buckingham, trans criber. *Rudo Ensayo, tentativa de una prevencional descripcion geographica de la provincia de Sonora, sus terminos y confines; ó mejor, Coleccion de materiales para hacerla quien lo supiere mejor. Compilada así de noticias adquiridas por el collector en sus viajes por casi toda ella, como subministrdas por los padres missioneros y practicos de la tierra. Dirigida al remedio de ella, por un amigo del bien comun,* by Juan Nentvig. St. Augustine, Florida: 1863.

Sommer, Doris. *Foundational Fictions: The National Romances of Latin America*. Berkeley, CA: University of California Press, 1991.

Soria Ortega, Andrés. "Ganivet y los costumbristas granadinos." *Cuadernos de Literatura* 13–15 (January–June 1949): 205–38.

Stavans, Ilán, et al., eds. *The Norton Anthology of Latino Literature*. New York: W. W. Norton & Company, 2010.

Stebbins, Consuelo. *City of Intrigue, Nest of Revolution. A Documentary History of Key West in the Nineteenth Century*. Gainesville, FL: University Press of Florida, 2007.

Stepto, Robert B. "Distrust of the Reader in African-American Narratives." In *Reconstructing American Literary History*, edited by Sacvan Bercovitch, 300–22. Cambridge, MA: Harvard University Press, 1986.

St. John, Rachel. *Line in the Sand. A History of the Western U.S.-Mexico Border*. Princeton, NJ: Princeton University Press, 2011.

Stubbs, Jean. *Tobacco and the Periphery: A Case Study in Cuban Labour History, 1860–1958*. New York: Cambridge University Press, 1985.

Ticknor, George. *History of Spanish Literature*. 3 vols. New York: Harper and Brothers, 1849.

Tinajero, Araceli. *El lector de tabaquería: historia de una tradición cubana*. Madrid, Spain: Editorial Verbum, 2007.

Tolón, Miguel Teurbe. *Compendio de la historia de los Estados Unidos, ó, República de América por Emma Willard. Traducido al Castellano por Miguel T. Tolón*. New York: A.S. Barnes and Co., 1853.

Tolón, Miguel Teurbe. *The Elementary Spanish Reader and Translator* (1853). New York: D. Appleton & Co., 1865.

Tolón, Miguel Teurbe. *Flores y espinas*. Matanzas, Cuba: Imp. de la "Aurora del Yumuri," 1857.

Tolón, Miguel Teurbe. *Leyendas cubanas*. New York: Mesa and Familton, 1856.

Tolón, Miguel Teurbe. *Lola Guara. Novela cubana*. Matanzas: Imp. del Gobierno y Marino, 1846.

Tolón, Miguel Teurbe. *Poesía reunida*, edited by Diego Ropero Regidor. Moguer, Spain: Junta de Andalucía, 2004.

Tolón, Miguel Teurbe. *Los preludios. Rimas de Don Miguel Teurbe Tolón*. Matanzas, Cuba: Imp. del Gobierno y Marina, 1841.

Torre Molina, Mildred de la. *El autonomismo en Cuba, 1878–1898*. Havana: Editorial de Ciencias Sociales, 1997.

Torres, Lourdes. "Latinx?" *Latino Studies*. 16.3 (2018): 283–5.

Travieso, Antonio Hernández. *El Padre Varela. Biografía del forjador de la conciencia cubana*. Havana: Jesus Montero, 1949.

Travieso, Antonio Hernández. *Varela y la reforma filosófica en Cuba*. Havana: Jesús Montero, 1942.

Trujillo, Enrique. *Apuntes históricos; propaganda y movimientos revolucionarios cubanos en los Estados Unidos desde enero de 1880 hasta febrero de 1895*. New York: Tip. De "El Porvenir," 1896.

Trujillo-Pagán, Nicole. "Crossed Out by LatinX: Gender Neutrality and Genderblind Sexism." *Latino Studies* 16.3 (October 2018): 396–406.

Ucelay da Cal, Margarita. *Los españoles pintados por sí mismos. Estudio de un género costumbrista*. Mexico City: Fondo de Cultura Económica, 1951.

Urrea, Luis Alberto. *The Devil's Highway. A True Story*. New York: Little, Brown and Company, 2004.

Vallejo, Catherine. "José Martí y su *transpensamiento* de *Ramona* por Helen Hunt Jackson: un diálogo de sustancia y estilo." *Revista Iberoamericana* 79.244–45 (July–December 2013): 777–95.

Vallejo, Mariano Guadalupe. *Recuerdos históricos y personales tocante á la Alta California; historia política del país, 1769–1849. Costumbres de los Californios; Apountes biográficos de personas notables* (1875). 5 vols. TS. BANC MSS CD17-21. Berkeley: Bancroft Library, University of California, Berkeley.

Van Tine, Mary Lindsay. "Translated Conquests: Archive, History, and Territory in Hemispheric Literatures, 1832–1854." Dissertation, Columbia University, New York, 2016.

Varela, Félix. *Cartas a Elpidio. Sobre la impiedad, la superstición y el fanatismo en sus relaciones con la sociedad* (1835, 1838), edited by Humberto Piñera. Epilogue by Raimundo Lazo. 2 vols. Havana: Universidad de la Habana, 1944.

Varela, Félix. *Félix Varela. Obras. El que nos enseñó primero a pensar* (1997), edited by Eduardo Torres-Cuevas, Jorge Ibarra Cuesta, and Mercedes García Rodríguez. 3 vols. Havana: University of Havana, 2001 (Digital Reprint).

Varela, Félix. *El Habanero: papel politico, científio y literario* (1824–26). Miami: Ediciones Universal, 1997.

Varela, Félix. *Jicoténcal*, edited by Luis Leal and Rodolfo Cortina. Houston: Arte Público Press, 1995.

Varela, Félix. *Letters to Elpidio*, edited by Felipe Estévez, translated by John Farina, et al. New York: Paulist Press, 1989.

Varela, Félix. *Manual de Práctica Parlimentaria: para el uso del Senado de los Estados Unidos por Tomas Jefferson: al cual se han agregado el reglamento de cada camara y el comun a mabas; traducido del ingle y anotado por Felix Varela*. New York: H. Newton, 1826.

Varela, Félix. *Xicoténcatl. An Anonymous Historical Novel about the Events Leading up to the Conquest of the Aztec Empire*, translated by Guillermo I. Castillo-Feliú. Austin, TX: University of Texas Press, 1999.

Varon, Alberto. *Before Chicano: Citizenship and the Making of Mexican American Manhood, 1848–1959*. New York: New York University Press, 2018.

Venuti, Lawrence. *The Scandals of Translation: Toward an Ethics of Difference*. New York: Routledge, 1998.

Venuti, Lawrence, ed. *The Translation Studies Reader*. New York: Routledge, 2000.

Venuti, Lawrence. *The Translator's Invisibility*. New York: Routledge, 1995.

Vidal-Ortiz, Salvador and Juliana Martínez. "Latinx Thoughts: Latinidad with an X." *Latino Studies* 16.3 (October 2018): 384–95.

Villaverde, Cirilo. *Cecilia Valdés o La Loma del Angel* (1882), edited by Jean Lamore. Madrid, Spain: Cátedra, 1992.

Vitier, Medardo. *Las ideas y la filosofía en Cuba*. Havana: Editorial Ciencias Sociales, 1970.

Volk, Kyle. *Moral Minorities and the Making of American Democracy*. New York: Oxford University Press, 2014.

Weikhart, Richard. "Progress through Racial Extermination: Social Darwinism, Eugenics, and Pacifism in Germany, 1860–1918." *German Studies Review* 26 (2003): 273–94.

Willard, Emma. *Abridged History of the United States or Republic of America*. Philadelphia, PA: A. S. Barnes & Co. 1844.

Willard, Emma. *Abridged History of the United States or Republic of America* Philadelphia, PA: A. S. Barnes & Co. 1850.

Willard, Emma. *Abridged History of the United States or Republic of America*. Philadelphia, PA: A. S. Barnes & Co. 1852.

Willard, Emma. *Abridged History of the United States or Republic of America*. Philadelphia, PA: A. S. Barnes & Co. 1860.

Willard, Emma. *History of the United States or Republic of America*. New York: White, Gallaher, White, 1828.

Willard, Emma. *History of the United States, or Republic of America*. New York: A. S. Barnes & Co., 1848.

Willard, Emma. *Last Leaves of American History: Comprising Histories of the Mexican War and California*. New York: George P. Putnam, 1849.

Willard, Emma. *Via media: A Peaceful and Permanent Settlement of the Slavery Question*. Washington: C. H. Anderson, 1862.

Williams, Lorna V. *The Representation of Slavery in Cuban Fiction*. Columbia, MO: University of Missouri Press, 1994.

Zamora, Javier. *Unaccompanied*. Port Townsend, WA: Copper Canyon Press, 2017.

Zenea, Juan Clemente (Adolfo de la Azucena). *Lejos de la patria. Memorias de un joven poeta*. Havana: Imp. "La Charanga," 1859.

{ INDEX }

Page numbers followed by "f" indicate illustrations.